BAR

NOPI

EST 1798

Clove
Store

Kitty Fisher's Jago

CINNAMON
Kitchen

BRASSERIE
ZÉDEL

LYLE'S

Pitt
-Cue-
Co.

BENARES

terroirs

ANDREW
EDMUNDS

BREAD AHEAD

THE MODERN

DIS

terroirs

DISHOOM

The Delaunay

NE

BR

na G

BREAD AHEAD

FERNANDEZ & WELLS

INA

na GYMKHANA

TOMs KITCHEN DA

AFE

INA

42 ALBEMARLE STREET
MAYFAIR

42 trullo Little SOCIAL

J. SHEEKEY

H

CAFE MURANO Towpath

TAPAS

BOCCA DI LUPO BIS

Y

KOYA

BRINDISA

LA FRO

Honey & Co.

Clos Maggiore GELUPO

DUC

BISTROT

THE

THE CLOVE CLUB

wahaca

DUC

LA FROMAGERIE

SMOKING GOAT

SPRING

THE IVY

José

DUCKSOUP

MORO

The River Café

sē

MISSION

L

KOFFMANN'S

SMOKEHOUSE

QUO VADIS

Zetter

TRASHED

GINGER & WHITE
LONDON

Rules

DF/MEXICO

RAW DUCK

THEO RANDALL

EST 1798

THE
CINNAMON
CLUB

St. JOHN

T

NOPI

Grain
Store

Pitt
-Cue-
Co.

BAR

CINNA
Kitch

CINNAMON
Kitchen

Kitty Fisher's Jago

LYLE'S

BREAD AHEAD

BENARES

terroirs

BRASSERIE
ZÉDEL

ANDREW
EDMUNDS

THE MODERN
PANTRY

DISHOO

OIrs

NEWMAN
SREET
TAVERN

BREAD

HOOM

The Delaunay

EAD AHEAD

DO

barrafina

GYM

FERNANDEZ & WELLS

GYMKHANA

TOMs KITCHEN DABBOUS

ALBEMARLE STREET
MAYFAIR

42 trullo Little SOCIAL

MU

42

The London
COOKBOOK

The
London
COOKBOOK

RECIPES FROM THE RESTAURANTS, CAFES, AND HOLE-IN-THE-WALL GEMS OF A MODERN CITY

Aleksandra Crapanzano
Photography by Sang An

TEN SPEED PRESS
BERKELEY

43

INTRODUCTION vii

INTRODUCTION

It begins on a walk. This walk happens to be one that I make whenever I'm in London. It begins at Books for Cooks, a cozy Notting Hill bookshop for serious cooks that is as packed with books as it is with enthusiasm and knowledge. It is here that I always learn that such and such a dish at so and so's new restaurant is not to be missed and that the new restaurant in Chiswick is worth the fifty-minute tube ride; that Patricia has just received her stock of Mrs. Kirkham's Lancashire at La Fromagerie and to make sure to buy the Ardraham from County Cork too, as it always disappears quickly; or that Yotam is almost out of tahini cookies, so I'd better hurry. And hurry I do, because my next stop is always the Ottolenghi on Ledbury Road, just off Westbourne Grove and only a few minutes walk from Books for Cooks. His tahini cookies are a sophisticated riff on peanut butter cookies that are on the savory side of sweet and therefore offer the illusion of being healthy.

And so it is that I find myself stepping out of Books for Cooks and into the sunshine—yes, the sun does shine in London—of Blenheim Crescent, jotting down at a furious rate all that I have learned in the shop before making my way down Portobello Road and across on Lonsdale to Ledbury. I turn the page of my notebook, only to realize that I've come to the last page. Somehow my random notes on food in London have filled a book. The rest of the day's walk, I confess, is a bit of a blur; something has begun here and I can't stop thinking about it.

Returning, finally, to my friend's house on Talbot Road, I fire off an email to my most discerning food-loving London friends, asking them all to write back with their five favorite restaurants and their favorite dishes in those restaurants—the dishes, I add, that they crave, dream about, and always order because they are quite simply irresistible. The response is immediate, eclectic, and overwhelming, confirming my sense that London has become a city of passionate eaters and beloved restaurants. It is, to my mind, the most exciting restaurant city in the world. But how did it get that way? And when?

It's no secret that for years, centuries actually, British food was the stuff of ridicule, particularly if you were French or Italian. Think of all those literary references to stringy mutton, gray vegetables, and soggy potatoes. If you were part of the castle set, you might have avoided this abomination by hiring a French chef. The British aristocracy feuded over the best French cooks throughout the eighteenth and nineteenth centuries. Those who won the culinary jackpot ate much better and more elaborately than even, it's said, the royal family; no stringy mutton for them. The chefs, meanwhile, charged more than double their rate at home, where their talents were not considered quite so rare. The rest of Britain made do with little to tease the palate.

Baking was the exception, and elevenses (a late morning snack) and teatime were clearly when joy was permitted on and at the table: scones, clotted cream, sweet jams and rich butter, biscuits, honey, the first sandwiches (cheers to Earl Sandwich), and the first Earl Grey tea (and to you too, Earl Grey), the good stuff. And, in fact, if you look back on those books we love—the Austins, Brontes, Trollopes, for instance, you'll see that the good things (the marriage proposals, the appearance of a beloved or a handsome new neighbor) happen at tea time. Supper clearly held little romance, but why? Why is that, when the English countryside is green and fertile, its pastures filled with cows and sheep, the milk as thick as cream, and France only a channel away? Moreover, how did a country that for so long had enjoyed the reach of Empire not savor the very spices that helped make it rich? Had years of industrialization and colonial expansion so entirely obscured the desire for good food? Sure, there was Anglo curry, bottles of Claret, and pasta on continental tours or holidays in Tuscany. But, really, did no one think of bringing it home?

In 1938, a young woman by the name of Elizabeth Gwynne ran off with a married actor. The scandalous pair sailed on a small boat across the channel and down the canals of France, arriving finally at Antibes. There, Elizabeth met the writer Norman Douglas, who taught her to "search out the best, insist on it, and reject all that was bogus and second-rate." He was speaking of food, and he was speaking to the woman we now remember by her married name, Elizabeth David. For nearly a year, Elizabeth gathered and collected the recipes of Southern France before setting sail once more with her paramour, this time on an ill-fated voyage to Sicily. It was, by now, 1940 and not a good time for romantic jaunts in Europe or for showing up unannounced on foreign shores. The Italians decided Elizabeth and her lover must be spies and tossed them in jail. Elizabeth was carrying, you see, a notebook of recipes that made her arrival appear highly suspect. What could all those numbers, quantities, and lists be but a secret code? By the time they were released and had crossed the border to Yugoslavia, the recipes were long gone, as was the boat and all their money. *A Book of Mediterranean Food* would not be published for another ten years, but when it did appear in the changed world of 1950, it started a culinary revolution that I believe is finally, today, coming to fruition.

To be fair, an interest in cooking had sprung up after the First World War, when Britain saw a massive social shift with the burgeoning rise of the middle class. Suddenly women were cutting their hair, seeking independence, and, ironically, getting bored as those in the middle classes now had nannies, housekeepers, and maids to do the house work. It was no longer acceptable to get your hands dirty, but it was acceptable to learn a bit about cooking. And, of course, the chic and scandalous denizens of Bloomsbury were already busy in their gardens, planting, picking, and eating, not to mention keeping journals that turned social norms topsy-turvy, given that no one could blame their taste for freedom on either their upbringing or their education. And, as it happened, the very first serious cookbooks in Britain were written by women most decidedly

on the upper floors of the upstairs–downstairs divide. As my friend Jeremy Lee, the chef at Quo Vadis, said of these early food writers: "They were very funny, very smart, and very, very grand. I think they were all terrifying."

Elizabeth David came out of that tradition as the grand-daughter of a viscount and baron and the daughter of an MP. She was regarded as shockingly elitist, sun-drenched, and spoiled. The writing was terrific, but the recipes were meant for the well-traveled cognoscenti. It would be decades before her Mediterranean diet was in fact found to be simple and sensible and decades before extra-virgin olive oil and fresh garlic would become pantry staples.

In the 60s, Julia Child appeared on screen with a great big bang and a loud chop. She was huge—literally, figuratively, and internationally. The British adored her. Her food was a marriage of indulgence and practicality. Nothing went into her books that hadn't been tested and retested. The recipes worked. It was back to basics, but the basics were French and fabulous and rich, drenched in butter and bathed in cream. It's no wonder that after years of gorging and gout, cooks would discover or rediscover, as the case may be, Elizabeth David and her vegetables, lightly dressed in good olive oil and a squeeze of lemon juice.

The restaurant world, meanwhile, was hardly thriving in those post-war decades. There was rationing in the 50s and seemingly endless recession. Dining out was an extravagance and a formal one, at that. You might dress up and go to the Savoy for dinner or perhaps the more intimate Rules, but apart from the national pastime of fish and chips on greasy paper, the idea of grabbing a casual bite to eat is a relatively modern one. The rise of curry houses offered a cheap alternative, but the gap between the Savoy and a curry house remained wide.

Until that is, Terrance Conran opened Bibendum in 1987 in the old Michelin tire building on Fulham Road in Chelsea. Conran had fallen in love with France and with Elizabeth David's books, most particularly her *French Provencal Cooking*. That was a devotion shared by Simon Hopkinson, Bibendum's chef. Known as Hop or Hoppy among his friends, Hopkinson filled his kitchen with like-minded cooks, all of whom went on to cook at rather exceptional restaurants of their own. There was Bruce Pool, who opened Chez Bruce; Henry Harris of Racine; Phil Howard of the Square; and the aforementioned Jeremy Lee. Hop spawned a generation of great London cooks, while Conran effectively brought about a new breed of restaurant. According to Jeremy, "Terence put great food on a good table in a beautiful room." It sounds simple, but the elegance of his simplicity was groundbreaking. The dining room was filled with natural light. He took away the fuss, the frills, and the flowers and made it clean and bright. Artless, unstarred food on plain white plates—it was a revelation. And it was, more or less, affordable. Conran had cracked the supremacy of the Michelin starred oligarchy and ushered in an era of beautifully cooked simple food.

At roughly the same time, Marco Pierre White, a chef of startling if not disturbing energy, had become London's favorite *enfant terrible* and pocketed three Michelin stars. But, while his food and personality rocked the city, and his protégés, Gordon Ramsey among them, proved wildly successful, his legacy burned up in its own fire. When it came to the way Londoners now wanted to eat, it wasn't in a storm of high temper and cocaine-fueled adrenaline. That was the stuff of gossip columnists and tabloids, whereas dinner at Rowley Leigh's Kensington Place or Alastair Little's eponymous restaurant in Soho, both known for their simple, delicious fare, could become a weekly ritual. People with incomes, not private inheritances—and, frankly, those inheritances were dwindling—wanted a place they could pop into after work. The very purpose of a restaurant had changed.

In 1987, the very same year that Bibendum opened, Rose Gray and Ruthie Rogers started the River Cafe, which was to prove as influential, as delicious, as gorgeous, and far sexier—not to mention enduring. It remains one of the great restaurants of London, and I must here confide that it is probably my favorite restaurant anywhere in the world. It began as little more than a canteen, albeit a terribly well-designed one. Ruthie is married to Richard Rogers, the great architect of the Centre Pompidou in Paris and the iconic Lloyd's of London. When Richard moved his architectural practice to a warehouse in Hammersmith Wharf, overlooking the Thames, he envisioned more than an office—he envisioned a community. The logical next step was a canteen of sorts at which Richard and his colleagues could eat, drink, and gather. Having grown up in Florence, Richard craved the food of his childhood, and Ruthie knew how to cook it.

Over a pot of coffee with her friend Rose Gray, Ruthie proposed the idea of opening a restaurant. Rose replied: "Let's do it," and the River Cafe was born. The two women had studied art, lived in Italy, and shared an aesthetic. They were also fast on their way to becoming the closest of lifelong friends. Richard designed the restaurant, creating a wall of glass doors opening onto the wharf and the restaurant's herb garden and outdoor seating. By day, the room is flooded with natural light; by night, the room has a cool, modernist sensibility. It is chic and, in its brilliance, timeless.

It's nearly impossible to describe the enormous influence that the River Cafe has had on food these last three decades. Perhaps its easiest to compare Ruthie and Rose to Alice Waters. They are her British counterpoints. I'd go so far as to suggest that Ruthie and Rose got London to eat their greens—no, not just to eat them, but to seek them, crave them, and understand them. Flown in from the markets of Milan a few times a week, the ingredients used at the cafe are staggeringly good and wisely allowed to shine unburdened by fuss and fancy. And yet Ruthie and Rose's influence has as much to do with the food, as it does with the generation of cooks they nurtured. And nurture, they did. Until Rose's death in 2010, the two friends brought an exquisite maternal focus to the educating of their protégés, and the list of River Cafe alumnae reads like a Who's Who of the culinary world.

In 1994, on the opposite side of town, a bon vivant with a degree in architecture and a fervent belief that the better parts of the animals we eat were being tossed in the rubbish—to his mind, both a sacrilege and a terrible waste—opened St. John Bread and Wine. Fergus Henderson famously said: "If you kill an animal, you should eat all of it. It's only polite." His "nose to tail" cooking sprung from this philosophy and set a whole generation of cooks making offal and pig's head and trotters and tripe. Fergus is pleased that the days of being greeted on the streets of London by strangers with offal puns have come to an end, as he feels himself simply to be a cook, no more no less. But what a cook at that! And what a spirit! He calls himself "quite a happy chap," which doesn't begin to do justice to his jolly generosity and affectionate wit. It's little surprise then that his influence has also extended far beyond his own talents as a cook. He is, at heart, a teacher. He is exacting with good cheer, careful never to offend, and yet too watchful to let a lesson go unlearned. His food is both traditional and utterly contemporary, and whether it is braised squirrel or a comforting slice of apple cake, it is meant to please in some very substantial, loving way.

If Conran made simplicity chic, and Ruthie and Rose made it sexy, Fergus pared it to down to whitewashed walls. It is functional by design. When the sun shines through the skylight of St. John's, it's a terrifically cheerful place, and when the clouds are dark and glooming, a lunch of roasted marrowbones will make you feel that much better. If a restaurant's purpose is indeed functional, then its primary function must be to make its guests happy. This, as much as "nose to tail," is at the heart of St. John's mission. (Fergus would hate

my use of the word *mission*, as he insists his restaurant is just a place to eat a good lunch. Apologies, Fergus.)

What you have at St. John's is heaping portions of beautifully crafted humble food served without the slightest pretension within those bright, clean, undecorated white walls. Thirty years ago, even twenty, this would have been unthinkable. Today, it is mimicked all over the world. Its utter and complete lack of affectation has, of course, become a statement, at best, and, at worst, an affectation among the many who have tried to copy it.

As restaurants became less stuffy and more fun, traditions toppled. Food was suddenly exciting, something to talk about, to read about, even to attempt at home. In 1997, Jamie Oliver blasted the then staid world of food television with *The Naked Chef*. He made it cool to cook and cool to eat organic. The exquisite writer Nigel Slater then detailed a year of cooking at home in *The Kitchen Diaries*, focusing a gentle spotlight on this quiet, sensual pleasure. Nigella Lawson reinvented the Julia Child role, this time as a lusty domestic goddess. Porn moved out of the bedroom and into the kitchen. If the country had been a food virgin, it was no longer. That much was certain. All that was needed was a heady dose of exoticism, which Yotam Ottolenghi brought to town, drenching sweet loaves in orange blossom syrup and scattering pomegranate seeds like red rubies across the plate.

I like to think that good food is contagious. It spreads with unstoppable vitality and cannot be contained. It trickles up. It trickles down. It trickles into the countryside, circling back quite literally to whence it came. Artisan dairies throughout the United Kingdom are making small batch cheeses, farmers are raising heritage breeds, and farmer's markets are filled with fresh herbs and heirloom vegetables. The reason remains quite simple. Anyone who has tasted good food will want it again. And so it is that food in London at every level, from the corner sandwich shop to the organic gastropub to Dinner by Heston Blumenthal at the Mandarin Oriental, has upped the ante.

With this relaxing of the reins, this flexibility and appetite for new tastes, came an opening of the culinary borders. London has long been the most international city in the world, and the food finally reflects that paradigm. While New York, for instance, has tremendously good ethnic food—the gift of waves of immigration—the food in London seems more, finally, to reflect the country's history of colonization. The best chefs in London now pick and choose from a global pantry, defying classic rules and recipes with confidence and yes, perhaps, a deep-rooted sense of entitlement. It is this extraordinary boldness of flavor that has put the city at the epicenter of the culinary map. The spirit is very much "out with the old, in with the new," the old being stodgy and tasteless, and the new, seasoned and spiced. There's a great feeling of discovery right now, as if the city has suddenly woken up hungry and adventurous. No doubt because its restaurants were so ghastly for so long, it has welcomed this culinary revolution with fervent gratitude. It may be that the British, exhausted by centuries of expansion and power, were more than ready to tuck into a good meal at home.

And so it was that I found myself two years ago walking to Ottolenghi in search of tahini cookies, only to find myself instead embarking on this book. I scoured the city high, low, east, and west for the best restaurants and recipes, tested them and retested them and narrowed them down from nearly three hundred to a highly curated hundred or so. If any part of the process was painful, it was this—and stopping. There are new restaurants opening weekly, many good, some fabulous. Seek them out. The vibrancy of London restaurants will continue to astonish. In the meantime, start cooking. It's my hope that the pages to follow will soon be dog-eared and stained and turned to again and again for years to come. More than anything, this is meant to be a working cookbook. I've included only recipes that are easily made at home. Some are quick, some take a bit longer, but not a single one is fussy. That would be terribly old-fashioned and dull of me. I never did make it to Ottolenghi that fateful day, but Yotam took pity and sent me the recipe. Here it is.

TAHINI COOKIES

Preheat the oven to 400°F. Place ⅔ cup of sugar and ⅔ of unsalted butter in a mixing bowl or stand mixer and beat on a medium speed for 1 minute, until just combined but not aerated much. Keeping the beaters running, add ½ cup light tahini paste, ½ teaspoon vanilla extract, and 5 teaspoons heavy cream and then add 2 cups plus 1½ tablespoons all-purpose flour and beat for about 1 minute, until the dough comes together. Transfer to a work surface and gently knead until smooth.

Pinch off a spoonful of dough and roll into a ball between your palms. Use the back of a fork to push down lightly on top of the ball so that it flattens just slightly and takes on the marks from the tines. Place on a baking sheet lined with parchment paper. Continue with the rest of the dough, spacing the cookies a little over an inch apart. You may need two baking sheets. Sprinkle cookies with 1 teaspoon ground cinnamon and bake for 15 to 17 minutes, until golden brown. Transfer to a wire rack to cool before serving. The cookies will keep in a sealed container for roughly a week.

THE LONDON CULINARY TREE

ST. JOHN
Fergus Henderson

ANNA HANSEN, the chef and owner of The Modern Pantry, was made a Member of the Order of the British Empire in 2012 for her outstanding service to the restaurant industry. (Ginger and Cilantro Spiced Cod with Cauliflower "Couscous," Molasses Cake with Garam Masala Ice Cream and Mulled Autumn Fruits, Black Sesame Panna Cotta)

JONATHAN JONES is the chef and co-owner of the gastropub Anchor & Hope.

TIM SIADATAN is the chef and owner of Trullo. (Mussel Fennel Sourdough Soup, Pork Shoulder, Black Pepper and Mascarpone Ragu, Marsala Raisin Ice Cream)

TOM PEMBERTON, the chef and owner of Hereford Road in Notting Hill, makes sweetbreads nearly as well as his mentor.

JAMES LOWE opened Lyle's in Shoreditch with a clean white-washed look that pays homage to St. John. (Chocolate Squares)

KARL GOWARD is now the head chef at Shepard's of Westminster.

KEVIN MCFADDEN hails from both St. John and Anchor & Hope, and his food at Abbeville Kitchen in Clapham is among the best in the neighborhood.

SHAUN KELLY and EDWARD DELLING WILLIAMS both moved to Paris consecutively to be the head chefs at Au Passage.

LEE TIERNAN'S Black Axe Mangal (BAM) has received the sort of stellar reviews that make Fergus the proud mentor he is, but Lee serves his offal with flatbread and chile, taking nose-to-tail global.

JOHN OGIER, a former manager at St. John's, is now a co-owner of Lyle's.

DAN WILLIS and JONNY SMITH helped ISAAC MCHALE open Clove Club.

JOHN ROTHERAM and TOM HARRIS opened The Marksman with funding from River Cafe alum Jamie Oliver.

JUSTIN GELLATLY started Bread Ahead, a bakery school, and sells at Borough Market to those who arrive early enough to score a loaf of sourdough. (Saint Clement's Posset, Ginger Spice Steamed Puddings with Rum Syrup.)

RIVER CAFE
Ruth Rogers

HUGH FEARNLEY-WHITTINGSTALL started River Cottage, which spawned everything from a cooking school and a bestselling cookbook series to a revolution in animal husbandry and farm-to-table eating. He says he was fired from the cafe for being sloppy. I say, it forced him to rethink his habits.

APRIL BLOOMFIELD With every year, it seems April circles back closer and closer to the ingredient-driven sensibility of the café. Her New York gastropub The Spotted Pig is nothing short of an institution.

JAMIE OLIVER is possibly the most famous of cafe alumni. Few people have done more on a global scale to inspire better eating. He was discovered by the BBC in 1997 during a film shoot at the cafe and the rest, as they say, is history.

BEN O'DONOGHUE, with the help of fellow cafe alum Jamie Oliver, took his cooking skills to the screen, becoming a fixture on Australian television.

STEVIE PARLE traveled the world between his tenure at the café and opening the global-inspired Dock Kitchen at the age of 24, but his second restaurant, Rotorino in East London, marks a return to the Italian food that was his first passion. (Korean Steak with Shoestring Fries)

GILLIAN HEGARTY returned to Ireland after her tenure at the café to become one of two head chefs at Ballymaloe House, the culinary heart of Ireland.

STEVE BEADLE is the head chef at Portrait Restaurant in the National Portrait Gallery, which floats high above Trafalgar Square with breathtaking views from Nelson's Column to the Houses of Parliament.

THEO RANDALL'S Italian fare at his eponymous restaurant is true to his training. (Risotto di Peperoni)

ANNA TOBIAS is the head chef at Rochelle Canteen, owned by Margot Henderson, wife of Fergus—and so the worldw grows smaller.

ED BAINS is the chef and co-owner of the Soho fish restaurant, Randall & Aubin.

DAVID STAFFORD was brought to Rules, the oldest restaurant in the city, on something of a diplomatic mission to honor the classics and surreptitiously nudge them forward. He has done just that—beautifully. (Potted Shrimp, Bakewell Tart)

RONNIE BONETTI moved to the ever-chic Soho House.

SAM CLARK has spawned a generation of extraordinary chefs at Moro, including Jacob Kenedy, Stevie Parle, and Bob Cairns. (Summer Chopped Salad, Sea Bass with Hot Paprika Vinaigrette)

TOBIE PUTTOCK hooked up with fellow cafe alum Jamie Oliver to set up Fifteen, a training restaurant for underprivileged teenagers. He then returned to native Australia to start Fifteen Melbourne.

JORDAN FRIEDA co-owns Trullo with St. John Alum TIM SIADATAN.

A NOTE ON INGREDIENTS

I am not a fussy cook but I do believe with a great big ferocity that a few details make the difference between good food and great. One of them is homemade stock. Make it in big batches and keep a few containers on hand in the freezer. The other is Parmesan. Buy it in large wedges and grate it, as needed, in the food processor. And while I haven't fallen into the current obsession with having dozens of salt varieties, I do keep a jar of fleur de sel, a jar of Maldon sea salt flakes, and a grinder of pink Himalayan salt on hand. Use what and how much feels right to you. A basic sea salt is, of course, fine for salting water and stock, but that last pinch or grinding of good finishing salt should elevate a dish. I do love Meyer lemons, not only for their taste but because their slightly sweet side allows you to use them in abundance to perk up all manner of food. I use a microplane grater for zesting as well as for mincing garlic. If you have ready access to milk and cream that is not ultra-pasteurized, do use it—it will be fresher and creamier than those with far-reaching expiration dates. But I do realize that this luxury isn't always available. When baking, I fluff up the flour a bit before measuring it. When precision is called for, I've added weights. But, for the most part, these recipes are forgiving and meant to be cooked with confidence and pleasure. Unless otherwise noted, assume the following ten commandments hold sway.

Salt is sea salt, either Maldon or fleur de sel.

Pepper is black pepper, freshly ground.

Eggs are large and organic.

Butter is unsalted.

Stock is homemade.

Parmesan is freshly grated.

Olive oil is extra-virgin.

Sherry and balsamic vinegars are aged and unadulterated.

Lemons are organic, whenever the zest is needed, and Meyer, whenever possible.

Cooking wine is good enough to drink.

LIGHT FARE

The River Cafe Ruth Rogers and Rose Gray	CRAB AND RAW ARTICHOKE SALAD 2
Rules David Stafford	POTTED SHRIMP 6
Tom's Kitchen Tom Aikens	POTTED KILN SALMON 8
DF/Mexico Thomasina Miers	SHRIMP AGUACHILI CEVICHE WITH JALAPEÑO AND CITRUS 11
Kitty Fisher's Tomos Parry	GRILLED LEEKS, CHÈVRE, BROWN BUTTER, AND SMOKED ALMONDS 12
Terroirs Dale Osborne	MORELS WITH JERSEY ROYALS, WILD GARLIC, AND LARDO 14
Ottolenghi Yotam Ottolengh	MUNG AND HARICOTS VERTS 16
Moro Sam and Sam Clark	SUMMER CHOPPED SALAD 18
Caravan Miles Kirby	CORN AND CHORIZO FRITTERS WITH SMOKED PAPRIKA CRÈME FRAÎCHE 20
St. John Fergus Henderson	WELSH RAREBIT 22
Quo Vadis Jeremy Lee	BEETROOT AND A SOFT-BOILED EGG 24
Duck and Waffle Daniel Doherty	DUCK CONFIT OR PORK BELLY CONGEE 28
Berners Tavern Jason Atherton	ROAST CHORIZO IN A BUN WITH ONION MARMALADE AND PAPRIKA AIOLI 30

CRAB AND RAW ARTICHOKE SALAD

Every morning, Ruthie sits down with one of her head chefs, Joseph Trivelli or Sian Wyn Owen, at a round table by the window. In front of Ruthie will be an oversized notebook open to the day's page, and on it, she will have listed everything that has come in fresh that morning. They will discuss the particularities of the ingredients, the weather, and what people will want to eat, even the political climate of London, and Ruthie will write, then and there, the day's menu. She'll hand it over to be photocopied for guests and cooks alike, and then the day really begins.

Having shadowed Ruthie over several mornings, I've gotten to know her kitchen and her staff. She wouldn't call them *staff.* They are family to her. And the atmosphere is unlike any other restaurant kitchen I've ever visited. An air of ease and affection and democracy permeates the place. Cooks laugh, and they work hard. There's no shouting, no swearing, no fear. Ruthie works with tireless focus, but despite the absolute precision of her craft, she moves through the room with a maternal, nurturing, and demonstrative loyalty. She teaches. She corrects. She touches shoulders. She makes sure everyone is well. She is the restaurant's mother, supervising her children with what educators like to call positive reinforcement, but which is really quite simply love.

I'm not surprised when she gathers the team for the prelunch meeting and mentions that so-and-so is bringing her children and to feed the kids first and that X will want his usual table and that Y is just married and to send over Champagne and that Z has just gotten separated and may be feeling a bit fragile.

When Rose Gray, Ruthie's founding partner in the restaurant and closest friend, died in 2010, the staff gathered round Ruthie and stayed close. This is a tight-knit family. Come late night, the cooks will push tables together to make one very long one. Wine, dessert, espresso—everyone will come round, everyone will dig in. At the center will be Ruthie, making sure her brood is fed and happy.

This recipe is classic River Cafe in the brilliance of its simplicity. The crab and artichoke play so well together. One from the sea, one from the earth—each draws out the other's inherent sweetness. Ruthie's gift has always been in unmasking the beauty of ingredients, and here, all she needs to do that is a touch of lemon juice and a drizzle of olive oil.

A few notes on ingredients: Blue crabs, spider crabs—ask your fishmonger to recommend a sweet variety. The brown crabmeat refers to the darker meat from the head of the crab. It is quite rich, so a little goes a long way. Ruthie imports violet artichokes from Venice for this recipe, but any small to medium artichokes will work, so long as they are fresh and firm enough to snap easily. Don't be tempted to use a mandoline, as the dish has more texture if every slice is not uniform, and too thin a slice will lead only to a soggy slice.

Continued

Continued

CRAB AND RAW ARTICHOKE SALAD

SERVES 2

2 artichokes

1 lemon, halved

7 ounces white crabmeat, cooked

2 teaspoons brown crabmeat, cooked

2 tablespoons extra-virgin olive oil

2 teaspoons coarsely chopped flat-leaf parsley

Salt and pepper, to taste

Clean and prepare the artichokes by removing the tough outer leaves, leaving only the pale, tender center leaves. Trim the tops of the artichokes, exposing the choke, and remove with a teaspoon. Trim the stalk and peel with a potato peeler. Rub with half of the lemon to stop them from discoloring.

Combine the white and brown crabmeat with the olive oil, the juice of ½ the lemon, and parsley. Season with salt and pepper. Slice the artichokes lengthwise as thinly as possible and add to the crab, stirring gently to combine. Season again, transfer to a serving plate, and finish with a drizzle of olive oil.

POTTED SHRIMP

SERVES 8

12 ounces peeled tiny shrimp

4 oysters (optional)

1⅓ cups unsalted butter,
at room temperature

Zest of ½ lemon

Juice of 1 lemon

¼ teaspoon ground mace

⅛ teaspoon freshly
grated nutmeg

Large pinch of
cayenne pepper

Sea salt and ground
white pepper

¼ cup clarified butter, melted

Toast or crackers, for serving

Watercress, as garnish
(optional)

James Bond is rarely seen eating—ordering a martini, yes, and even occasionally sipping it while his eyes survey friend and foe. But he shares with his creator, Ian Fleming, a fondness for potted shrimp. This may sound rather quaint, but it is, of course, the juxtaposition that sets both off so splendidly. Potted Shrimp is traditionally made with the tiny brown shrimp native to Morecambe Bay, in northwest England, and nutmeg-scented butter. The butter acts as a preservative—at least a temporary one—and the mixture is stored in a covered pot to later be spread on brown toast.

Often made with a touch of Gentelman's Relish anchovy paste, Rules chef David Stafford instead uses oysters and their liquor to bring that briny note. "Whilst not traditionally part of the dish, I feel they bring a real salinity, or flavor of the sea, on board to balance out the natural sweetness of the shrimp," he explained. And brown shrimp are indeed sweet, much more so than their larger cousin, the prawn. These flotsam were once considered poor man's shrimp, as they would be dredged up in nets along with pricier, larger catch and ignored by all but the fishermen.

Boil the shrimp for 3 minutes, 4 if they are larger. Drain immediately and pat dry with paper towels. Remove and discard the heads and tails. If you haven't found tiny shrimp, cut larger ones into pieces no longer than ⅓ inch. Or pulse them in a food processor for a smoother texture.

If you wish to include the oysters, shuck them carefully. Remove each oyster from its shell, reserving the liquor.

Take two-thirds of the room-temperature butter and put it into a food processor along with the oysters and their liquor (if using) and roughly 1 tablespoon of the boiled shrimp. Process thoroughly.

Transfer the butter mixture to a large bowl and add the remaining shrimp, room-temperature butter, lemon zest and juice, mace, nutmeg, and cayenne. Use a wooden spoon to combine well. Season with salt and white pepper. Transfer to small ramekins or canning jars. Cover the shrimp with a thin layer of clarified butter, close the lids, and refrigerate for a few hours to set.

To serve, take the potted shrimp out of the fridge and let sit at room temperature for a half hour or so, until the mixture is spreadable but still faintly chilled. Serve with toast or crackers and a few watercress leaves, nothing more. The potted shrimp is best eaten within three days.

POTTED KILN SALMON

SERVES 4

½ to 1 teaspoon freshly squeezed lemon juice, plus a bit more for poaching

Salt and pepper

A few sprigs dill for poaching, plus 3 sprigs dill, minced

8 ounces kiln or cedar-smoked salmon, flaked

6 ounces fresh salmon fillet

Scant ½ cup mayonnaise

4 tablespoons unsalted butter, at room temperature

2 tablespoons crème fraîche

2 tablespoons horseradish sauce, drained

2 teaspoons fresh horseradish, grated

Zest of 3 lemons

6 chives, thinly sliced

¼ teaspoon smoked paprika

1 tablespoon diced shallots

Clarified butter, for storing

Toast, gherkins, watercress, for serving

Salmon makes for a less traditional pot than shrimp, but set one on the table and watch the contents be devoured within minutes. Spread on a thin crisp of toast, this is, for me, a lighter version of Sunday lox and bagels. It is picnic fare, brunch food, hors d'oeuvre, appetizer, and midnight snack. It looks quaint in a covered glass canning jar, but it adores a glass of Champagne. The only drawback is that it doesn't keep as well as the Potted Shrimp, as the horseradish seems to take over if given half a chance. So do eat this within a day of being made.

Fill a skillet or braising dish with three inches of water and bring to a boil over high heat. Reduce the heat to a simmer and add a squeeze of lemon juice, salt, pepper, and a few sprigs of dill. Poach the fresh salmon until cooked. The salmon is done when it is a uniform color and easily flaked. Leave it to cool and then flake.

Have the ingredients at room temperature. Mix everything but the poached salmon, butter and garnishes together in a bowl. Gently fold in the flaked salmon.

Transfer to small lidded ramekins or canning jars and smooth the top. Cover with a thin layer of clarified butter, close the lids, and refrigerate for at least 2 hours to set.

Remove from the refrigerator 30 minutes before serving. Serve with toast, sliced gherkins, and a few watercress leaves.

SHRIMP AGUACHILI CEVICHE WITH JALAPEÑO AND CITRUS

SERVES 4 TO 6 AS A STARTER

Juice of 4 limes

Juice of 1 pink grapefruit

2 or 3 jalapeños, seeded and chopped

2½ tablespoons demerara sugar

2 tablespoons 100 percent agave tequila, blanco or reposado

1 teaspoon Asian fish sauce

1 teaspoon flaky sea salt, such as Maldon

1 small or ½ large Lebanese cucumber, unpeeled

1 pound large shrimp, unpeeled

2 shallots, finely chopped

A handful of chopped fresh assorted herbs, such as chervil, cilantro, and mint

2 cups cherry tomatoes, quartered

1 Hass avocado, pitted, peeled, and diced

Tortilla chips, for serving (optional)

DF stands for *Distrito Federal*, another name for Mexico City. That the restaurant DF/Mexico is situated right off Brick Lane in East London is oddly fitting, given that Brick Lane has long been a hub of immigrant cuisine, whether it be Ashkenazi delis or the more prevalent Bengali curry houses. Mexican food, I believe, is a first for the street, but Brick Lane has undergone many a change in recent years, spawning nightclubs and art galleries. Today, even the graffiti on Brick Lane is signed by famous street artists, and the lane is routinely closed for the filming of music videos. Every hipster seems to want to make reference to this ever-changing icon of immigrant energy—or, at least, to pay it a visit. DF/Mexico fits right into the hood's contemporary vibe. It pays homage to diner culture with a wink and a grin and really good food.

In a blender, combine the lime and grapefruit juices, 2 jalapeños, sugar, tequila, fish sauce, salt, and one-third of the cucumber. Blend until smooth and adjust the seasoning. Taste and decide if you want to add the third jalapeño.

Peel and devein the shrimp. Remove and discard the heads and tails and slice in half lengthwise. Transfer to a bowl with the citrus mixture and the shallots. Refrigerate for 15 to 45 minutes to let the citrus juice "cure" the shrimp, but be careful not to let them cure too long or the shrimp will turn rubbery. Tommi (Thomasina) cures hers for 15 minutes, but anything up to 45 minutes is fine.

Just before serving, cut the remaining cucumber in half lengthwise, scoop out the seeds, and cut into thin slices. Stir most of the herbs into the aguachile, along with the tomatoes, cucumber, and avocado.

Serve in small bowls, spooning the sauce over the shrimp. Sprinkle with the remaining herbs. Serve with tortilla chips.

GRILLED LEEKS, CHÈVRE, BROWN BUTTER, AND SMOKED ALMONDS

SERVES 2

4 leeks

12 tablespoons unsalted butter

1 or 2 sprigs thyme

¼ cup fresh (young) chèvre

4 teaspoons whole milk

Sea salt and white pepper

1½ ounces smoked almonds, finely chopped

NOTE Choose leeks that are not too thick and not too dirty.

London has gone char-grilled, barbecued, and smokin' crazy, from Jamie Oliver's "cathedral to fire and food" Barbecoa to Smokehouse, where the short ribs in the *boeuf bourguignon* are cooked in the smoker. At Kitty Fisher's, in the tiniest kitchen ever, Tomos Parry works his magic over a wood grill. When I asked him why he chose a wood grill for his kitchen, Tomos laughed and reminded me that there was no room for a proper stove. Out of limits comes brilliance, as this simple salad more than proves. When Tomos gave me this recipe, he urged me not to be afraid of blackening the leeks. And so I offer his same advice to you.

Preheat the oven to 325°F.

If the leeks are dirty, slice down the green stalk and flush the entire leek by holding it under a faucet of running cold water. Don't worry too much if there's still a bit of dirt as the outer leaves will be discarded before serving.

Grill the leeks over a very hot grill, turning them often, until completely burnt; they should be black all over. This will take about 20 minutes.

Melt the butter in a frying pan over medium heat until it turns a rich brown. Immediately remove the brown butter from heat and add the thyme. Set aside somewhere warm to allow the thyme to steep. You may need to reheat the butter slightly before serving it. The thyme and milk solids may be discarded.

Bake the leeks until cooked, about 12 minutes. The leeks should be tender but not mushy. Set aside for a few minutes to cool the leeks slightly.

Using a fork, lightly whisk the chèvre and the milk together and season with salt and white pepper.

Peel the blackened outer layers of the leeks back to reveal the smoky, silken tender interior. You can either discard the blackened layers or serve the leeks with them still attached for dramatic effect.

Top the leeks with the chèvre, drizzle liberally with the brown butter, and sprinkle generously with the smoked almonds.

MORELS WITH JERSEY ROYALS, WILD GARLIC, AND LARDO

SERVES I

3½ ounces tiny potatoes, such as Jersey Royals

3½ ounces fresh morel mushrooms

3½ tablespoons Madeira

3½ tablespoons unsalted butter

Sea salt and black pepper

3 wild garlic leaves (only the smallest, most tender leaves)

3 slices of lardo (sliced as thin as possible on a meat slicer)

Pinch of piment d'Espelette

A few wild garlic flowers, for garnish

———

NOTE This recipe is easily double or tripled.

This recipe is an ode to the ephemeral romance of spring. Hidden under a warm, transparent veil of lardo rest morel mushrooms, the leaves and tiny flowers of wild garlic, sweet Royal Jersey potatoes, and the faint perfume of Madeira—an exquisite bouquet of tastes and textures. Put it on your calendar for late April, or remember that when the daffodils bloom, the ingredients for this dish will ever so briefly appear on the menu at Terroirs *and* at your farmers' market. It is, I realize, the least practical recipe in this book. But there are times when a three-season suit is rather less appealing than hand-stitched linen.

Jersey, the largest of the Channel Islands, has a surprisingly temperate climate. Having belonged at times to the French and at times to the British, it is best known by historians of that enduring feud. For the gourmand, however, it is known for the rich milk produced by Jersey cattle and for the tiny, ever-so-sweet spring potatoes known simply as Jersey Royals—today, the island's largest export. Not to worry if you can't source these beauties. I've found peanut-size Yukon golds and tiny baby reds quite easily, and they both work well here. Do make sure your lardo is sliced very thin.

At Terroirs, this dish is paired with a 2013 Irancy "Les Mazelots," produced by Vini Viti Vinci, the project of winemaker Nicolas Vauthier. This young red Burgundy has an energetic palate and fits in well with the extensive list of natural and organic wines for which Terroirs is known.

Scrub the potatoes clean and boil them until easily pricked with a fork.

If necessary, lightly wash the morels, as they will most likely hold some dirt in their pocket. Do not brush them and do try to use as little water as possible. Gently pat dry with paper towels.

Combine the Madeira and butter in a saucepan over medium-low heat and cook, stirring, until an emulsion forms.

Add the morels and cook in the Madeira butter until tender, about 1 minute. Add the potatoes, cook until heated through, and season with salt and pepper.

To assemble, place the morels and potatoes in the middle of an ovenproof plate and coat with a few spoonfuls of the Madeira butter.

Lay the wild garlic leaves on top of the morels and potatoes.

Cover the wild garlic with the slices of lardo.

Place the plate under the broiler for a couple of seconds just to warm and soften the lardo. It will become translucent, and you will see the wild garlic leaves just underneath.

Sprinkle with piment d'Espelette and scatter with wild garlic flowers.

MUNG AND HARICOTS VERTS

SERVES 4

⅓ cup white wine vinegar

2 tablespoons sugar

1 small red onion, thinly sliced

1 cup dried green mung beans

1 pound haricots verts, trimmed

½ cup olive oil

2 cloves garlic, thinly sliced

1 red chile, such as a Fresno, thinly sliced, with seeds

1 tablespoon grated fresh ginger

2 teaspoons black mustard seeds

1 teaspoon cumin seeds

1 teaspoon fennel seeds

2 sprigs fresh curry leaves

1 lime, the zest cut into a few long strips

½ cup chopped fresh cilantro, chopped

Salt and pepper, to taste

A few years ago, my mother, Jane Kramer, wrote a remarkable profile of Yotam in the *New Yorker*. The profile was titled "The Philosopher Chef," and it began, not with a description of his food, but with mention of his master's thesis in the "genius program" at Tel Aviv University. When he sent the manuscript to his parents, Yotam attached (or rather buried) a note that read: "Here is my dissertation. I've decided to take a break from academia and go to cooking school." When my mother met him, years later, he wore the "happy smile of a man who has left behind the life of the mind for baked eggplants with lemon thyme, za'atar, pomegranate seeds, and buttermilk-yogurt sauce." This smile is same one I see on Ottolenghi customers. It is a smile that comes from seeing the vivid colors of his salads and the tender crumb of his cakes, from sniffing the exotic spices that season his grains and the hints of rose and orange blossom that perfume his sweets.

This salad is very Ottolenghi in that it marries a world of ingredients into a seamless whole. The mung beans are Asian, the haricots verts French, the spices Indian. The flavor is bold. And it is with this boldness that Yotam has redefined London food, perhaps more than any other chef in the past decade.

Place the vinegar and sugar in a small saucepan over medium-high heat. Cook for about 2 minutes, until the sugar has dissolved. Stir in the onion, remove from the heat, and set aside to cool for at least an hour.

Place the mung beans in a medium saucepan with plenty of water. Bring to a boil, lower the heat, and simmer for 25 minutes, until the beans are soft but still retain a bite. Drain, refresh in cold water, and set aside.

Bring a pot of salted water to a boil. Add the haricots verts and cook for 4 minutes, until just short of tender. Drain, refresh in cold water, and set aside to dry.

Heat the oil in a sauté pan, add the garlic, chile, ginger, mustard seeds, cumin, fennel, curry leaves, and lime zest. Sauté over medium-high heat for 4 to 5 minutes, until the garlic is golden brown. Discard the curry leaves and lime zest, and pour the spice mixture over the mung beans.

Strain the onions and fold them into the salad, along with the haricots verts and cilantro. Season as needed and serve immediately.

SUMMER CHOPPED SALAD

There are few chefs spoken of with the sort of affectionate reverence that husband Samuel and wife Samantha inspire. The restaurant Moro feels young and of the moment, as do Sam and Sam, but that belies the enormous influence it has had since opening in 1997. It all began when Sam and Sam met, fell in love, got married, bought a camper, and spent three months driving and eating their way through Spain, Morocco, and the Sahara. They returned to London and opened what must have been the first Moorish restaurant in the city in the then backwater of Exmouth Market. They were not, exactly, without culinary experience. Samantha had cooked at the River Cafe, cutting her teeth with the likes of Jamie Oliver and Theo Randall. And Samuel had cooked at the Eagle, one of the earliest and most admired gastropubs. Perhaps it was being so well mentored that has led Sam and Sam to spawn their own generation of wonderful and devoted cooks, including Stevie Parle of Dock Kitchen and Jacob Kenedy of Bocca di Lupo.

Now, about this Summer Chopped Salad. I say *summer*, but there's always a chopped salad at Moro. The ingredients simply shift with the seasons. What makes this salad compelling is that it has three dressings, each adding a dimension that gives the salad character and substance. The salad is first tossed with a vinaigrette, then drizzled with a garlic yogurt dressing, then drizzled with an Aleppo-infused browned butter. The two Sams may include a few pickled vegetables for a note of zing and surprise, sometimes in the form of pickled chiles. I like to add a few sliced cornichons, which isn't very Moorish of me. Pickled beets, carrots, or cabbage—use what you have.

There's no need for a proper recipe here. Simply toss a bounty of chopped cucumbers, tomatoes, sweet onions, wild arugula, parsley, mint, radishes, and whatever greens you find at the market in a big salad bowl. Make more if you are wildly hungry, less if you are not.

For the first dressing, toss the salad with a really good extra-virgin olive oil, freshly squeezed lemon juice, and season to taste with a bit of Maldon sea salt and freshly ground pepper. Divide among your serving plates.

For the second dressing, crush a small clove of fresh garlic with a ½ teaspoon salt. Whip this into a cup of Greek yogurt. I add table-spoon of olive oil to loosen it a bit. Drizzle as much of it as you'd like onto the salad. The idea here, of course, isn't to drown the greens in yogurt but rather to give them a nice tangy edge, so do be sparing.

For the third dressing, melt ¼ cup of unsalted butter in a saucepan over medium heat. When the butter starts to turn a lovely golden brown and gives off a nutty aroma, remove it from heat and stir in 1 teaspoon ground Aleppo chile or ½ teaspoon cayenne pepper. Drizzle a bit of this lovely red butter over the yogurt dressing. The salad will be quite pretty, wearing its hat of yogurt and ribbon of chile.

CORN AND CHORIZO FRITTERS WITH SMOKED PAPRIKA CRÈME FRAÎCHE

SERVES 4

FRITTERS

7 ounces fresh Spanish chorizo or morcilla sausages

1½ cups all-purpose flour

½ cup polenta

2 teaspoons sea salt

1½ teaspoons baking powder

½ teaspoon sugar

¼ teaspoon smoked paprika

1 cup whole milk

⅔ cup full-fat Greek yogurt

2 eggs

1 cup fresh or frozen corn kernels

½ bunch scallions, white part only, thinly sliced

2 tablespoons finely chopped fresh cilantro

Vegetable oil, for frying

Caravan was one of the first places in London to serve serious coffee. In the basement is a working coffee roastery, providing a sensory lifeline to those waiting for their caffeine fix. Walk inside and you will find people sniffing the air in anticipation. Situated on a busy corner in Farringdon's Exmouth Market, Caravan helped turn this neighborhood into the trendy one it is today. Of course, being a five-minute walk from the great restaurant Moro didn't hurt. If the roastery made Caravan a coffee destination, it was the food that made people stay. Miles may hail from New Zealand, but his menu can only be described as global. The last time I visited, I saw Nepalese Vegetable Momo, Miso-Cured Salmon, Egyptian Tagine, and these Spanish-American fritters on the menu.

These fritters are for hangovers and lazy Sundays and hungry kids just home from soccer practice. For vegetarians, cook them without the sausage; simply increase the amount of smoked paprika. For the more adventurous, try making them with morcilla sausage, which is what is used at the restaurant. This Spanish blood sausage is dark—dark in color and dark with the ritual slaughter that is integral to its production. I prefer the brighter notes of chorizo on a Sunday morning.

If you've moved past morning coffee, I recommend a margarita. Top the fritters with sliced avocados, a squeeze of lemon, a drizzle of olive oil, snipped chives, a scattering of cilantro, a dusting of paprika, and a dollop of smoked paprika crème fraîche.

To make the fritters, either remove the casings and crumble the meat of the sausages or chop them into dice. Fry the sausage pieces in a frying pan over medium-high heat until they've rendered much of their fat and have started to color. Remove to a paper towel–lined plate to drain.

In a large bowl, combine the flour, polenta, salt, baking powder, sugar, and paprika. In another bowl, combine the milk, yogurt, and eggs, giving the eggs a little beating with a fork. Pour the milk mixture into the flour mixture and stir together with a wooden spoon until combined. There should be no dry, floury pockets. Fold in the sausage, corn, green onions, and cilantro.

PAPRIKA CRÈME FRAÎCHE

1 tablespoon olive oil

1½ teaspoons sweet
smoked paprika

1 cup crème fraîche

1 tablespoon fresh chives,
chopped

Salt and pepper

ACCOMPANIMENTS

2 ripe avocados

Freshly squeezed lemon juice

Olive oil

Chopped fresh chives

Chopped fresh cilantro

Salt and pepper, to taste

Sweet smoked paprika

If possible, let the batter sit for 10 minutes at room temperature or up to an hour or two in the fridge. (This is a good time to prepare the crème fraîche.)

To make the paprika crème fraîche, gently warm the oil in a small saucepan over medium heat and then add the paprika and stir. This allows the paprika to dissolve and sets its aroma free. Remove from the heat after 1 minute and set aside to cool. Stir the paprika oil into the crème fraîche and season to taste with salt and pepper.

To cook the fritters, heat a little vegetable oil in a nonstick pan or well-seasoned cast-iron frying pan over a lively heat. When the oil is hot but not smoking, spoon in fritter-size dollops of batter, about ¼ cup per fritter. Cook until the bottoms are golden, then flip and cook the second sides. Remove to a paper towel–lined plate. Repeat with remaining batter. These do need to be eaten right away, so hurry everyone to the table.

To serve, divide the fritters between serving plates. Add a dollop of the crème fraîche and half an avocado, peeled and sliced, to each plate. Give the avocado a squeeze of lemon juice and a drizzle of olive oil. Scatter everything with the chives and cilantro and sprinkle with salt and pepper and smoked paprika.

WELSH RAREBIT

SERVES 4

A knob of unsalted butter

1 tablespoon all-purpose flour

1 teaspoon English mustard powder

¼ teaspoon cayenne pepper, or to taste

⅞ cup Guinness stout

A very long splash of Worcestershire sauce (and set the bottle on the table)

1 pound mature, strong cheddar cheese, grated

4 large pieces of good toast

Lunching at St. John last fall, I looked over to the next table and found two gentlemen tucking—and that really is the precise word here—into their five-course lunch. They were both portly, somewhere around sixty, and might have been brothers. They were served without ordering, and so I assumed they were regulars. Both wore bowties that were soon covered by the napkins they'd hung from their shirt collars. Classic eaters, I'd call them, and what better place to show their bona fides as gourmands than at St. John, which truly is a classic London restaurant if ever there was one. In my experience, diners at St. John attend to their meals with absolute seriousness and joy, and in this way, my two gentlemen fit right into the worldly jeans- and T-shirt-wearing crowd around them.

Fergus, with whom I was lunching that afternoon, clearly adored these two regulars, although not a word was spoken between them. All was proper, formal, and discreet. But when, after several courses had come and gone, the gentlemen were served Welsh rarebit and glasses of port, Fergus motioned me to observe. He wanted me to appreciate the fact that some old-timers still have their rarebit and port at lunch as a final savory course. Moreover, he wanted me to note that they cut their rarebits the correct way—by first scoring the rarebit with crisscrossing diagonal lines, creating channels for Worcestershire sauce. Seeing the delight in Fergus's eyes, I realized that he took far more pleasure in watching these two men eat their lunch than he would ever take in his extraordinary success. I've included this iconic recipe, which also appears in his book *The Whole Beast: From Nose to Tail Eating.*

Melt the butter in a saucepan over a lively heat, stir in the flour, and let the mixture cook until it smells biscuity but is not browning. Add the mustard powder and cayenne pepper, stir in the Guinness and Worcestershire sauce, and then gently melt in the cheese. When it's all of one consistency, remove from the heat, pour out into a shallow container, and let set. Spread a ½ inch thick layer on the toast and place under a broiler. Eat when bubbling golden brown. If you like, drizzle a bit of Worcestershire sauce over the top.

BEETROOT AND A SOFT-BOILED EGG

SERVES 6

4½ pounds assorted small
beets of every color
and variety

⅔ cup sugar

1 cup very good red
wine vinegar

1 cup of water

6 eggs

2 tablespoons sugar

2 tablespoons white
wine vinegar

2 teaspoons good
Dijon mustard

6 tablespoons heavy cream

Salad leaves

Salt and pepper, to taste

A stick of fresh horseradish

Chopped fresh chives

Don't assume this is just another beet salad. It's not. It's better. Jeremy gives the beets a very light pickling of sugar and white wine vinegar, which draws forth the natural sweetness of the beets and counters the sharp grating of fresh horseradish he showers on the salad immediately before serving it. With a creamy Dijon dressing and a soft-boiled egg or two, it has an appealing medley of textures, color, and flavor. As I find Jeremy's writing completely irresistible, I've left the recipe exactly as he emailed it to me, only adding U.S. measurements:

Beetroot and a soft boiled egg. A cheery salad. It is certainly worth seeking out a purveyor of fine vegetables who may well have several differing varieties and colors of beetroot to jolly up this salad even more. These quantities will feed 6 folk happily.

Trim and wash well the beetroots. Place in a suitable pot to steam until quite cooked through and tender. When done, remove them to a bowl and when cooled slightly, rub the skin away from the beetroot. When all are peeled, cut the beetroots into large pieces, of roughly the same size.

In a bowl, whisk together the ⅔ cup of sugar and the red wine vinegar until the sugar is dissolved and add the cup of water. Pour this light pickle over the beetroots and cover well. Refrigerate for a few hours. These pickles will happily last a week in the fridge.

Place a bowl of ice water next to the stove. Bring a pan of water to a furious boil. Drop in the eggs and let cook for 3 minutes once the water returns to a boil. Transfer the eggs to the bowl of ice water, and once cooled, peel carefully, storing them in another bowl of ice water.

To make the dressing, dissolve the 2 tablespoons of sugar and the white wine vinegar in a bowl. Stir in the mustard until smooth, then add the cream. Cover, and refrigerate.

Peel the horseradish and keep covered until needed. Wash the salad leaves, dry well, and keep covered. Should chives be at hand, slice them very thinly in readiness.

For each serving, tumble the salad leaves onto a plate and then heap the beetroots thereon. Cut one egg in half and lay upon the beetroots, seasoning with a little salt and pepper. Liberally spoon over the mustard dressing then grate horseradish all over swiftly, followed by the chives.

DUCK CONFIT OR PORK BELLY CONGEE

SERVES 4

CONGEE

1½ cups short-grain rice

7½ cups water

2 knobs fresh ginger, peeled and crushed or pounded

3 cloves garlic, peeled

1½ teaspoons salt

TOPPINGS

A knob of unsalted butter

4 to 8 eggs, depending on the crowd's hunger

1½ pounds of your favorite leftover meat, such as confit duck legs, cooked duck breast, cooked pork belly, sliced

Soy sauce, for drizzling

Crushed roasted hazelnuts, for topping

1 bunch scallions, sliced (white and a bit of the palest green)

A small knob fresh ginger, peeled and julienned

Leaves from 1 bunch cilantro

Sriracha sauce, for drizzling

Duck and Waffle is unlike any other restaurant I know in London. It sits high in the sky on the fortieth floor of the Heron Tower in the City of London, as the financial district is known. It is open 24-7 and the views, particularly at sunrise and sunset, are spectacular. At 11 p.m., you may find the entire Arsenal Football Club drinking to victory and feeding postgame hunger. At 4 a.m., you may find Chinese businessmen eating lunch in a fog of jet lag. At 7 a.m., you may find a film crew desperate for Daniel's comforting fare after a night of shooting in the rain. There's something very *Lost in Translation* about the place. And then there is the food, which is anything but lost.

Daniel makes the food we crave. His menu reads like a GPS diagram of our internal longings. There is, of course, the eponymous Duck and Waffle, a leg of duck confit served on a waffle with a fried duck egg and drizzled with mustard maple syrup. For the sake of our collective health, I am not including the recipe. There's a rib eye with Marmite hollandaise. Try it, and you may fall in love with Marmite in a way you never could have imagined. Then there are meatballs and spicy ox cheek doughnuts with apricot jam and smoked paprika sugar and, a cult favorite, the foie gras crème brûlée.

But the recipe I include here has become a favorite at home, as it adapts well to a variety of leftover meats and makes good use of pantry items. For anyone under the weather, suffering a hangover, or seeking the comfort of rice, the shock of hot sauce, the warmth of ginger, the protein of a fried or poached egg, and the freshness of cilantro in one brothy bundle, this is your dish. Daniel occasionally makes it with smoked haddock or with duck hearts skewered on rosemary sprigs, but I prefer the succulence of pork belly or duck confit. Occasionally, if I have a good, rich stock on hand, I'll add a ladleful. This is excellent with leftover Kakuni (page 171). Don't limit yourself. This is meant not so much as a recipe, but as an invitation to assemble a bit of this and a bit of that. Adapt it to your liking.

Place the rice in a fine sieve and rinse it under cold running water, gently swishing the rice around occasionally, for 5 minutes. Transfer the rice to a bowl and add water to cover by a few inches. Set aside for 10 minutes, then drain.

Combine the washed rice with the water, ginger, garlic, and salt in a medium pot. Bring to a boil, then cover, lower the heat, and simmer for 15 to 20 minutes, until the grains start to break down and overcook slightly. Resist the urge to remove the rice from the heat too early. You actually want the rice to be overcooked and soupy when making congee.

Set aside and keep warm. Just before serving, discard the ginger and garlic.

When the congee is almost done, melt the butter in a frying pan over medium heat. When the butter is foaming, fry the eggs to your liking. Reheat your meat, whether it be duck or pork. It should be hot.

To assemble, ladle generous portions of congee into 4 warmed, wide, and shallow soup bowls. Drizzle with soy sauce to taste. Working in a circle so that each topping is well displayed, arrange your meat, fried eggs, hazelnuts, scallions, ginger, and cilantro over the top. Give the whole thing a good drizzle of Sriracha and serve immediately.

ROAST CHORIZO IN A BUN WITH ONION MARMALADE AND PAPRIKA AIOLI

SERVES 4

MARMALADE

4 tablespoons unsalted butter

3 Spanish onions, thinly sliced

¾ cup red wine

½ cup sugar

5 tablespoons good sherry vinegar

Salt and pepper, to taste

AIOLI

2 egg yolks

2 tablespoons white wine vinegar

1 tablespoon Dijon mustard

2 teaspoons smoked paprika

1½ cups vegetable oil

Salt and pepper, to taste

2 tablespoons butter at room temperature

4 brioche hot dog buns

4 fresh chorizo sausages, cooked

Jason is a tightly wound, very controlling, and superb chef. Nothing escapes his notice. Chatting one afternoon at Pollen Street Social, the most formal of his London restaurants, he told me that his dream was to have a publicly traded restaurant company. He wants to see his name on the stock exchange. Whenever I interview chefs, the conversation most often turns (rather too predictably, at times) to the beauty of seasonal produce, to heritage breeds of cattle, and to the soulful pleasures of craftsmanship. Rarely does a chef admit to the kind of striving, personal ambition that Jason described to me so bluntly. I immediately understood why he is admired, but perhaps not always beloved, by his colleagues. Yet the next evening, at a fund raiser at the River Cafe for underprivileged children, it was Jason who pushed some of the best-known chefs in the UK to donate more of their time and resources to this underserved community. This was a man, I realized, who had lifted himself by his bootstraps out of a rather bleak childhood to become a phenomenal success, with restaurants in Shanghai, Hong Kong, Sydney, and Dubai. While he does not tolerate failure in himself and is known to wield a fairly Machiavellian rule in his many kitchens, I detected a deep well of compassion, borne of memory, for those truly in need. Of the many chefs I've met over the years, he is the most driven, the most haunted, and the most determined.

What does all this have to do with a hot dog? you must be asking. This: Inherent in Jason's ambition is a very keen eye. He has clearly spent years watching what people like to eat, what they crave, and what makes them return again and again to a restaurant. Here, he nails it. The spicy chorizo, the slippery, sweet-and-sour marmalade, and the decadent, smoky aioli make this dish imminently crave-worthy. When convenient, grill the chorizo. In winter, however, it can be roasted in a hot oven, then broiled or even pan-fried. Whatever your source of fuel, do make sure the sausage is browned, not boiled, and serve it piping hot. Save some of the marmalade to add dimension to almost any meat sandwich. But do remember to warm it up. It's not good straight out of the fridge. Jason uses the oil that the chorizo has rendered in cooking to make his aioli.

I've tried to replicate that effect with smoked paprika, as it isn't always possible, let alone safe, to catch drippings while working over a hot grill. For the risk takers among you, gather what chorizo drippings you can and reduce the amount of oil I've listed in the recipe.

To make the onion marmalade, melt the butter in a wide skillet over medium-low heat. Add the onions, reduce the heat to low, and cook for 45 minutes, stirring occasionally, until the onions are meltingly soft and caramelized.

Stir in the wine, sugar, and vinegar, and give the bottom of the pan a scraping with a wooden spoon to get any good bits unstuck.

Cook 20 to 30 minutes longer, until the liquid evaporates. Season with salt and pepper. Keep warm or reheat just before serving.

To make the aioli, use a balloon whisk to whisk together the egg yolks, vinegar, mustard, and paprika in a bowl. Very slowly pour in the oil, whisking constantly, until it has the texture of mayonnaise. Season with salt and pepper.

To assemble the hot dogs, butter and toast the brioche buns to your liking. Fill each bun with a chorizo sausage, a good lathering of marmalade, and a slick of aioli. Serve immediately with plenty of napkins.

SOUPS

SOUP OF PEAS AND BEANS

SERVES 4

9 ounces little haricot beans, Navy beans, or Alubia blanca beans

1 bay leaf, preferably fresh

2 thick slices smoked, streaky bacon

1 pound peas in their pods or 1 cup shelled peas

9 ounces waxy potatoes, peeled and cubed

1 bunch mint

1 clove garlic, unpeeled

½ cup freshly grated Parmesan

⅓ cup excellent extra-virgin olive oil

Salt and pepper, to taste

Jeremy's cooking is not fancy, but it is superbly crafted, even at the level of this simplest of soups. And by crafted, I do not mean artfully composed, although it is clearly that, but rather that it reflects an understanding of his ingredients which, over years has become intuitive. Jeremy is both precise and fluid, cooking with the casual wisdom of a master. I include this soup because it is so much more delicious than other seemingly similar soups and because I learn something from every one of Jeremy's recipes and believe you might as well. It is really no more than a bean soup with a mint version of pistou swirled in at the end. Jeremy makes it with the tiny little haricot beans of Spain, known in the United States as navy beans, and I make it with Alubia blanca, a little white bean from Steve Sando of Rancho Gordo that has become a favorite. I call Steve every time I cook anything with beans. I'm entirely dependent on his knowledge and his heirloom bean company. He found these beans growing in the shade of a volcano just outside of Mexico City. They are delicate, and when cooked low and slow, they hold their shape until they melt in your mouth.

Soak the beans overnight in plenty of water. The next day, drain the beans, discarding the soaking water. Rinse the beans and put them in a large heavy pot with plenty of water and the bay leaf. Bring the beans to a boil and lower the heat to the barest of simmers. Add the bacon and leave the soup to cook for a couple of hours, until just tender. Do not add salt as it will toughen the beans.

Pod the peas, if needed, and rinse. Rinse the potatoes under cold running water until all traces of starch have been washed away. Add the potatoes to the beans, together with more water, if required. (If there is too little liquid in the pot, it will cloud up and turn starchy.) When the potato is almost cooked, add the peas and, again, more water, if required. Cook the soup for 15 to 20 minutes longer, until all is cooked to your liking.

Meanwhile, pick and chop the mint. Peel and chop the garlic. Stir together the mint, garlic, Parmesan, and olive oil.

When all of the soup's ingredients are soft and yielding to the tongue, season with salt and pepper. Discard the bacon slices and bay leaf. Ladle into warmed bowls and swirl with a generous spoonful of the mint pistou.

FENNEL AND WATERCRESS SOUP

SERVES 4

SOUP

2 tablespoons unsalted butter

1 tablespoon olive oil

3 bulbs fennel or 5 small bulbs wild fennel, coarsely chopped, feathery fronds reserved and snipped

2 stalks celery, finely chopped

2 yellow onions, finely chopped

Sea salt

3 tablespoons Pernod

4 cups vegetable or chicken stock, preferably homemade

Leaves from 2 bunches watercress

CRÈME FRAÎCHE

½ cup crème fraîche

Juice of ½ lemon, or to taste

Salt and pepper

1 tablespoon chopped fresh chives, snipped

I confess to being highly partial to all things fennel. It is, for me, a green candy. In New York, I've been known to walk through near blizzard conditions for the fennel juice at City Bakery. It is the color of health—in other words that of spinach—but it is really no more than fennel, cold-pressed sugarcane, and Kirby cucumber. It tastes of the brightest candy in the world. You might, then, imagine that the sight of this soup on the menu at Newman Street Tavern had me at its first word. It is, of course, not a sweet soup, but the licorice note is enticing and the watercress an excellent peppery addition. Garrick, my son, was almost entirely through a bowl before he noticed he was eating something green, at which point, with a rather dramatic flourish, he suddenly dropped his spoon.

If you can find small, young bulbs of wild fennel at a farmers' market, you will be in for a real treat, but any very fresh, seasonal fennel will do. The restaurant uses vegetable stock, but I prefer the less intrusive taste of a homemade chicken stock. I also have a rather liberal hand with the Pernod. Do save some of the fronds to use as a garnish. And try to avoid making this soup in advance. Time diminishes its vividness. Cook it only as long as is needed and serve immediately.

To make the soup, in a large skillet with a lid, warm the butter and oil until the butter melts. Add the fennel, celery, and onions and stir to coat with the fat. Season with salt. Cover the skillet and sweat the vegetables for 10 minutes, until just soft. Raise the heat to medium high, add the Pernod, and cook, stirring for a minute or two, until the alcohol evaporates. Add the stock and simmer, uncovered, for 15 minutes, until the vegetables are tender.

While the soup is cooking, whisk the crème fraîche, lemon juice, salt, and pepper together and fold in the chives. Just before serving, add the watercress to the hot soup. Using caution and working in small batches, puree the soup in a blender until it is as smooth as silk. Transfer each batch back to the pot, as you go, and give the whole thing a stir and a taste before serving. If needed, season with salt and pepper. Ladle into warmed bowls, dollop with the crème fraiche, and lightly sprinkle with the fennel fronds. Serve immediately.

SMOKED PAPRIKA, PIQUILLO PEPPER, AND TOMATO SOUP WITH CHÈVRE TOASTS

SERVES 4

28 ounces canned San Marzano plum tomatoes

2 or 3 tablespoons olive oil, plus more for the crostini

1 or 2 red chiles, or to taste

14 ounces jarred piquillo peppers

1 teaspoon smoked paprika

Pinch of sea salt

1 clove garlic, finely chopped

2 tablespoons excellent balsamic or sherry vinegar

2 cups homemade chicken stock, vegetable stock, or water

1 or 2 handfuls cooked chickpeas, if desired

Half a baguette

Velvety chèvre of your choice, for spreading

This is a fiery winter soup that will banish any chill. But it is not without dimension. The vinegar provides a raisiny sweet-and-sour note, and the chèvre brings richness. Josep serves it with floating toasted slices of baguette topped with Monte Enebro, a Spanish goat cheese, but I also like to drop in bits of chèvre rather unceremoniously. Stirred into the soup, the cheese enriches the texture and mellows the chiles. If you're particularly hungry or want to turn the soup into a main course, a handful or two of cooked chickpeas will provide substance and protein.

In a food processor, pulse the canned tomatoes until they are somewhere between diced and pureed.

Warm the olive oil in a stockpot over medium heat. Finely dice the chiles. (For a milder soup, use only one chile and don't include the seeds.) Add the chiles to the warm oil. While the chile is cooking, slice the *piquillo* peppers into strips and add to the pot, followed by the paprika and a pinch of salt. Sauté for 5 minutes, then add the garlic, and cook 2 minutes longer. Raise the heat to high, add the vinegar, stir a moment, then add the tomatoes, and simmer for 10 minutes. Add the stock, bring the soup to a boil, and simmer for 15 minutes longer. Add the chickpeas, if using, during the last 5 minutes of cooking.

Meanwhile, prepare your crostini by lightly brushing slices of the baguette with olive oil and cooking them over a grill or toasting them. Make however many meet your fancy, but do count on at least two per serving. Spread the chèvre onto the crostini.

Ladle into warmed bowls and either float the crostini on top of the soup or serve them on the side. Alternatively, drop bits of chèvre into the soup and swirl through just before serving. Serve immediately.

FARRO AND PORCINI SOUP

SERVES 4

3 cups dried porcini mushrooms

¼ cup olive oil

2 stalks celery, diced

1 white onion, finely diced

4 cloves garlic, finely diced

1 tablespoon finely chopped fresh rosemary

5 ounces cremini mushrooms, thinly sliced

⅔ cup pearled farro

1 tablespoon fine chopped rosemary

4½ cups homemade chicken or vegetable stock

3 to 4 tablespoons amontillado sherry, Marsala, or port

NOTE It's best to eat farro soup as soon as it's ready, as the grains continue to absorb liquid long after they're fully cooked. Still, up to an hour off the heat won't hurt. Simply add some stock when reheating the soup and adjust the seasoning, if needed.

Andrew Edmunds is as timeless as any restaurant in London. It is not really that old, having been established in its present incarnation only in 1986, but the storefront exterior, wood plank floors, low ceilings, candles in wine bottles, chalkboard, and handwritten menu all conspire to keep this eighteenth-century town house feeling like it's a long-held secret. It is the place for a tryst. It is also the place for an exceptional bottle of wine. When Andrew bought the place, it was a wine bar, a bit seedy but with a surprisingly decent cellar. An art dealer, Andrew owned the print shop next door and would bring artists and collectors by when the occasion called for, as it often did, a drink.

Andrew is rather humble about the beginnings of his restaurant and perhaps with good reason. "I took over a junked-up wine bar painted pink with a waitress and someone who put tinned chili con carne in the microwave. From there, it drifted into its present form," he explained. Drifted, it must be said, under Andrew's spirit and good taste, which he described as being straight out of Elizabeth David. Andrew himself is something of a relief in what is now a high-powered media neighborhood. When I saw him last, he was wearing what looked like a Savile Row cashmere sweater, a bit worn by time and a moth, and was navigating the many dusty artworks in his shop, his wit biting and his taste for life fierce and generous. He knows art. He knows wine. He knows food. And after almost thirty years, he's finally installed a proper restaurant kitchen and has a winner of a chef in Bob Cairns.

I love this soup. It is at once elegant and rustic, healthy and rich. Bob adds a few potatoes, peeled and cubed, as is the tradition in so many peasant dishes. He also serves it with grated Parmesan. I prefer it without the distraction of either, and that is how the recipe is presented here. I also often swap the sherry for Marsala or port, the latter being particularly good with morels instead of porcinis.

Continued

Continued

FARRO AND PORCINI SOUP

At least half an hour before you start to prepare the soup, reconstitute the dried porcini mushrooms in 1 cup boiling water.

Warm the olive oil in a wide pot over medium-low heat. Add the celery and onion and cook for 10 minutes until the onions start to soften. Add the garlic and rosemary and continue to cook for a minute or so longer.

Raise the heat to high, add the cremini mushrooms and cook for 5 minutes, stirring occasionally so that they do not stick to the bottom of the pan. Add the farro and cook, stirring, for about a minute to infuse it with flavor.

Remove the porcini mushrooms from the soaking liquid, give them a rough chop, and add to the pot. Strain the soaking liquid through a fine-mesh sieve and pour into the pot, along with the stock. Bring to a boil and then turn down the heat and simmer for 35 to 40 minutes, until the farro is cooked but still al dente.

Add the sherry, adjust the seasoning, and cook for another minute or two to boil off some of the alcohol. Serve immediately.

SWEET POTATO, BACON, AND SAVOY CABBAGE SOUP

SERVES 4

6 thick slices bacon

Extra-virgin olive oil, for cooking, if needed

1 yellow onion, chopped

2 cloves garlic

1 large or two small sweet potatoes, peeled

Pinch of freshly grated nutmeg

½ savoy cabbage, finely sliced or chopped

2½ cups homemade chicken stock

Salt and pepper, to taste

2 cups whole milk

3 tablespoons quick-cooking rolled oats, if so desired

―――――――――

NOTE If you'd like to get a head start, prepare the bacon, onion, and garlic in advance, but wait to add the sweet potatoes or they will get mushy.

It's quite possible to see the same Hampstead locals day in, day out at Ginger and White. It is more than a neighborhood café—it is a hub. This is in large part to do with the cheery menu. Muffins and scones, heaping mounds of homemade roasted peanut butter churned with honey and demerara sugar, the ubiquitous mac and cheese, steak for the very hungry, and pearl barley salads for the parents.

My son Garrick adores this soup, possibly because he adores all things bacon. Here it provides a bit of smoky meatiness that is particularly welcome in the winter months. But everything in this soup pleases: the palette of vivid orange and green, the gentle murmur of nutmeg and cloves, the milky broth, the flecks of oats.

To an American, it may resemble a chowder; to a Scot, however, the use of oatmeal as a thickening agent will conjure memories of mussel brose, a traditional mussel stew made with milk and oatmeal. There's little need to follow this soup with a main course. It is perfect for a night at home when warmth and comfort are required but a long, rich meal is not.

Slice the bacon into lardons. In a heavy soup pot with a lid, sauté the bacon over low heat until it has rendered much of its fat. Add a splash of olive oil, if needed.

Add the onion and garlic and toss to coat with the bacon fat. Cover the pot and sweat the onion and garlic for 10 minutes, until soft. Check every now and then to make sure they aren't coloring.

Meanwhile, cut the sweet potatoes into ½-inch cubes. Add to the pot along with the nutmeg. Cover and cook for 5 minutes longer.

Uncover the pot, toss in the cabbage, and cook, stirring, until it has wilted. Pour in the stock and bring to a boil. Season with salt and pepper. Add the milk and bring it to a simmer, watching to make sure it doesn't boil over. Remove from heat and taste.

If the soup's consistency is already to your liking, check only to make sure that the vegetables are tender and the soup well seasoned. For a thicker soup, whisk the oatmeal. Simmer 5 minutes longer.

Ladle into warmed bowls. Serve immediately.

ROASTED CORN AND CHORIZO CHOWDER

SERVES 4

3 cups fresh or thawed
frozen corn kernels

2 tablespoons olive oil

1 pound fresh Spanish
chorizo sausage

1 cup peeled and diced potato

4 cups chicken or vegetable
stock, preferably homemade

2 cups sofrito (see recipe
on page 46)

1/2 cup coarsely chopped
roasted piquillo peppers

1 cup crème fraîche

3 tablespoons chopped
fresh chives

½ clove garlic, minced

Hot paprika or sweet
smoked paprika, to taste

Red chile flakes, to taste

Salt and pepper, to taste

It's only 9:30 in the morning, and I've already got a cup of this fiery soup on my desk. The forecast described today's weather, accurately, as "a freezing precipitation of ice pellets." In other words, it's a day for a smoky, peppery, hearty chowder that will warm you straight to the bones. I also crave this Spanish chowder at the end of summer, when the corn and tomatoes are at their peak and the evening wind holds a faint chill.

This chowder is almost a meal in and of itself. A loaf of crusty bread, a glass of Rioja, maybe a salad are really all that's needed. To my mind, the perfect dessert would be another thick slice of crusty bread, this time grilled and topped with dark chocolate, a drizzle of olive oil, a few flakes of Maldon sea salt, and maybe a grating of orange zest or a pinch of red chile flakes.

I often cook this soup in two steps, making the *sofrito* in advance. Any leftover *sofrito* is delicious stirred into scrambled eggs, as a base for eggs *en cocotte,* or simply topped with poached eggs for a simple lunch.

Preheat the oven to 425°F.

Line a rimmed baking sheet with aluminum foil. If using thawed frozen corn kernels, pat them dry with paper towels. Toss the corn with 1 tablespoon of the olive oil and then spread out in a single layer on the baking sheet. Roast the corn for about 10 minutes, until the edges are starting to turn a golden brown. Remove from the oven, transfer to a plate, and set aside.

Slice the chorizo or remote from its casing and crumble. Warm the remaining 1 tablespoon of olive oil in a soup pot over medium-high heat. When hot, add the chorizo and sauté until browned. Transfer the chorizo to another plate. If it has rendered a lot of fat, discard some and leave roughly 2 tablespoons. Toss the potato into the pot and cook, stirring, letting it absorb some of that chorizo goodness. Add the stock, *sofrito, piquillos,* and roasted corn and bring to a boil. Lower the heat and simmer about 20 minutes, until the vegetables soften but haven't yet lost their texture.

Continued

Continued

ROASTED CORN AND CHORIZO CHOWDER

Meanwhile, in a small bowl, stir the crème fraîche with a fork to loosen it up a bit. Stir in the chives, garlic, paprika, and chile flakes. Season with salt and pepper.

Slide the chorizo into the soup, stir in half of the crème fraîche mixture, and cook for 5 minutes longer. Ladle into warmed bowls, dollop with some of the remaining crème fraiche, and lightly dust with paprika.

SOFRITO

MAKES 2 CUPS

3 tablespoons olive oil, plus more as needed

2 pounds yellow onions, thinly sliced

4 cloves garlic, thinly sliced

2 red bell peppers, peeled and thinly sliced

2 cups fresh or canned whole tomatoes

1 fresh or dried bay leaf

Pinch of sugar

Salt and pepper, to taste

Warm the olive oil in a large skillet. Toss in the onions and garlic. Cook gently, stirring often, for about 20 minutes, until the onions are soft and translucent but not colored. Peel the bell peppers with a vegetable peeler and add them to the onions. Continue to sauté for another 20 minutes, until they too are soft.

If you are using fresh tomatoes, grate them on the largest holes of a box grater. If you are using canned tomatoes, pulse them in a food processor until they are somewhere between diced and pureed.

When the bell peppers are soft add the tomato and bay leaf and cook at the merest simmer for 25 minutes longer. Add the sugar, season with salt and pepper, and give the *sofrito* a final stir.

If you are making the *sofrito* ahead, let it cool completely. Pour into a jar, cover with a thin layer of olive oil, close the lid, and refrigerate for up to 10 days.

CELERIAC AND CHANTERELLE SOUP

SERVES 4

5 ounces pancetta or guanciale, cut into lardons

Olive oil, for cooking, if needed

4 large shallots, thinly sliced

1 stalk celery, sliced

1 leek, white part only, thoroughly cleaned and thinly sliced

2 cloves garlic, finely chopped

1 tablespoon fresh thyme leaves

1 celeriac, peeled and cut into cubes

Salt and pepper, to taste

4 cups homemade chicken stock

4 ounces chanterelles, wiped clean and sliced

1 tablespoon minced flat-leaf parsley

This soup is the taste of late fall—earthy, smoky, rooty. It has none of the vibrancy of a spring velouté, nor any of the pretty shades of summer. Instead it has a deep, lingering flavor. When I make it, I'm reminded that the cold months offer their bounty in camouflage—chanterelle mushrooms from the forest floor, dirty grotesque celeriac—but offer them, they do. When it's time to open your fireplace's flue, it's time to make this soup. Serve it in warmed earthenware bowls, followed by a winter salad of bitter greens, and then a rustic apple-and-pear crisp.

In a heavy soup pot with a lid, sauté the pancetta over low heat until it has rendered much of its fat and gotten crispy. Add a splash of olive oil, if needed. Using a slotted spoon, transfer the pancetta to a paper towel-lined plate. Pour out 1 tablespoon of the rendered fat and reserve for cooking the chanterelles. Leave the remaining rendered fat in the pot.

Add the shallots, celery, leek, garlic, and thyme to the pot and toss to coat with the pancetta fat. Cook over low heat for about 10 minutes, until the shallots and leek soften and become translucent. Add the celeriac and season with salt and pepper. Cover the pot and sweat the vegetables for 10 to 15 minutes, until the celeriac is soft. Check every now and then to make sure they aren't coloring. Uncover the pot, pour in the stock, and bring to a boil. Lower the heat and simmer until the celeriac is completely tender.

Using caution and working in small batches, puree the soup in a blender until it is smooth as silk. Make sure to cover the top of the blender with a dish towel as the heat of the soup may cause the top to pop off. Transfer the soup to a large bowl as you go, then stir it all together.

Warm the reserved 1 tablespoon bacon fat in a saucepan. Add the chanterelles and fry over high heat. Once they lightly colored, add the pancetta and cook to warm through and crisp up.

Ladle the soup into warmed bowls, garnish with the chanterelles and pancetta, and sprinkle with parsley. Serve immediately.

MUSSEL, FENNEL, AND SOURDOUGH SOUP

SERVES 2

1 pound mussels, cleaned
and debearded

Extra-virgin olive oil

½ cup dry white wine

2 cups fish stock or
clam broth

2 bulbs fennel, or 4 small
bulbs wild fennel, sliced;
fennel fronds reserved
and chopped

1 clove garlic, thinly sliced

½ teaspoon fresh red chile,
such as Fresno, finely
chopped and seeds discarded

Salt, to taste

Juice of ½ lemon

A handful of good sourdough
bread, torn up a bit

I readily confess to being a Jamie Oliver fan. He's as warm and affable offscreen as he is on, which, it has to be said, is rare. But it's what he did with Fifteen that I really admire. When Jamie decided to teach fifteen teenagers how to run a restaurant and partner with Channel Four to film the process, it sounded like nothing more than a publicity stunt, albeit one for a good cause. Well, it turned out to be a godsend for many of those kids, and especially for Tim. One of fourteen children, Tim worked after school four days a week to help his family make ends meet. When he was nineteen, Jamie chose him out of more than fifteen thousand applicants to become one of his trainees. One spoonful of this nuanced soup, and you'll realize it was a good move for everyone.

This thick Mediterranean soup is almost more of a stew, and as such, it feels like a main course. Serve it with thick grilled slices of sourdough bread rubbed with garlic and olive oil, as you'll want to soak up every last bit of the broth.

Discard any mussels that are open and won't close when tapped on a work surface. Place a colander over a bowl.

Place a saucepan with a lid that's big enough to easily fit all the mussels on the stove and warm over high heat. When the pan is hot, pour in a nice glug of olive oil, quickly followed by the mussels. Toss for 30 seconds. Add the wine and let reduce for 30 seconds; then add the stock and bring it to a boil.

Cover the saucepan with the lid and turn down the heat to medium. Cook for 4 to 5 minutes, until the shells open. If any are still closed at this point, chuck them.

Pour the mussels into the colander set over a bowl, which will catch all the mussel juice. Strain the mussel juice through a fine-mesh sieve. Now, you have two choices. Either pick the mussels out of their shells and coarsely chop the meat, discarding the shells or, alternatively, keep the mussels attached to their shell and serve as is. This is a more dramatic look and, I think, outweighs the inconvenience at the table.

Warm another saucepan with a lid and add a glug of olive oil. Add the fennel and sauté until just golden. Add the garlic and chile and sauté

for 2 to 3 minutes longer. Add the mussel juice and be sure to scrape up the sticky fennel goodness from the bottom of the pan. Cover the pan with a lid and cook over low heat for 30 minutes, until the fennel softens. Check every now and then to see if you need to add more water or stock. Taste and cautiously season with salt, as the mussel juice may already be quite salty.

Add the lemon juice, torn sourdough, and chopped or whole mussels and stir to combine. The consistency should be quite thick, like porridge. If it's too thick, add a splash of water. Ladle into warmed bowls, drizzle with good olive oil, and scatter with chopped fennel fronds.

PASTA, RICE, AND GRAINS

SUMMER PASTA WITH CRÈME FRAÎCHE, ARUGULA, AND LEMON

SERVES 4

1 cup crème fraîche

1 cup freshly grated Parmesan, plus more for serving

Zest of 2 organic lemons, preferably Meyer

¼ cup freshly squeezed lemon juice, preferably Meyer

½ teaspoon sea salt

Freshly ground pepper

6 ounces baby or wild arugula, the more peppery the better

1 pound dried egg pasta or fresh tagliatelle

This recipe requires no cooking, other than boiling the pasta. It takes five minutes and one bowl. It is a perfect recipe. Great ingredients are key, so make this only when you can source wild or baby arugula, juicy lemons, and excellent Parmesan. I usually make this with Cipriani dried egg tagliatelle or fettuccine. If you can't find Cipriani, look for an artisanal egg pasta, dried or fresh, long and flat. Or do as the restaurant does and make your own. For those of us stateside, Meyer lemons are the closest approximation to Amalfi lemons. A touch sweeter than the standard Eureka, they can be used generously without the risk of too much pucker.

When I asked Ruthie about the recipe, she spoke of receiving an abundance of fabulous lemons from the Amalfi coast one day. Crème fraîche offered the ideal rich, tangy match for the bright citrus, and the sharp notes of arugula gave it a good kick. And so a favorite was born.

Start heating the pasta water, as this is a quick sauce to prepare.

Scoop the crème fraîche into a large bowl and stir it with a fork to loosen it up a bit. Add the Parmesan, lemon zest and juice, and the salt. Season with pepper and stir well to combine. Adjust the seasoning. You should have a lemony, creamy well-seasoned sauce.

Slice the arugula into slivers with a sharp knife or scissors. Stir into the sauce.

Cook the pasta in generously salted boiling water. Drain and toss with the sauce. It will be warm and silky. Serve immediately.

LINGUINE WITH CLAMS, JAMÓN SERRANO, GARLIC, AND THYME

SERVES 4 AS A TAPAS COURSE, 2 FOR A MORE SUBSTANTIAL COURSE

¼ cup extra-virgin olive oil

1 small yellow or red onion, finely chopped

3 cloves garlic, finely chopped

1 small fresh or dried bay leaf

Sea salt and freshly ground black pepper

1 pound clams, preferably Manila

8 ounces dried linguine

1½ cups dry sherry (such as manzanilla or fino)

4 ripe plum tomatoes, peeled, seeded, and finely diced

5 ounces jamón serrano, cut into lardons

Leaves from 2 sprigs thyme

Really good extra-virgin olive oil, for drizzling

———————

NOTE My mother puts her clams in a large bowl of salted ice water, sprinkles them with cornmeal or polenta, and lets them sit for an hour. I don't know the science behind this, but it seems to clean them well, ridding them of any lingering sandiness.

José, despite his many years in London, still speaks with a lilting Spanish accent that infuses his words with the promise of a never-ending good time. His restaurants are like that too. These are not places you go for quiet, somber conversation, but to be drawn into the fray.

The first thing I ever ordered at Pizarro was spaghetti with chorizo and mussels. The heat of sausage, the brininess of the sea, and the comfort of the pasta united Spain and Italy in a dance. When I next returned to the restaurant, José made this similar pasta, which is now my favorite. The flavors are subtler and the sherry provides an intriguing note. If using chorizo, simply switch from sherry to white wine.

Start heating the pasta water, as this is a quick sauce to prepare.

In a large skillet with a lid, over medium-low heat, warm 3 tablespoons of the olive oil, toss in the onion and garlic, and add the bay leaf. Cook, stirring frequently, until the onion is soft and translucent. Discard the bay leaf. Season with salt and pepper. Transfer to a plate so that you can reuse the skillet.

Wash the clams and discard any that are open and won't close when tapped on a work surface.

Cook the linguine in generously salted boiling water, draining it when it is still al dente, or more fitting here, *al punto*.

While the linguine is cooking, warm the skillet over high heat. When hot, add the clams and sherry, cover the pan with a lid, and cook, shaking the pan now and then, for 2 to 3 minutes, until the clams just open. If any are still closed at this point, chuck them. Transfer the clams and their juice to a bowl and set aside.

Add the remaining 1 tablespoon of olive oil to the pan, followed by the tomatoes, flash-cooking them for a minute or two over high heat. Reduce the temperature, and return the onions to the skillet, add the jamón serrano and thyme, and cook to warm through. Add the just-drained linguine and toss for 30 seconds or so. Off the heat, add the clams and their juices, and fold into the pasta. If the sauce is too dry, drizzle with a bit of olive oil. Adjust the seasoning. Serve piping hot in warmed bowls.

YELLOWFIN TUNA SPAGHETTI PUTTANESCA

SERVES 2

1 (7-ounce) fillet
yellowfin tuna

2 tablespoons olive oil

2 cloves garlic, crushed

14 ounces canned whole San
Marzano tomatoes, chopped

5 salt-packed anchovies,
rinsed and patted dry

20 capers, rinsed

3 pinches of dried red
chile flakes

Salt and pepper, to taste

Aromatics, to taste (fresh
bay leaves, thyme, rosemary,
and garlic)

Vegetable oil, for cooking

12 ounces dried spaghetti

10 black olives, pitted and
chopped

2 tablespoons finely chopped
fresh flat-leaf parsley

½ cup freshly grated
Parmesan

————————

NOTE Some may look askance
at the very idea of serving
Parmesan with a fish sauce—
a definite no-no in some
parts of Italy, but Angela
does it and so do I. Why ever
not? Rules are meant to be
broken, when they are broken
themselves.

Angela was one of the first major female chefs in London. The number, at long last, is on the rise. But for much of the last twenty years, it was just Ruth Rogers, the late Rose Gray, Sally Clarke, Skye Gyngell, and Angela. The circle was indeed a tiny one, though it was also a very influential one. Angela's cooking is perhaps the most classic, if also—at Murano—the most elaborate . The food there is the kind of highly refined Italian that makes tossing a bowl of pasta with pesto seem almost savage. It is extraordinarily good. But at the more informal Café Murano, Angela lets down her guard and the food is livelier. This spicy, fiery puttanesca is paired with a beautiful confit of yellowfin tuna. Capers and olives give heat and texture, while the confit offers silken luxury.

Warm the olive oil in a large skillet or saucepan over a medium-low heat. Add 2 of the garlic cloves and sauté until golden, but not brown.

Add the tomatoes and simmer for 10 minutes. Add the anchovies, capers, and chiles, and simmer for 5 minutes longer. Season with salt and pepper and set aside, off heat.

Place the whole piece of tuna in another saucepan with a high rim and cover with aromatics. Pour in enough vegetable oil to completely cover the tuna. To confit the tuna, bring the oil to a simmer over low heat and gently cook until it flakes easily.

Transfer the tuna to a cutting board. Discard the vegetable oil.

Cook the spaghetti in generously salted water until al dente.

Reserve ¼ cup of the tomato sauce and set aside. Add the just-drained spaghetti to the pan with the remaining tomato sauce and toss over medium heat for 30 seconds or so.

Divide the pasta between two wide, warmed bowls. Cut the tuna in half and place a half atop each serving of pasta. Spoon the reserved tomato sauce over the top. Scatter with the black olives and parsley, and garnish with a grind of black pepper and a bit of the grated Parmesan. Serve immediately with the remaining Parmesan, if so desired.

CINNAMON-SCENTED PORCINI DUCK RAGÙ

SERVES 2 AS A HEARTY MAIN COURSE

2 duck legs, skin removed

Sea salt

1 tablespoon duck fat

1 carrot, peeled and finely diced

1 stalk celery, finely diced

2 shallots, finely diced

2 cloves garlic, grated

⅓ cup dried porcini mushrooms

1 bottle red wine, preferably Chianti, and another to drink

1 bouquet garni with rosemary, thyme, and a fresh or dried bay leaf

1 small cinnamon stick

28 ounces canned whole San Marzano plum tomatoes, chopped

3 cups chicken stock, preferably homemade

12 ounces fresh pappardelle

Freshly grated Parmesan, for serving

Mission is tucked into the railway arches at Bethnal Green in East London. In the middle of its bare-bones dining room, a palm tree holds court, offering a canopy of vivid green that is meant to conjure the Californian coast. Owners Charlotte and Michael Sager-Wilde spent two years in San Francisco studying wine, hanging out in the Mission District, working at Bar Tartine, and amassing the cellar that has put this rocking joint on the oenophile map of London. Don't go for a quiet conversation as you won't hear it. But do go for some of the best Californian wines to be had outside of the States and for food so good you might forget to drink them.

It comes then as no surprise that this recipe calls for one bottle of red wine for cooking and a second for drinking. It may, however, be surprising to see cinnamon on the ingredient list. In Italy, cinnamon is as commonly used in savory dishes as it is in desserts. Cinnamon is said to have been brought to Sicily during the Arab occupation of the tenth century and presumably traveled north. Here, a cinnamon stick adds a layer of almost woodsy warmth to the acidity of the wine and the richness of the duck. It accentuates the earthiness of the porcini, offering only the faintest hint of sweetness.

The scent of this ragù as it cooks will draw neighbors, wanted and unwanted, to your home. If you are in the mood for a quiet, intimate night, seal the windows. If not, double or triple the recipe. The ragù freezes well, protected by the duck fat. It is also better the next day, but I defy you to wait. It is truly sublime served with fresh pappardelle and no less than excellent served with most any dried pasta or even as the base of a lasagna.

Preheat the oven to 325°F.

Season the duck legs with salt. Warm the duck fat in a Dutch oven over medium-high heat and sear the legs until golden all over, Transfer to a plate and set aside. Reduce the heat to medium, add the carrot, celery, shallots, garlic, and porcini to the same skillet, and cook about 10 minutes, until sticky and sweet. Raise the heat to high; add the wine, bouquet garni, and cinnamon and cook until reduced by half.

Add the tomatoes and chicken stock and bring to a simmer. Add the duck legs and any accumulated juices. Cover and place in the oven for 3 hours.

Remove the duck from the sauce and set aside for a few minutes to cool a bit. Shred the meat with your fingers or a fork. Discard the bones. Return the shredded meat to the sauce and warm it up for a minute on the stove. If you prefer a thicker sauce, simply cook it a bit longer.

If you are making the ragù a day in advance, let it cool to room temperature and refrigerate overnight. An hour before serving, remove it from the fridge, scrape off and discard the layer of fat that will have formed on the surface. Bring the sauce to a simmer over medium heat.

Cook the pasta in generously salted water until al dente. Drain and toss with the ragù over a medium-high heat for 30 seconds or so. Check the seasoning. Serve immediately in warmed bowls and pass a bowl of Parmesan around the table.

PAPPARDELLE AI FEGATINI DI POLLO E SALVIA

**SERVES 2 OR 3
AS A FIRST COURSE**

6 ounces chicken livers

2 tablespoons vegetable oil

1 shallot, finely chopped

¼ cup Cognac

1 cup white wine

2 tablespoons heavy cream

1 cup unsalted butter, plus
1 additional tablespoon

Salt and pepper, to taste

10 fresh sage leaves

12 ounces fresh pappardelle

3 tablespoons freshly
grated Parmesan

When I first met Giorgio, it was not at his exquisite restaurant but at the River Cafe, and not in the dining area or the kitchen but in the cheese room. Giorgio and his wife, Plaxy, were in the refrigerated glassed-in storage room that cheese lovers seek out for the glorious smell and tantalizing display of the best Parmigiano and Pecorino, sweet pungent Gorgonzola, and briny ricotta salata. Together, we sniffed until we were in a state of euphoria, three people silent in culinary dreamland. And then we started talking.

Giorgio is one of the great Italian chefs in London, and Locanda Locatelli is well known for its highly refined cuisine. His is not the rustic, peasant fare that is now synonymous with Italian cooking, but a more formal, nuanced cuisine, befitting his training at the Savoy and La Tour d'Argent. This is quite the opposite of the man himself. Giorgio is gregarious and convivial and happiest, one imagines, chatting with friends and family over a big bowl of pasta and a bottle of wine. His two books, *Made in Sicily* and *Made in Italy*, are classics.

This is an honest recipe, by which I mean not that its ingredients were sourced locally, but rather that Giorgio openly admits to the extravagant quantity of butter that makes this pasta sauce so fine. There is more butter, more olive oil, more duck fat, and more cream in restaurant food than we should ever know—unless, that is, we want to cook with as much sublime extravagance as may be found at Locanda Locatelli.

This is not a recipe for every day, but it is an easy one to prepare. Serve it as a first course with fresh pappardelle; it is simply too rich to be a main course. Forget the fact that it is made with chicken livers for, in Locatelli's hands, they have more in common with delicate foie gras mousse than with those odd, unappealing slippery things so often discarded when you roast a chicken. The sauce is cooked in two steps, carefully strained and flambéed, and is an altogether elegant affair, replete with Cognac, wine, butter, and copious amounts of fresh sage. There is nothing rustic about it, and its success, I'm afraid, depends on following the instructions precisely. Do so, however, and you will be amply rewarded.

In the center of each chicken liver is a white filament. Carefully remove it with a sharp knife and reserve. Finely dice the livers.

Warm 1 tablespoon of the vegetable oil in a saucepan over high heat. Add the reserved liver trimmings, spreading them out over the bottom of the pan. Cook, without stirring, for 2 minutes. The trimmings will have stuck to the bottom of the pan. Gently scrape them up with a spatula and flip them over. Let them cook for 2 minutes more, until sticking to the bottom of the pan again, then scrape them up and flip. They should color but not burn. Lower the heat and smash the trimmings with the back of a spoon.

Add the shallot and cook for 3 minutes. Raise the heat to high, add 2 tablespoons of the Cognac. Turn off the stove and carefully ignite. Flambé until the alcohol evaporates and the flames subside. Turn the burner back on. Add the white wine and cream and cook for a couple of minutes, until the sauce has reduced to a voluptuous consistency. Turn the heat to a low simmer.

Cut all but 3 tablespoons of the butter into cubes, then slowly whisk it in, one cube at a time, to form an emulsion. While whisking the sauce, slightly raise the temperature to prevent the sauce from separating; then when all of the butter is incorporated, turn down the heat for the same reason. Strain the sauce through a fine-mesh sieve, pressing down on the solids. Set aside someplace warm.

Warm the remaining 1 tablespoon vegetable oil in a sauté pan over. Add the diced chicken livers, season with salt and pepper, and flip them over. Add the remaining 2 tablespoons of Cognac, take off heat, and carefully ignite. Flambé until the alcohol evaporates and the flames subside. Season. Add the remaining 3 tablespoons of butter followed by the sage. Let the butter melt and get foamy, lightly crisping up the sage. Remove from the heat.

Cook your pappardelle in generously salted water, reserving a spoonful or two of pasta cooking water.

Off the heat, add the reserved pasta cooking water to the chicken livers and whisk to emulsify the sauce. Then add the just-drained pappardelle and toss all together. Do not heat the sauce, or the butter will separate. Add the Parmesan, toss again, and serve immediately.

CHESTNUT STRACCETTI WITH MUSHROOMS AND CHESTNUTS

SERVES 4

PASTA

1 cup chestnut flour

2½ cups "00" flour, plus more for rolling

5 eggs

SAUCE

4 ounces guanciale or pancetta, cut into small lardons

5 tablespoons unsalted butter, cut into cubes

7 ounces vacuum-packed cooked whole chestnuts, cut into ¼-inch slices

30 fresh sage leaves

12 ounces Chanterelle mushrooms, cut into ¼-inch slices

½ cup heavy cream

1 cup freshly grated Parmesan

A handful of fresh flat-leaf parsley, chopped

NOTE You may also use one pound of dried pasta with this sauce.

If you've never made fresh pasta or seen anyone make it, this is the moment for a YouTube demonstration.

This dish is, quite simply, a knockout. When the weather turns cold, the thought of chestnuts, pancetta, sage, and mushrooms is a seductive one. Add cream and homemade chestnut pasta to the mix and you may race to your kitchen. Here is what Jacob has to say: "Straccetti, little rags, are the easiest pasta to make at home and are best with the heartiest of sauces such as the current example. This is mountain fare, the warm cushion it provides against a cold autumn or winter's day will last a lifetime . . . on the hips." There, you've heard it from the master.

I wasn't at all surprised when Jacob sent me this recipe to find that it is pitch-perfect. After all, he's the author of two excellent cookbooks, *The Geometry of Pasta* and *Bocca*. Jacob is one of those extraordinarily well-educated chefs who now populate many of London's best restaurants. He read history and the philosophy of science in his second year at St. John's College, Cambridge, moving on to Disease, Society, and Sexuality in his third year. Summers he worked at Moro, the groundbreaking Moorish restaurant belonging to Sam and Sam Clark. Bocca is often filled with paintings by Jacob's mother, the artist Haidee Becker. Situated on a tiny street, it is a well-guarded Soho secret. Lunch is most fun at the bar.

I so love the combination of flavors in this sauce that I make it often using dried pasta, when there's no time to make fresh. Made this way, it's ideal last-minute dinner party fare.

To make the pasta, bring together the two flours on a working surface. Make a well and crack the eggs into this well. Draw the flour into the eggs with a fork until combined and then knead for a good 10 minutes. Roll into a ball, wrap in plastic, and refrigerate 15 minutes.

On a well-floured surface, roll out the dough until it's ¹⁄₁₆-inch thick ("like a tuppenny piece") with a floured roller, and then let it partially dry on your work surface for about 20 minutes. Cut it into rough shapes—triangles, rhombi, and trapezoids—that are ½ to 2½ inches wide and 2 to 6 inches long. "Imagine the skin of Edward Scissorhands's lover," Jacob advises.

Continued

CHESTNUT STRACCETTI WITH MUSHROOMS AND CHESTNUTS

Continued

Before you start the sauce, have a tall pot of well-salted water already at a boil. If using dried pasta, you will want to cook it while the sauce is cooking. If using fresh pasta, wait to cook it until the sauce is almost finished.

To make the sauce, fry the *guanciale* or pancetta in a wide skillet over high heat until well browned. Add the butter and allow it to melt and then add the chestnuts and sauté them for 5 minutes, until the edges of the nuts are crispy and browned. Add the sage leaves and sauté for 2 minutes; then add the mushrooms and sauté for another 2 minutes. Maintain a high heat and stir occasionally.

If using homemade pasta, you'll want to cook it as soon as the mushrooms start to brown convincingly. The straccetti will only take two minutes cooking to be firm and al dente.

While the pasta is cooking, add the cream, ⅓ cup of the Parmesan, the parsley, and a touch of pasta water, if necessary, to emulsify the sauce. Shake the pan or use a wooden spoon to combine. Add the just-drained pasta and toss over high heat for 30 seconds or so.

Divide the pasta among four warmed bowls. Serve immediately with the remaining Parmesan.

PORK SHOULDER, BLACK PEPPER, AND MASCARPONE RAGÙ

SERVES 4

2½ pounds boneless pork shoulder

Sea salt and black pepper

1 carrot, peeled and finely chopped

1 stalk celery, finely chopped

½ yellow onion, finely chopped

2 cloves garlic, finely chopped

5 fresh or dried bay leaves

20 black peppercorns

½ teaspoon ground mace

1 glass dry white wine

Roughly 3 to 4 cups homemade chicken stock or water

1 pound dried pasta, such as pappardelle

2 tablespoons mascarpone

1 lemon, halved, plus lemon wedges for serving

Trullo has Islington all abuzz. This northern area of London has slowly but very surely landed on the city's culinary map. Trullo, with its roughhewn industrial integrity, fits right in to the scene. Co-owner Jordan Frieda is a River Cafe alumnus and, surprisingly, the son of shampoo titan John Frieda. The chef, Tim Siadatan, was another of those teenagers Jamie Oliver plucked off the proverbial street and made a trainee at Restaurant Fifteen. If curious, go back and watch the first season of the TV series *Jamie's Kitchen*. You'll see Tim's talent all over the screen, a talent he then honed at St. John. His food is a bold ode to his mentors—the attention to ingredients that so marks the River Cafe, the big, generous spirit of Jamie Oliver, and the expert craft and appetite of Fergus Henderson all play into this rustic fare.

This isn't the prettiest of dishes, but the comfort it offers on a cold winter's night will not disappoint. Unlike most of its saucy cousins, what with their red tomatoes and parsley garnishes, this ragù appears bare bones. It's just shredded pork, with no colorful adornment. But the pork is cooked long and low until tender and deeply flavored. Lemon juice cuts the richness, mascarpone gives it a bit of luxury, and mace and peppercorns provide intrigue. Tim braises the pork in water, but when I have homemade chicken stock on hand, I use that instead.

If you do have the time, now is the moment to make homemade pasta. Or, then again, buy it—just stay away from any pasta that is too delicate. This is a rustic dish, and the pasta should offer a bit of resistance. Something long and thick, like pappardelle, seems to envelop the sauce quite beautifully. Serve with a wedge of lemon, a heavy shower of black pepper, and bowlfuls of Parmesan and mascarpone.

Preheat the oven to 325°F.

Pat the pork dry with paper towels and season it with salt and pepper. Warm a heavy skillet over medium heat. When the pan is hot, sear the meat until it's a deep golden color on all sides. Transfer the pork shoulder to a Dutch oven or other wide pot with a lid.

Using the same skillet, add the carrot, celery, onion, garlic, bay leaves, peppercorns, and mace in the rendered pork fat and sauté over medium-low heat. Add a pinch of salt to help the onions give up their water. Cook, stirring more or less continuously (for about 25 minutes) until the vegetables are nicely colored and one happy vegetal mass. Don't take any shortcuts—patience, here, is an amply rewarded virtue. Once the vegetables tender and golden, transfer them to the pork pot.

Over high heat, deglaze the skillet with the wine, scraping up any good bits stuck to the bottom. Pour these juices over the pork and then add enough stock to cover a third of the pork. Cover pot with the lid. Roast the pork for a good, solid 4 hours. Check every now and then to see if you need to add more water or stock.

Have a large pot of generously salted water in a boil and cook the pasta as you finish the sauce.

Once cooked, the pork should easily fall apart. Remove the pork from the sauce, let cool, shred the meat with your fingers or a fork, and transfer to a big serving bowl. Stir in the mascarpone and the juice of one lemon. Season with salt and pepper. If you like your sauce saucy, add some of the cooking liquid from the pot, being sure to discard any peppercorns and bay leaves. Italians prefer to be sparing with the sauce, but the point is to do as you like best. Toss in the cooked pasta. Serve immediately.

RISOTTO DI PEPERONI

**SERVES 4 TO 6 AS A
FIRST COURSE OR 2 TO 4
AS A MAIN COURSE**

4 bell peppers in assorted
colors (such as orange,
yellow, and red)

4 ripe plum tomatoes

5 to 6 cups homemade
chicken stock

2 tablespoons extra-virgin
olive oil

3 stalks celery,
finely chopped

1 yellow onion,
finely chopped

2½ cups Carnaroli rice

1 glass dry white wine

1 cup freshly grated
Parmesan, plus more
for serving

A handful of fresh basil
leaves, finely sliced

¼ cup unsalted butter,
cut into pieces

Salt and pepper, to taste

NOTE Carnaroli rice is
preferable, but Arborio may
be substituted. Keep extra
chicken stock on hand, in case
the rice absorbs more of it
than you expected.

Proving yet again the extent to which the River Cafe has spawned an extraordinary list of alumni, we have Theo Randall and his eponymous restaurant. Theo's cooking is light, fresh, and often vibrantly hued, like this risotto with red, orange, and yellow bell peppers and basil confetti. Broiling or grilling the peppers gives them a smoky flavor that pairs beautifully with the creaminess of the rice and the richness of the Parmesan.

And to borrow from another River Cafe alumnus Jamie Oliver, add a final ladle of chicken stock to the finished rice off the heat, then cover the skillet, and call everyone to the table. That last bit of stock keeps the rice moist while everyone assembles. To make this recipe truly easy, cook the risotto in a pressure cooker, which is what everyone not intimidated by tradition seems to be doing now in Italy. But these are my words, not Theo's. With a glass of wine, good music, and friends about, stirring risotto has its pleasures.

Preheat the broiler or a gas or charcoal grill. Broil or grill the bell peppers until charred on all sides. The trick is to char the pepper skins but not to scorch the flesh. Cook them with a watchful eye, turning them as soon as one side starts to blacken. To make peeling the charred peppers a breeze, transfer them to a large bowl and cover tightly with plastic wrap. Let sit for 10 minutes before scraping off the charred skin with a small serrated knife. Slice the peppers in half and remove the stem, pith, and seeds. Rinse the peppers with water, if needed, and pat them dry with paper towels. Dice the peppers and set aside.

Bring a wide pan of water to a boil. Score the bottom of each tomato and then dunk them into the boiling water for a scant minute before transferring to a cutting board. Peel off the tomato skins, which should now slip off easily. Halve the tomatoes, scoop out the seeds, and finely chop the flesh. Set aside.

Bring the chicken stock to a gentle simmer in a separate saucepan and keep warm over low heat.

In a large skillet or saucepan over medium-low heat, combine the olive oil, celery, and onion. Cook, stirring regularly, about 5 minutes, until the onion is soft but not colored.

Raise the heat and add the rice. Stir the ingredients together for a few minutes to coat the grains in the oil and marry the flavors. Once the rice starts to look translucent, raise the heat a tad more and add the white wine. Cook, stirring, until the wine has almost evaporated and then start adding the hot stock, one ladleful at a time, stirring continuously and letting each addition be absorbed by the rice before adding more. When cooked, the rice should still have bite but no crunch. It usually takes about a half hour to cook risotto, but taste it repeatedly as you get close and don't rely on the clock.

When the risotto is a minute or two away from being fully cooked, add the chopped peppers, tomatoes, Parmesan, basil, and butter and stir vigorously until the butter melts and the risotto is a lovely creamy consistency. Season with salt and pepper. Add a ladleful of stock, cover the saucepan, and call everyone to the table. Serve immediately in warmed shallow bowls and pass additional Parmesan at the table.

WATERCRESS RISOTTO

**SERVES 4 AS A FIRST COURSE
OR 2 AS A MAIN COURSE**

3 cups watercress leaves

1 cup spinach leaves

4 cups homemade vegetable
or chicken stock

¼ cup olive oil

4 large shallots, finely diced

3 sprigs thyme

2 cloves garlic,
finely chopped

1 fresh or dried bay leaf

Salt and pepper, to taste

1¼ cups Carnaroli or
Arborio rice

1 cup white wine

½ cup freshly grated
Parmesan, plus more
for serving

½ cup crème fraîche,
or to taste

1 lemon, halved

When Tom closed his Michelin-starred eponymous restaurant some
years back, it was sorely missed in the food world, so it's not surprising
that when he opened Tom's Kitchen, a casual neighborhood restaurant
in Chelsea, I worried it might be a mere stop-gap enterprise—something
along the way to another serious restaurant. Then I went for dinner
and immediately understood why it quickly became a beloved Chelsea
institution. The menu is one of the most appealing I've ever seen. The
food is generous, indulgent, and comforting. It may not surprise, but it
will keep you coming back for more.

This risotto caught my eye as a waiter was serving it to, alas, someone else
(you can see it pictured on page XV). It is startlingly green. Watercress
is an ingredient I most often use as a counterpoint to something rich and
creamy; its sharp, peppery notes need to be offset. Here, a classic risotto
provides the perfect foil. If, like me, your spirit sags at the thought of
picking the leaves off a great number of watercress stems, take heart.
The watercress puree may be made in advance and frozen. In other
words, pluck those leaves over a Netflix binge and a glass of wine one
quiet night, blitz in a food processor, and freeze.

Place your food processor or blender blade in the freezer until cold,
about 15 minutes. Bring a pot of salted water to a boil. Add the watercress
and spinach and cook for only 2 minutes, then drain immediately,
pressing down on the greens to squeeze all the liquid out. (If you
haven't enough stock, reserve this cooking liquid for the risotto.)

Remove the blade from the freezer and reinstall. Combine the watercress
and spinach in the food processor or blender and puree until smooth. If
you're preparing the watercress and spinach leaves in advance, transfer
the mixture to a freezer-safe container and freeze. The puree may be
kept frozen for a few days. Let it come back to room temperature before
adding it to the risotto.

Bring the stock to a gentle simmer in a saucepan and keep warm over low
heat. In another large skillet or saucepan, over medium heat, combine
the oil, shallots, thyme, garlic and bay leaf. Sauté for 2 minutes, until
the shallots are tender but not colored. Add the rice and cook, stirring
to coat the grains in the oil, for 2 minutes. Add a ½ cup of the wine and

cook until it has been absorbed, stirring all the while. Add the remaining ½ cup of wine, followed by the stock, one ladleful at a time, until the stock has been absorbed and the rice is just shy of tender.

When cooked, the rice should still have a bite but no crunch. It usually takes about a half hour to cook risotto, but taste it repeatedly as you get close and don't rely on the clock.

Just before serving, discard the bay leaf and thyme sprigs and season as needed. Stir in the watercress puree followed by the Parmesan and the crème fraîche. Adjust the seasoning and squeeze lemon juice over the top. Serve immediately in warmed bowls and pass additional Parmesan.

RISOTTO ALL'AMARONE DELLA VALPOLICELLA WITH SPICED PUMPKIN

SERVES 6 AS A FIRST COURSE, 2 OR 3 AS A MAIN COURSE

1 pound pumpkin

1 dried red chile

3 tablespoons extra-virgin olive oil

1 tablespoon dried oregano

Salt and pepper, to taste

2 cups chicken stock, preferably homemade

⅔ cup unsalted butter, at room temperature

2 red onions, chopped

2 cups Carnaroli rice

1 bottle Amarone della Valpolicella wine

1 cup freshly grated Parmesan

Splash or two of heavy cream

When I was growing up, my experience of pumpkins was threefold. In New York, they were something to carve on Halloween, and their seeds were toasted. In Paris, they were small and appeared magically filled with hot soup and a dollop of crème fraîche. And then, for a short while, there was my nanny, whose self-inflicted nickname was Pumpkin. (She wore only tight-fitting orange polyester over her ample frame.) Before Pumpkin entered my life, I'd had a Swedish au pair who made pancakes filled with lingonberries and dusted in confectioners' sugar. Such culinary treats, I'm sad to report, were quite foreign to Pumpkin. The first time my father discovered her cooking, she'd poured dry spaghetti straight from the box into a pan of boiling ketchup and set the smoke alarm off. Pumpkin's tenure ended none too soon, when my parents discovered she was taking me to a seedy betting ring after school instead of ballet class. She'd set me up as clairvoyant and was charging for my so-called premonitions.

Not to get too deterministic about the whole thing, but it was a full twenty years before I could bring myself round to the culinary pleasures of pumpkin. Had I tasted this stunning risotto a bit sooner, my aversion would have been corrected instantly. Here, the risotto is rich with stock and wine, the pumpkin roasted with chile and oregano, the final stir, one of butter and cream. It is a therapeutic recipe. But for anyone with their own unresolved pumpkin trauma, butternut squash may be used with no loss in flavor.

Preheat the oven to 400°F.

Peel the pumpkin and cut into ½-inch cubes. Crumble the chile. Combine the pumpkin, chile, olive oil, and oregano in a large bowl. Season with salt and pepper and toss. Line a baking sheet with aluminum foil, rub it with more oil, and spread out the pumpkin in a single layer. Bake for about 20 minutes, shaking the baking sheet from time to time to turn the pieces, until tender and crisp around the edges. If the pumpkin starts to burn, turn down the heat.

Continued

Continued

RISOTTO ALL'AMARONE DELLA VALPOLICELLA WITH SPICED PUMPKIN

Bring the stock to a gentle simmer in a separate saucepan and keep warm over low heat.

Heat the chicken stock and adjust the seasoning.

Melt two-thirds of the butter in a large skillet or saucepan. Add the onions and gently sauté for about 20 minutes, until just lightly colored. Add the rice and cook, stirring to coat the grains, for 1 minute.

Raise the heat and pour in a glass of the wine. Cook until the wine reduces to a syrup. Add the hot stock, a ladleful at a time, stirring all the while, only adding more when the rice has absorbed the previous addition.

When all of the stock has been absorbed, gradually add the remaining wine. The rice should immediately take up the color of the wine. Continue adding wine in the same manner as you added stock.

When cooked, the rice should still have bite. It usually takes about a half hour, but taste it repeatedly.

Add ½ cup of the Parmesan, the remaining butter, and cream, if you like. Season with salt and pepper. Fold in the pumpkin, taking care not to stir too much as you want to keep the pieces mostly intact. Serve immediately in warmed bowls and pass the remaining Parmesan at the table.

VEGETARIAN

Andrew Edmunds Bob Cairns	SPICED HERITAGE CARROTS, FREEKEH, AND LABNEH 81
Rawduck Tom Hill	ROASTED SQUASH, BRAISED LENTILS, SOFT-BOILED EGG, GARLIC YOGURT, AND DUKKA 84
NOPI Yotam Ottolenghi and Ramael Scully	PURPLE SPROUTING BROCCOLI WITH OLIVE OIL MASH 86
Gymkhana Karam Sethi	POTATO CHAAT WITH POMEGRANATE, MINT, AND ROSE RAITA 89
The Three Crowns Lee Urch	POLENTA WITH CHESTNUTS, RICOTTA, SQUASH, AND FRIED SAGE 91
Fernandez and Wells Dee Rettali	TAKTOUKA 95
La Fromagerie Patricia Michelson	ALPINE FONDUE 97

SPICED HERITAGE CARROTS, FREEKEH, AND LABNEH

**SERVES 2 AS A MAIN COURSE
AND 4 AS A FIRST OR
SIDE COURSE**

LABNEH

2 cups full-fat Greek yogurt

Good pinch of sea salt

CARROTS

1 pound heritage carrots,
preferably of different colors

12 cardamom pods, crushed
and husk removed, or
1¾ teaspoons ground
green cardamom

1 teaspoon cumin seeds

4 whole allspice

Splash of extra-virgin olive oil

¼ to ½ cup chicken or
vegetable stock

Few splashes of
Moscatel vinegar

FREEKEH

1½ cups freekeh

3¾ to 4 cups chicken or
vegetable stock,
preferably homemade

Leaves from 1 bunch cilantro,
plus sprigs for garnish

2 lemons, for juicing

Maldon sea salt

Ground black pepper

Black onion seeds (also called
nigella seeds), for sprinkling

Aleppo pepper flakes,
for sprinkling

I've got a thing for cardamom and have been known to open a jar of the green pods randomly throughout the day to inhale their scent. They are said to be a stimulant and, if so, I'm clearly hooked. Moreover, they're also said to combat depression and, in fact, they do seem to produce a happy, contented feeling. This might account for the great popularity of chai. For coffee drinkers, adding a cardamom pod to the pot is a favored Middle Eastern tradition well worth adopting when an extra lift is needed. Doing a bit of research on the spice recently, I read that, in small amounts, it is considered an aphrodisiac but that in large doses, it produces, well, rather the opposite outcome. The article neglected to mention exactly how much is too much, leaving many a poor reader, as it were, betwixt and between. Whatever the case may be, I still remember walking into Andrew Edmunds' one day and nearly swooning at the scent of this dish. I took a seat immediately and made it my lunch.

Carrots and cardamom are as well matched as a pair can be. The spice draws the root's natural sweetness to the fore. Here they're roasted together and served with freekeh, a nutty, chewy, and enormously healthy grain, and labneh for a cool, tangy counterpoint. Treat the recipe as a blueprint and double or triple the amounts as needed. And if you forgot to make the labneh, never fear. A good thick Greek yogurt seasoned with a bit of salt will do the trick effortlessly. Likewise, if you haven't a bag of freekeh on hand, simply use farro or even Israeli couscous. And the carrots needn't be heritage and of different hues, but they are sweetest and prettiest that way. That said, do use fresh green cardamom pods, as once ground, the seeds lose their heady aroma and, I imagine, their magical properties. To make the labneh, you'll need a small square of muslin cloth, some string, and a little space in your fridge to hang it.

Continued

Andrew Edmunds O Bob Cairns

Continued

SPICED HERITAGE CARROTS, FREEKEH, AND LABNEH

To make the labneh, season the yogurt with salt and place in the center of a square of muslin cloth. Tie the bundle and hang it over a bowl. Refrigerate overnight. The following day, remove the labneh from the muslin and discard the liquid that has dripped into the bowl.

To cook the carrots, preheat the oven to 350°. Peel the carrots. Cut in half crosswise and then lengthwise.

Grind the cardamom, cumin, and allspice together in a mortar and pestle or spice grinder.

Place the carrots in a roasting pan, add the olive oil and the spice mixture, and season with salt and pepper. (Carrots bleed when cooked, particularly the darker purple ones. If you don't like the look of this, roast the carrots of each color separately.)

Toss the carrots until they are well coated in the oil and spices. Add a little stock to the roasting tray, just enough to cover the bottom. Cover the roasting tray with aluminum foil and bake for about 30 to 40 minutes, until the carrots are just tender but retain a bit of bite. Remove the foil and roast until most of the liquid evaporates.

Remove from the oven, add a few splashes of Moscatel vinegar, and shake the tray so the carrots take on its flavor. Season and set aside.

To make the freekeh, put it in a fine-mesh sieve and rinse it under cold running water until you are happy that all of the dust has been removed. Transfer the freekeh to a medium-sized lidded pot and cook over low heat for 1 minute, until toasted. Add enough stock to cover the freekeh by a few inches and stir together. Bring to a boil, cover, and then lower the heat. Simmer for about 20 minutes, until the freekeh is tender. Drain.

In a bowl, toss together the carrots and their juices, the freekeh, and the cilantro. Add a generous squeeze of lemon juice and season to taste with Maldon sea salt flakes and coarsely ground black pepper. Spoon onto plates, top with a good spoonful of labneh, and sprinkle with onion seeds and Aleppo pepper. Garnish with a few cilantro sprigs.

ROASTED SQUASH, BRAISED LENTILS, SOFT-BOILED EGG, GARLIC YOGURT, AND DUKKA

SERVES 6

DUKKA

1 tablespoon ground
Isot chile

2 fresh or dry bay leaves

1 cup toasted almonds,
chopped

1 cup toasted hazelnuts,
chopped

⅓ cup toasted sesame seeds

3 tablespoons toasted
coriander seeds

3 tablespoons toasted
cumin seeds

3 tablespoons ground sumac

1 tablespoon Maldon
sea salt flakes

1½ teaspons freshly
ground black pepper

1 tablespoon dried thyme

This is what I like to eat in the fall and winter when I'm taking a break from meat. It's not the least bit difficult to make, but it does have multiple components. This layering of flavors and textures is, I believe, the key to vegetarian food. Here, roasted squash offers a sweet note that offsets the earthy lentils. A soft-boiled egg adds protein and comfort. The garlic yogurt and dukka give the dish tang and spice. And, once you've got a jar of dukka in your fridge, you'll be able to whip this up anytime the craving strikes.

Dukka is an Egyptian blend of toasted nuts, seeds, and spices. The varieties are many, so don't hesitate to play with the recipe. Pistachios, cashew nuts, and even dried coconut often make appearances. Sumac, coriander, and sesame seeds tend to be the one constant. Dukka can be crushed, pounded with a mortar and pestle, or (cheating!) chopped up in a food processor using the pulse button. This particular dukka is so good, I keep a jar in the fridge and routinely sprinkle it on all sorts of dishes, from salads to soups to grains to plain Greek yogurt. It's wonderful on a piece of grilled bread drizzled with olive oil. Sometimes I just eat a spoonful for a bit of crunch and energy, as it's packed with protein. On the subject of spices, Isot chile, also called Urfa Biber, is common in Turkey and a bit harder to find elsewhere. It's worth seeking out, as it adds as much smoky depth as it does heat. Aleppo pepper from neighboring Syria, is the closest substitute.

After being open only five months, Rawduck literally collapsed. The whole building came tumbling down. Had it not been for food this good, that might have been the last we'd see of the place. But the locals wouldn't stand for that, and they pushed the Hackney Council to find Tom and his partners a new site, on neighboring Richmond Road, where it thrives today.

GARLIC YOGURT

3 cups whole milk
Greek yogurt

2 cloves garlic, crushed

Juice of ½ lemon

Maldon sea salt flakes

¼ cup extra-virgin olive oil

SQUASH

Grapeseed oil, for cooking

3 pounds butternut squash or
pumpkin, peeled and cut into
2-inch chunks

1 tablespoon cumin seeds

1 tablespoon black onion
seeds (also called
nigella seeds)

⅔ cup extra-virgin olive oil

2 yellow onions, diced

2 large cloves garlic, chopped

1 tablespoon paprika

4 pounds plum tomatoes,
peeled and chopped

1 pound Le Puy lentils, cooked

6 eggs, soft-boiled for
6 minutes and peeled

Really good olive oil,
for finishing

To make the dukka, lightly crush all of the ingredients together using a mallet, a mortar and pestle, or a mini food processor on pulse.

This recipe yields enough to also keep a jar on hand for future use. It will stay fresh in the cabinet for a month, in the fridge, for two months.

To make the yogurt, whisk all of the ingredients for the garlic yogurt together in a small bowl and refrigerate until needed. Remove from the refrigerator about twenty minutes before serving.

To make the squash preheat the oven to 425°F.

Warm a touch of grapeseed oil in a heavy skillet over a lively heat. Add the squash and cook until it has a bit of color all over. Transfer to the oven and bake 8 to 10 minutes, until just tender.

Meanwhile, in a frying plan, over medium-low heat, temper the cumin and onion seeds in the olive oil for 5 minutes to release their aroma. Add the onions and cook until soft and translucent. Add the garlic and paprika and cook for 5 minutes longer.

Raise the heat and add the tomatoes. Cook for a minute or two and then add the lentils and simmer for 15 minutes, until everything is well married and hot. Off heat, add the roasted squash and gently fold into the lentils.

To serve, divide the lentil-squash mixture among six warmed wide pasta bowls. Cut the eggs in half and place two halves cut side up atop each serving of lentils. Spoon on a bit of garlic yogurt, shower liberally with dukka, and drizzle with a really good olive oil, for finishing.

PURPLE SPROUTING BROCCOLI
WITH OLIVE OIL MASH

**SERVES 4 AS A FIRST COURSE
OR 2 AS A MAIN COURSE**

1 pound purple sprouting
broccoli or broccolini, leaves
and woody ends trimmed

2 pounds Yukon gold
potatoes, unpeeled

1 head garlic

1 red chile

3 long shaved strips of
lemon zest

½ cup olive oil, plus more
as needed

1 tablespoon freshly
squeezed lemon juice

Salt and pepper, to taste

4 lemon wedges, for
squeezing

You may well wonder why I've included a recipe here for what is essentially mashed potatoes and grilled broccoli. The answer is simply Yotam. When Yotam cooks vegetables, magical things happen. With slight additions or minute extra steps here and there, something as simple as mash becomes exponentially better. And isn't this, really, what we all wish we could do, in the kitchen and everywhere? I confess to being a bit underwhelmed when Yotam first suggested I include this dish. We'd been bouncing ideas back and forth and when this recipe appeared in my in-box, my response was clearly reticent. Yotam jumped on the phone in surprise. "You didn't like it?" he asked, with genuine concern. I confessed to not yet having tested it and promised to do so straightaway. I called a few hours later, tail between my legs, having made it and, of course, I loved it. I think you will too.

A note on ingredients: Yotam uses purple sprouting broccoli. This leafier, deeper hued cousin of your standard green broccoli is quite similar to broccolini. It is often available in farmers' markets from February until April. Broccoli rabe is also an excellent option, if slightly sharper in taste. At NOPI, this is served as a first course, but I think it is a wonderful and substantial supper.

And the answer to a much-asked question: NOPI is the acronym for "North of Picadilly."

Preheat the oven to 350°F.

Bring a large pot of water to a boil and parboil the broccoli for 3 to 4 minutes, until it is cooked but retains its bite. Shock it with a blast of very cold water, drain, and set aside to dry.

Arrange the potatoes on a large baking sheet. Slice the top off the garlic head and discard it. Wrap the remaining garlic in aluminum foil and place it alongside the potatoes. Bake for 50 to 60 minutes, until the potatoes are cooked through.

Thinly slice the chile at an angle and place it in a small saucepan with the lemon zest and olive oil. Warm over medium heat for 3 minutes and then remove from the heat and set aside to cool. Discard the lemon zest.

Peel the warm potatoes and press them twice through a potato ricer or use a masher. Transfer to a medium saucepan. Unwrap the garlic and squeeze to release the cooked cloves, adding them to the mash. Whisk the mash well over medium heat as you add ¼ cup of the chile oil, lemon juice, 1 teaspoon of sea salt, and a good grind of black pepper. Whisk until smooth and silky; add some water and more oil if the mash is too thick and then use a spoon to stir and cook another minute. Set aside somewhere warm until ready to serve.

Place a ridged grill pan over high heat and leave it to heat up well. Toss the cooked broccoli with the remaining chile oil and a pinch of salt. Grill in batches until the stems just start to color.

Serve the broccoli atop a generous serving of mash. Drizzle with olive oil and a further squirt of lemon.

POTATO CHAAT WITH POMEGRANATE, MINT, AND ROSE RAITA

SERVES 4 AS A FIRST COURSE OR SIDE DISH

1 pound baby new potatoes, boiled until just tender

Grapeseed oil, as needed

1 cup cooked chickpeas

1 yellow onion, finely chopped

¼ cup minced fresh ginger

1 green chile, minced, seeds included for extra heat, removed if a milder taste is preferred

A good handful of fresh cilantro leaves, chopped

Salt or black salt

⅓ cup whole plain yogurt

Honey, for drizzling

⅓ cup tamarind chutney

1 teaspoon chaat masala mix (see page 90)

2 tablespoons clarified butter or ghee

Continued

This is as impossible to resist as a plate of perfect french fries, and let's face it, there are times in life when nothing short of a fried potato will do. Imagine now, that said fried potato has been seasoned with chiles and ginger, drizzled with sweetened yogurt, drizzled again with tamarind chutney, and served with a beautiful raita garnished with pomegranate seeds and ground rose petals. Now you will understand why almost everyone who walks through the door of Gymkhana orders this potato chaat before even being shown to a table.

Karam named Gymkhana, his second restaurant, after the gentlemen's clubs in India. Originally started by the British, gymkhanas were places of assembly and sport. Many centered around equestrian events, tennis, golf, cricket, and, of course, bridge. Inside there would be a formal dining room, a bar, and several drawing rooms. Long after colonial rule, the gymkhanas continue to thrive. Karam wanted to draw on the idea that Gymkhana was more than a restaurant, that it was really a place of gathering and feasting. Indeed, if you take a walk through Gymkhana, you'll discover several rooms, including a dark, sexy bar downstairs. An ideal afternoon, to my mind, would be a late lunch in the dining room, a visit to the Marlborough Gallery just across the street in the afternoon, a return to the restaurant for a dessert of mango kheer and perhaps, early evening, a quinine sour in the bar. Something about the place saps one's sense of industry and ambition, or maybe it is merely the happy satiation brought on by this potato chaat.

When the boiled potatoes are cool enough to handle, flatten each potato with the palm of your hand and then cut in half crosswise. Thinly coat a frying pan with grapeseed oil and heat it to medium high. Fry the potatoes until golden brown and then flip and repeat on the other side.

Transfer the potatoes to a bowl, along with the chickpeas, onion, ginger, chile and most of the cilantro. Gently toss together and season with sea salt, if needed.

Continued

Continued

POTATO CHAAT WITH POMEGRANATE, MINT, AND ROSE RAITA

POMEGRANATE, MINT, AND ROSE RAITA

2 cups full-fat Greek yogurt

Leaves from 8 sprigs mint, finely chopped

3 tablespoons dried rose petals, ground in a coffee or spice grinder and a bit more for sprinkling

3 green chiles, seeds removed and chiles minced

2 teaspoons fresh ginger, grated

Sea salt

Black salt, if available

A good handful or two of fresh pomegranate seeds

MAKES ABOUT 3 TABLESPOONS

1½ tablespoons chaat masala

1 tablespoon amchoor powder

1½ teaspoons black salt

Pinch of dried fenugreek

In a small bowl, sweeten the yogurt with a drizzle of honey.

In a separate bowl, stir together the tamarind chutney and chaat masala mix; then stir in the clarified butter.

To make the raita, whisk together the yogurt, mint, half of the ground rose petals, the chiles, and ginger together in a bowl. Season with sea salt and, if available, black salt.

To serve, arrange the potato mixture on a platter and drizzle with the sweetened yogurt and the tamarind chutney mixture. Scatter the remaining cilantro on top. Scatter with fresh pomegranate seeds and a dusting of ground rose petals.

Serve immediately with the raita on the side.

CHAAT MASALA MIX

Put all the ingredients in a small bowl and stir to combine.

POLENTA WITH CHESTNUTS, RICOTTA, SQUASH, AND FRIED SAGE

SERVES 4 TO 6

POLENTA

3 quarts chicken stock or vegetable stock, preferably homemade, or water, at room temperature

2 cups polenta

6 tablespoons butter, at room temperature, cut into pieces

7 ounces vacuum-packed cooked whole chestnuts, coarsely chopped

A ladleful of whole milk (optional)

1½ cups freshly grated Parmesan, plus more for serving

A handful of chopped flat-leaf parsley

RICOTTA

1 cup good artisanal fresh ricotta, at room temperature

Olive oil, as needed

Salt and pepper, to taste

SAGE

1 or 2 bunches sage

1 tablespoon flour

Olive oil, for frying

SQUASH

1 red kuri squash or small butternut squash, peeled and cut into ¼-inch slices, each about 2 inches long

Olive oil for frying

Sea salt

Apologies to the chef are in order. A few years ago, a friend showed me how to make polenta without stirring, and now I can't bring myself to make it any other way. You start with room-temperature water, broth, or milk, add the polenta, and pop the pot in the oven. You are then free to do the eighteen other things requiring your immediate attention. At the Three Crowns, of course, the polenta is made with water and stirred, as befits tradition and authenticity. It can be served warm and soft, or it can be allowed to set, sliced, and either grilled or fried.

Lee's simple cold-weather pairing is an inspired one. A dollop of fresh ricotta offers a cool, tangy note that plays well with the crisp sage. In spring, I swap in asparagus for the chestnuts and squash and omit the sage. A few fresh chives, chervil, or tarragon add an herbaceous edge. In autumn, wild mushrooms are wonderful with the polenta and ricotta, particularly if thickly sliced. And in summer, there's always zucchini, perhaps sautéed with a sliced Vidalia onion or two and maybe a hint of mint. The one necessity here is to use a good fresh artisanal ricotta, as it will be immeasurably creamier than anything you'll find in a supermarket.

To make the polenta, preheat the oven to 350°F.

Pour the stock into a large heavy stockpot. Add the polenta and 3 tablespoons of the butter. Give it a little stir. Put the pot in the oven and bake, uncovered, for 1 hour and 10 minutes.

Give the polenta a thorough stir, then add the remaining 3 tablespoons of butter and the chestnuts. If the polenta seems dry, add a ladleful of milk, broth, or water. Bake for 10 minutes longer.

Remove the pot from the oven and stir in the Parmesan and parsley.

Grease a rimmed baking sheet. Pour the polenta onto the prepared sheet and smooth the top with a spatula. Cover with parchment paper and refrigerate until set, at least 2 hours and up to 24.

Continued

Continued

POLENTA WITH CHESTNUTS, RICOTTA, SQUASH, AND FRIED SAGE

Once set, cut the polenta into squares. Let your hunger dictate the size. There will be leftover polenta; save it for tomorrow, freeze for another day, or even thinly slice and deep-fry it as polenta french fries.

Now that you have your polenta squares, you can either fry them, place them under the broiler, or grill them. Be sure to cook until crisp on both sides and heated through.

To prepare the ricotta, combine the ricotta with a little olive oil and salt and pepper in a bowl. Set aside until needed.

To fry the sage, pluck the leaves from the sage sprigs. Pat the sage leaves dry with paper towels if they are at all moist. A trick to frying very fresh sage—and I do mean sage that you've picked yourself only moments before—is to give it the barest coating of flour. Shake off any excess and proceed.

Line a plate with a few layers of paper towels. Heat a good-sized glug or two of olive oil in a frying pan. Carefully drop the sage leaves into the hot oil and fry for 20 seconds. The leaves should sizzle and curl slightly. Remove them with a slotted spoon and check to see if they are crisp. If not, fry them a few seconds longer, but do not let them burn—no one enjoys burnt sage! Transfer to paper towels to drain.

To make the squash, line a plate with a few layers of paper towels. Warm another good-sized glug of olive oil in a large frying pan until hot, but not smoking. Working in batches, add the squash and fry until lovely and golden on both sides. Transfer to the paper towels to drain and season to taste.

To assemble, place the polenta, whether grilled or fried, on warmed plates and top with a good dollop of the ricotta followed by a generous pile of your fried squash. Finish with a flourish of the fried sage. If you like, add a shower of freshly grated Parmesan and several grindings of black pepper.

TAKTOUKA

SERVES 4

2 to 3 tablespoons olive oil

1 small white onion,
finely chopped

4 cloves garlic, minced

2 teaspoons harissa paste

1 teaspoon ground cumin

½ teaspoon ras el hanout
(see pages 192-194)

2 or 3 large red tomatoes,
chopped

3 bell peppers in assorted
colors (such as orange,
yellow, red), grilled, skinned,
seeded, and sliced in strips

Sea salt

3 teaspoons chopped
fresh cilantro leaves, plus
a few extra whole leaves
for garnish

3 teaspoons finely
chopped fresh mint

½ teaspoon orange-blossom
water

4 eggs

Great olive oil, for drizzling

Thick grilled slices of
sourdough bread or
toasted pita, for serving

Perhaps it is my unabashed love for London that has put me in a state of denial, but I don't believe it rains more in London than, say, in Paris or New York. It is simply that the rain is different. It is truly a gray rain, not the New York rain that leaves the sky a crystalline blue or the Paris rain that, when it lifts, leaves a pink aura in its wake. I'm reminded more of Nantucket, which is called the "little grey lady by the sea" by locals because of the morning fog that sets in and blankets the sky in a cloak of soft gray.

When it rains in London, two things become immediately essential. The first is color; the second is a roaring fire in the hearth. Since one is so rarely seated before a roaring fire, I'd like to suggest food with a fiery bite. This *taktouka* delivers on both fronts. It is bright with red and yellow bell peppers and fiery with harissa. Served in the piping hot cast-iron skillet in which it is cooked, it is simple, rustic peasant fare at its most nourishing.

At Fernandez and Wells, I like to eat the *taktouka* when I'm perched at the bar with a view of hanging charcuterie and the tangy smell of cheese wafting through the space. It comes in its own small cast-iron skillet, but, as few of us have a supply of these at home, I've adjusted the recipe to fit a standard skillet. Dee's *taktouka* is ever so slightly different from others I've tasted. The touch of orange-blossom water she uses rounds the flavor beautifully, offering an elusive, seductive note that also appears in her harissa paste, which includes rose petals. This may sound strange, but it is quite traditional to Morocco, where Dee's husband was born.

Taktouka is actually a Berber word for *vegetable stew* and is thought to be Tunisian in origin. That said, it is now found throughout North Africa and much of the Middle East. Technically, *taktouka* becomes *shakshuka* when it includes a poached egg, but I won't change names on Dee. I will, however, offer a few notes. In a pinch, you may peel the peppers, slice them finely, and sauté them with the onion. They are softer if chargrilled, but perhaps brighter if not. If you desire more heat—and the harissa already provides a lot—add a whole dried chile and remove it before adding the eggs. And if you crave a bit of

Continued

Continued

TAKTOUKA

creaminess, toss in a few small nuggets of feta cheese. They will melt just enough to form pockets of richness. If you are too busy to stand by a hot stove, transfer the *taktouka* to a hot oven for ten minutes just after adding the eggs. They will bake rather than poach, but to no adverse effect. In Israel, this is considered a breakfast dish. But try it one cold rainy afternoon, and you will find yourself much fortified.

In a skillet, preferably made of cast iron, warm the olive oil and then sauté the onion until it is soft and transparent. Add the garlic and sauté 5 minutes longer at a gentle heat. Add the harissa, cumin, and ras el hanout and cook another minute or two. Give it a stir to help coat the onions with the spices. Stir in the tomatoes and bell peppers and simmer until soft, about 20 minutes. Season with salt. Stir in the cilantro, mint, and orange-blossom water.

Crack the eggs into the *taktouka*, evenly spacing them around the pan. Continue to cook at a gentle simmer the eggs are lightly poached.

Drizzle with a great olive oil and garnish with a few cilantro leaves. Serve immediately with crusty sourdough bread or toasted pita.

ALPINE FONDUE

SERVES 6

11 ounces Emmental
de Savoie

14 ounces Beaufort Alpage

11 ounces Comté d'Estive

½ ripe Reblochon, rind
removed (about 8 ounces)

5½ ounces Bleu de Gex,
rind removed

½ clove garlic

1 bottle white wine,
preferably from the Savoie

Pinch of freshly
ground pepper

Pinch of freshly
grated nutmeg

3 to 4 tablespoons kirsch,
to taste

Cornichons, pickled pearl
onions, a baguette torn
or cut into chunks, as
accompaniments

There is that moment when you walk into a cheese shop and the tangy, buttery aroma suddenly comes over you in a wave of pleasure. You ogle, you taste, you buy; but you don't want to leave. You want to sit right then and there, order a glass of wine and a cheese board, and eat while enveloped in that aroma. Scientists tell us that smell accounts for much of what we perceive as taste. This, then, is my rationale for making a habit of lunch at La Fromagerie: to bring another sense into the mix. The bars of artisanal dark chocolate, the hearty rounds of bread, the bottles of wine, the artfully assembled vegetables, the heady coffee beans, and the copious charcuterie offer the visual reassurance that you need, in fact, that you need never leave as all is provided.

I am not alone in this thinking. La Fromagerie has had an enormous influence on the way Londoners eat. Patricia opened the shop in 1992 when French cheese was something you only ate in France. Her influence has resurged in recent years, as she has been a great advocate for the artisanal small-batch cheesemakers now scattered throughout the British Isles. Having seduced Londoners with Continental cheeses, she has now convinced them to look to their own backyards as well. When I was last in the shop, two Scottish brothers showed up with a wheel of their homemade cheese for Patricia to taste and hopefully stock. Her passion for cheese made her eminently accessible, and the brothers were soon seated and a bottle of wine poured.

Patricia, not surprisingly, has a knack for fondue. For those who assume that this involves no more than melting cheese in a pot, think again. A great fondue is a balancing act, melding different varieties and keeping upstarts in check so that no single cheese claims center stage but instead offers shifting, surprising character. It is for this reason that I've included not only Patricia's ingredient list, but a list of possible substitutions using stateside artisanal cheeses on pages 98-99. This latter version is thanks to Matthew Rubiner, owner of Rubiner's Cheesemongers in Great Barrington, Massachusetts, and one of the very few Americans to be inducted into the Guilde Internationale des Fromagers. As both Patricia and Matthew write deliciously about cheese, I've left their words verbatim.

Continued

Continued

ALPINE FONDUE

—————

PATRICIA'S CHEESE NOTES:

Emmental de Savoie: "I find this has a lovely nutty flavour and is not too waxy."

Beaufort Alpage: "Such a wonderful floral richness."

Comté d'Estive: "Do try and get one that is aged eighteen months–plus."

Reblochon: "Remove the rind."

Bleu de Gex: "This is a Franche-Comté Blue, which will give the fondue a toasty sharp edge."

—————

MATTHEW'S CHEESE NOTES AND U.S. ALTERNATIVES:

Emmental de Savoie: "There are so many 'Swiss' cheeses made here, but only a few achieve the nutty complexity of the holey Swiss (and Savoyard) classic. Robinson Farm's Robinson Family Swiss from Hardwick, Massachusetts, is simple and sweet, a little farmy. Holey Cow, from California's Central Coast Creamery, is very mild, very rich. But only Wisconsin's Edelweiss Creamery makes a traditional Emmentaler, in wheels the size of truck tires, by hand in copper vats from the milk of grass-fed cows."

Beaufort Alpage: "Thistle Hill Farm and Spring Brook Farm, of North Pomfret and Reading, Vermont, respectively, each make a cheese called Tarentaise, inspired by French Beaufort and Abondance. They are both superb, big flat wheels with ridged, convex sides and tacky auburn rinds. They are similar in flavor—hazelnutty, gratinéed leeks—but Thistle Hill's is firmy, Spring Brook's more melty. Jasper Hill Farm's Alpha Tolman, a little more pungent, would work admirably."

Comté d'Estive: "Andy Hatch's Pleasant Ridge Reserve, from Uplands Cheese in Dodgeville, Wisconsin, should do the trick. Firmer, more crystalline, and more intensely flavored than our Comté, which we like sweet, but much like the more aged Comté that Patricia seems to favor."

Reblochon: "We are deprived of real Reblochon de Savoie in the U.S., but Sequatchie Cove's Dancing Fern from Tennessee is a dead ringer. Gushingly, I would say it is supple, more heaving from its soft pink flaky rind than flowing like a saucy custard; pungent but not so pungent as Époisses or Munster or the like, with a soft sour tang of cultured butter and onions slowly stewed in that butter."

Bleu de Gex: "There are not many U.S. blues with the firm but springy (and not terribly appealing) texture of Bleu de Gex. But there are so many good ones that should bring the same sort of spice that Patricia is looking for. Jasper Hill Farm's Bayley Hazen Blue from Greensboro, Vermont, is fudgy textured and anglophile. Rogue Creamery's Rogue River Blue is moister, sweeter."

Patricia, going against European tradition, likes to start a fondue dinner with a salad of winter greens and bitter chicory leaves. The sharp citrus tang to these leaves, she tells me, needs a nutty dressing—walnut or hazelnut oil with a mild white wine vinegar or verjuice, a spoonful of Dijon mustard, and a pinch of sugar, salt, and pepper. She then tosses in coarsely crushed toasted hazelnuts or walnuts. The salad is meant to whet the appetite, since the fondue is exceedingly rich. Of course, lots of cubes of crusty bread lightly dried out in the oven are essential here, but Patricia expands the accompaniments to include bits of smoked cooked ham, cured ham, salami, steamed skin-on small potatoes, and steamed broccoli florets, which I could do without. A bowl of cornichons keeps things perky. Matthew reminded me that the kirsch needs to be a good one, without any of that awful fake-cherry flavor that kills lesser bottles. And Patricia reminded me to choose a bottle of white Savoie—Chignin or Apremont or something similarly fresh and fruity (not a creamy white chardonnay!). You will probably not need the whole bottle for cooking, but the white Savoie is also a perfect wine to serve alongside the fondue.

Continued

Continued

ALPINE FONDUE

Grate all the cheeses on the large holes of a box grater—not too finely—and place in separate bowls. It is easiest to grate cheese if it is chilled. (It's perfectly fine to tear the Reblochon and Bleu de Gex into small pieces.) Set aside and let come to room temperature.

Start the fondue in a saucepan on the stove. You may later transfer it to a fondue pot at the table.

Choose a heavy saucepan that will conduct heat evenly, such as a Dutch oven. Rub the inside of the pan with the garlic, pressing hard to extract the juice. Discard the garlic.

Pour 2 glasses of wine into the pan and bring to a gentle simmer. Sprinkle a small handful of the Emmental into the pan. Stir briskly with a wooden spoon until the cheese has melted and then sprinkle in more Emmental a small handful at a time until all the Emmental has melted. Repeat with the Beaufort, followed by the Comté. If the consistency is too thick, add another glass or half glass of wine and whisk briskly with a balloon whisk.

Transfer the fondue to a warm fondue pot, if you have one, and bring it to the table. Just before serving, add the Reblochon (whisk briskly with a balloon whisk), followed by the Bleu de Gex. Add the pepper and nutmeg and, as a final flourish, pour in the kirsch.

Serve with bowls of the cornichons, onions, and baguette. The fondue will need to be stirred often at the table to maintain the creamy richness, so make sure there are a few wooden spoons for your guests to use.

SEAFOOD

RAZOR CLAMS WITH FAVA BEANS AND SERRANO HAM

**SERVES 4 AS A TAPAS,
2 AS A FULL COURSE**

2 pounds fava beans in their pods, shelled and peeled

½ cup olive oil

1 ounce sliced serrano or Iberico ham, cut into ½-inch strips

2 shallots, finely chopped

2 cloves garlic, finely chopped

¾ to 1 cup chicken stock, preferably homemade

Maldon salt and freshly ground black pepper

⅓ cup good-quality olive oil

20 small razor clams, thoroughly cleaned

Ajillo, for serving

AJILLO

⅓ cup extra-virgin olive oil

3 cloves garlic, finely chopped

A small handful fresh flat-leaf parsley, finely chopped

Catching razor clams is squirmy fun and embarrassingly funny thanks to its overt obscenity. On a summer's day on the beach, look for wiggly holes in the sand that resemble in shape a sperm on steroids. Pour a good amount of salt into the hole and pour on some seawater. In seconds a razor clam will come poking out, long and skinny. It will push up through the sand, the clam itself extending out of the shell and retracting with surprising vigor. In fact, if a clam doesn't do its in-out thing, it is a dud and should be tossed. Sadly, as of this writing, there is no Viagra for mollusks. Don't miss Shorehound's YouTube video, "How to Catch Razor Clams" set to Fats Waller's song "Hold Tight (Want Some Seafood Mama?)" for a laugh and a dance.

Back to the serious art of food: Nieves serves the razor clams simply prepared as a tapa with serrano ham and fresh fava beans, with a drizzle of what her staff calls "magic", otherwise known as ajillo, an infusion of garlic and parsley in extra-virgin olive oil. I like to extend this tapa into a meal by also serving thick, grilled slices of peasant bread, brushed, of course, with a bit of that magic and perhaps some sautéed cherry tomatoes, just bursting out of their skins.

Place a bowl of ice water next to the stove. Bring a large pan of salted water to a boil. Add the peeled favas and blanch for 1 minute. Drain and plunge the favas into the ice water for 2 minutes. Drain the favas again and pat them dry with paper towels. Set aside.

Warm ¼ cup of the olive oil in a large skillet over medium heat. Add the ham and cook gently for 30 seconds. Add the shallots and cook for 30 seconds, then add the garlic and cook for a couple of seconds longer. Add the remaining ¼ cup of olive oil as well as the stock and simmer until the liquid reduces by half. Add the favas, season with the Maldon salt and pepper, and cook until heated through, about 1 minute.

In a separate skillet, warm the good-quality olive oil over high heat until smoking. Add the razor clams and cook, tossing, until the shells open. Turn the razor clams flesh side down and cook for 1 minute longer, until the flesh is golden brown. If any are still closed at this point, chuck them.

To make the ajillo, stir together the olive oil, garlic, and parsley in a small bowl.

Divide the clams among plates and spoon the favas and ham over the top and into the shells. Drizzle with the ajillo and serve immediately.

SCALLOPS WITH RED NAM YUM

SERVES 2

6 large, fat fresh scallops in the shell

2 tablespoons finely chopped cilantro, stems and leaves, plus additional leaves for garnish

7 cloves garlic, peeled

4 fresh long Thai red chiles, seeded and coarsely chopped

Sea salt

3 tablespoons palm sugar (see note)

1¼ cups freshly squeezed lime juice, plus more if needed

Juice from 2 mandarins or small oranges

⅔ cup Asian fish sauce

NOTE Do buy the highest-quality palm sugar you can find, as it will have the lowest percentage of cane sugar.

Smoking Goat is a hole-in-the-wall Thai restaurant on the wrong side of the tracks, but it happens to have serious pedigree. Likewise, Denmark Street may not appear to be posh, but it discreetly houses the offices of some of the film industry's most wildly successful producers. (Just ask Harry Potter.) The street, nicknamed Tin Pan Alley, is still perhaps better known for once housing some of the most legendary recording studios and their stars. The Rolling Stones recorded at 4 Denmark Street, David Bowie frequented Gioconda Café at number 9, and the Sex Pistols lived at number 6.

Had Smoking Goat been around in the 60s and 70s, it would have fit right in. It has an insider feel to it and a cool authenticity. Ben came to the restaurant world already an accomplished graphic artist and interior designer. His life took a dramatic turn when he started cooking and found himself with an immediate following at Climpson's Arch, a pop-up for new chefs. Urged by friends like Tomos Parry of Kitty Fisher's to open a place of his own, Ben took the leap and did it with bold flavors on this storied street.

Ben is a grilling man. He tells me he likes the range of heat this fuel source can provide. To make these scallops on the half shell, he places them ever so briefly on white-hot embers. As the red nam yum sauce is irresistible, don't hesitate to serve it on pan-seared scallops whenever the desire strikes, even if grilling is impractical. Ben, himself, uses the red nam yum sauce liberally on everything from meat to vegetables, and I imagine you will too. The sauce is at once sweet, salty, sour, and hot. It is also bright red, and on a white shell with a scattering of coriander leaves, it makes a striking impression.

To grill the scallops on wood, wait until your fire has burned down to hot embers. Remove the skirt retaining the roe that is attached to the scallop muscle. Loosen the flesh of the scallop from its shell with a spoon. Roast the scallops on the half-shell directly on the embers for around 90 seconds. A short, sharp searing heat will just start to turn the flesh opaque, while the shell protects it. Remove from heat. Flip the scallop

Continued

Continued

SCALLOPS WITH RED NAM YUM

meat. The shell should have a dusting of golden brown. The residual heat in the shell will finish cooking the scallop.

Alternatively, heat a cast iron pan over high heat. Add a light touch of grapeseed oil. When the oil is smoking hot, sear the scallops (out of their shells), flipping them over mid-way through cooking, until just opaque, about three minutes total.

To make the red nam yam sauce, in a large mortar and pestle, pound the cilantro stems, garlic, and chiles into a coarse paste, using coarse sea salt as an abrasive if necessary. Add the palm sugar and pound it into the paste for a few more seconds. Just before serving, add the lime juice, mandarin juice, and fish sauce.

Dress the grilled scallop on the half shell with a spoonful of the sauce and garnish with a couple of cilantro leaves. Serve immediately.

SCALLOPS WITH CORN PUREE AND CHILE OIL

SERVES 4

CHILE OIL

1 fresh red chile

2 teaspoons olive oil

Pinch of salt

CORN PUREE

6 to 8 ears corn, husks
and silks removed

1 cup water, plus more
if needed

Two dried chiles, each cut
into halves

1 tablespoon sugar

6 tablespoons unsalted butter,
at room temperature

½ cup crème fraîche, at room
temperature

Salt and pepper, to taste

SCALLOPS

20 diver scallops

Sea salt and freshly ground
black pepper

1½ teaspoons olive oil

4 limes, for squeezing

As always, the apparent simplicity of Skye's recipes belies a highly
refined culinary aesthetic. Her food is a reminder that less is often more,
at least when it comes to the number of ingredients. As to amounts, well,
this corn puree is so good that I've doubled the recipe, as everyone who
tastes it wants more.

When Skye serves this, she uses the puree as a soft bed on which to
place the seared scallops. If you like your puree to be the texture of
crème fraîche, use six ears of corn. It will spread over your plate to form
said bed. If you prefer your puree a bit thicker, use eight ears, and it will
have the texture of polenta. Make this dish at the height of corn season,
and it will make you swoon. Don't be put off by the sugar, as it counters
the chile, yielding a subtle sweet-spicy accent to the corn.

To make the chile oil, slice the chile in half lengthwise and discard the
seeds. Chop the chile as finely as possible. In a small bowl, stir together
the chile, olive oil, and salt. Let infuse for an hour or two.

To make the corn puree, work with one ear of corn at a time, standing
it upright on a cutting board and using a sharp knife to cut the kernels
off the cob.

Put the kernels in a saucepan with the water, chiles, and sugar and
cook over medium heat for about 20 minutes, until the corn is tender.
Drain the corn, discarding the chiles. Put the corn and butter in a food
processor and puree until smooth. Set aside to keep warm while you
make the scallops. Just before serving, fold in the crème fraîche, season
with salt and pepper.

To cook the scallops, pat them dry with paper towels and season with
salt and pepper. Warm a nonstick frying pan over high heat. Add the
olive oil and let the pan become really hot. Working in batches so as not
to overcrowd the pan, sear the scallops for one minute, flip and sear for
another minute.

To serve, spoon the corn onto four warmed plates and lay the scallops
on top. Drizzle with the chile oil and squeeze the limes over them. Serve
immediately.

FISH AND CHIPS

SERVES 5

TARTAR SAUCE

4 egg yolks

1 teaspoon English mustard

½ teaspoon fine sea salt

¼ teaspoon freshly ground
black pepper

¼ teaspoon freshly ground
white pepper

1 tablespoon white wine
vinegar

2 teaspoons freshly squeezed
lemon juice

3 cups canola oil

2 tablespoons ice water,
if needed

1 tablespoon chopped
gherkins

1 tablespoons capers, rinsed

2 large shallots, minced

2 tablespoons chopped
flat-leaf parsley

Continued

They are indisputable. A fact of British life.

That, perhaps, is the most important thing you need to know about fish and chips. So essential to the happiness of Brits, fish and chips was one of the only foods not rationed during World War II. Perhaps Churchill was a devotee, or perhaps he simply knew that ravaged families needed foods that offered not only comfort, but a sense of national continuity. I wonder if he knew that Jewish refugees from Spain and Portugal, in flight from the Inquisition, first introduced fried fish to England in the early sixteenth century.

Since the days of Charles Dickens and his chips with "reluctant drops of oil," there has been both much evolution and none at all. Many a chipper or chippy, as fish and chip houses are called, still serve roughly the same recipe you might have found one or two hundred years ago. But then there are chefs like Tom, who have elevated the art and craft of fish and chips while preserving the beloved tradition to a T. To my mind, his version is the best in London. And while chips aren't as skinny as their French cousins, fries or *frites*, they are nearly as irresistible, doubly so, with this tartar sauce. Oh, and on the subject of origins, tartar sauce has nothing to do with the Tartars, save for the French predilection for adopting exotic names for their sauces, including *sauce tartare*. Too bad, as it would have made for a good story.

Here are a few pointers about heat and timing, as expertise in deep-frying isn't a given. If the oil isn't hot enough, your fish and chips will be soggy instead of crispy. Be patient in waiting for the oil to heat to the required temperature and work in batches so as not to overcrowd the fryer and lower the temperature of the oil. I suggest making the tartar sauce first and refrigerating it until needed. Then prepare the batter. And finally, heat the oil and set to frying, first the potatoes and then the fish.

Continued

Continued

FISH AND CHIPS

FISH AND CHIPS

1½ cups self-rising flour

2 tablespoons cornstarch

¾ teaspoon fine sea salt

½ teaspoon sugar

½ cup beer, preferably lager

½ cup sparkling water

2 pounds potatoes, such
as russets or Maris Pipers,
peeled

Oil for frying, such as canola,
safflower, or grapeseed

5 pieces cod fillets, roughly
5 ounces each

Malt vinegar, for serving

To make the tartar sauce, whisk together the egg yolks, mustard, salt, and pepper in a bowl until pale. Whisk in the vinegar and lemon juice. While whisking constantly, drizzle in the oil to form a mayonnaise-like emulsion. Only add the ice water as needed to loosen the consistency if too thick. Fold in the gherkins, capers, and shallots. Fold in the parsley just before serving.

To make the batter for the fish, combine the flour, cornstarch, salt, and sugar in a bowl. Make a well in the center of the flour mixture, then pour in the beer and sparkling water and whisk to combine. Set aside for 10 minutes, then whisk again until smooth. Set aside to rest for 15 to 20 minutes longer and then whisk again. There should be no lumps!

To make the chips. Wash the peeled potatoes and cut them into ½-inch wide batons. Rinse the potatoes under cold running water to remove excess starch.

Parboil the potatoes in abundantly salted boiling water until just short of tender. Drain and transfer immediately to a bath of ice-water.

Line a plate with paper-towels and place next to the stove. Heat the oil in a deep-fryer or high-sided saucepan to 280°F. Working in batches, drain the potatoes and plunge them into the hot oil to blanch for 2 minutes. Remove with a spider spoon and drain on paper towels. Increase the heat of the oil to 360°F, then plunge the chips back into the oil for 4 to 5 minutes longer, until golden brown and crispy. Remove immediately to drain on paper towels and sprinkle with sea salt.

To make the fish, line a plate with paper towels and set next to the stove. Using the same saucepan or fryer as you used to the make the chips, bring the oil to 360°F. Working in batches, dip the fish into the batter and, holding each piece up by its tail end, let the excess drip off. Gently place the fish into the hot oil and fry for about 8 minutes, until golden and crispy. Work quickly because the beer batter is best used as soon as it's ready. Transfer to drain on the paper-towel lined plate while you finish frying the remaining fish.

Serve the fish and chips immediately with the tartar sauce and malt vinegar.

SUGAR-BRINED SALMON WITH RADISH, CUCUMBER, AND PEA SHOOT SALAD

SERVES 4

SALMON

⅓ cup demerara sugar

2 tablespoons Maldon sea salt or coarse sea salt

Zest of 1 lemon

Zest of 1 lime

3 white peppercorns, crushed

4 skinless salmon fillets, about 6-ounces each, pin bones removed

Grapeseed oil, for cooking

DRESSING

½ cup mayonnaise

2 tablespoons crème fraîche

Juice of ½ lemon

Leaves from ½ small bunch flat-leaf parsley, finely chopped, plus more for garnish

Leaves from ½ small bunch tarragon, finely chopped, plus more for garnish

Leaves from ½ small bunch chervil, finely chopped, plus more for garnish

Leaves from ½ small bunch chives, finely chopped, plus more for garnish

Maldon salt flakes and freshly ground pepper

Continued

Of the handful of iconic restaurants in London, two boast stained glass windows—Bibendum and the Ivy. Bibendum's glass rendition of the Michelin man is instantly recognizable to locals and foreigners alike. The subtle diamond-mullioned stained glass windows at the Ivy are a better kept secret. On any given night, the restaurant is a veritable who's who of London's theater community. Actors come fueled by adrenalin, pumped with applause, or seeking solace, camaraderie, and drink after a tepid review. The privacy offered by the stained glass windows keeps predatory paparazzi at bay and, for those wanting further remove, there's now a private club upstairs. I've little doubt, however, that were it not for Gary's exceptional cooking, the A-list would find other watering holes.

The Ivy has been a success since it opened its doors in 1917, and Gary has had the good sense not to mess with the ever-popular classics, such as shepherd's pie and Bang Chicken. But his menu now includes a column called Asian Graze and Share, which threatens to upstage tradition, and I notice more and more hints of spice and zest and umami with every visit. When I mentioned this, he gave me a mischievous smile and whispered "baby steps."

This salmon is a favorite of mine, thanks to the dry brine of sugar, citrus, and crushed white peppercorns. I cook this salmon so often that I rarely get around to making the salad and green goddess dressing, but when I do, I am always glad. The brine is brushed off the salmon before cooking, but what remains of the sugar caramelizes in the pan to delicious effect. It's addictive.

To make the salmon, stir together the sugar, salt, lemon and lime zests, and peppercorns in a container or baking dish big enough to fit the salmon in a single layer. Place the salmon in the sugar mixture, turning and rubbing the salmon until it's coated on both sides and let it brine at room temperature for one hour. Don't brine the salmon for more than 2 hours, or the salmon will start to break down.

Continued

Continued

SUGAR-BRINED SALMON WITH RADISH, CUCUMBER, AND PEA SHOOT SALAD

SALAD

1 cucumber, peeled

1 bunch assorted radishes (such as rainbow and breakfast)

A handful of pea shoots

To make the dressing, stir together the mayonnaise, crème fraiche, lemon juice, parsley, tarragon, chervil, and chives in a bowl. Season with salt and pepper. Cover and refrigerate up to 2 hours.

To make the salad, julienne the cucumber and radishes. In a large bowl, toss the cucumber, radishes, and pea shoots with just enough of the dressing to lightly coat them. Save the remaining dressing to use within one day as a dip or salad dressing or sandwich condiment.

Remove the brine from the salmon. Gary advises rinsing the fillets and patting them dry with paper towels, but I like to brush off the brine, leaving a bit of the sugar stuck on. Just be sure to brush all of the salt away. Pat the fillets dry.

Warm a bit of the oil in a nonstick frying pan over high heat. When the oil is smoking, add the salmon and cook for 3 to 4 minutes, until you see a good charred color on the bottom. Flip the salmon and cook on the other side until done to your preference.

Transfer the salmon to plates and serve the salad alongside it. Top with a scattering of herbs, should you have some left.

PLAICE, SALSIFY, AND CAPERS

SERVES 4

1 pound salsify

3 pounds plaice, cut
into 4 portions

Olive oil for frying

10 tablespoons unsalted
butter

½ cup dry vermouth

4 lemons, 2 juiced and
2 halved

2 tablespoons capers, rinsed

Leaves from 1 small bunch
curly parsley, finely chopped

———————————

NOTE if you can't source
plaice, halibut and sole
are delicious alternatives.
Salsify looks rather like dirty
parsnips or even horseradish.
Once cleaned and cooked,
they have a delicious creamy
almost oystery taste. They
are a root vegetable and a
member of the dandelion
family.

Fergus has one of the great smiles. When something stirs his fancy, his face opens, like a child's, in gleeful delight. It is infectious and generous, and I challenge anyone to resist it. When I first met Fergus , it was a little before eleven on a weekday morning. He had asked me to join him for a meeting and then lunch at St. John Bread and Wine. I was about to ask for a cup of coffee, when I saw him enter the restaurant. He greeted me as if I were an old friend and handed me a glass of Champagne. When I opened my mouth to protest, he gave me that pink-cheeked smile and, kindly cutting me off, said simply: "because." "Because" to Fergus is because it is life, because it is good, because it can be even better with a glass of Champagne, because I am your host, because we will feast and be merry, because all will be well, because why not? I drank the Champagne, of course, and all was indeed as his smile had promised.

We were soon surrounded by a circle of friends—locals stopping by the bar, some after a morning yoga class at Fierce Grace down the street, others still in last night's party clothes. Two cooks had just gotten engaged to each other, and so another bottle of Champagne was opened. Three young Japanese women approached Fergus for an autograph, and drinks were sent to their table. At noon, Fergus led me up the stairs to lunch in the dining room with Trevor Gulliver, his longtime business partner.

Five hours later, we were still at lunch, still feasting, still drinking, and still very merry. We'd followed the Champagne with a crisp white and a full-bodied red and then vintage port to accompany the cheese course of Welsh Rarebit (page 22). Moreover, we'd eaten one of the great meals of my life, including this plaice with salsify and capers. Salsify makes Fergus smile that smile of his. When ordering, he promised it would have a "delicate and subtle, creamy flavor" that would make it "a perfect partner to plaice." Having learned that absolute submission was the wisest approach to this lunch, I nodded happily. Something of a salsify novice, I became a convert and now love its almost oystery taste.

By the time we'd moved on to Apple and Calvados Cake (page 215), my happiness held a sharp note of sadness. Fergus, as so many know, has

Parkinson's disease. It has neither dampened his public spirit nor curbed his immense talent, but it is a tragedy that a man of such luminous generosity should suffer. He no longer dances with Margot (his wife) on tables, as they are known to have done—this he told me, ever the stoic, making light of heartbreak for the sake of others. What effort this must take him. And all with that smile of his.

In the words of Fergus: First, prepare the salsify. It is grown in very sandy, light soil. To keep it straight, the end is often left on to protect the root. It should be handled with a degree of care and kept whole, roots on. Like beetroot, salsify will bleed during cooking, losing flavor. Lightly brush away the excess soil then remove the remaining dirt by immersing it in cold water and gently cleaning with a brush that is not too stiff.

Preheat the oven to 375°F.

Place the whole roots in a braising pan or small roasting pan and cover with water, add a little salt, and cover with foil. Either gently poach on the hob (stove) or cook in the oven. It will take 20 to 30 minutes. Test with a small knife, as you would potatoes. Remove from oven. Pour off the water and then cover the pan in plastic wrap so that the roots continue to steam. When cooled slightly, peel away the outer skin with a small knife, and cut into 2½-inch lengths.

In a large heavy frying pan, fry the plaice, skin-side down, in a little olive oil, until golden.

Place the pan in the oven for about 4 minutes. Turn the plaice over, and add the salsify batons to the pan. Return to the oven for about 3 minutes, although obviously this will be determined by the thickness of your plaice.

When just cooked, lift out the fish and place the pan back on a medium to high heat. Add the butter and sizzle until golden and nutty brown then stop the butter from burning by adding the vermouth, then the lemon juice. Add the capers and parsley to finish. Serve each piece of fish with a half lemon.

GINGER- AND CILANTRO-SPICED COD WITH CAULIFLOWER "COUSCOUS"

SERVES 8

MINT AND RAISIN CAULIFLOWER COUSCOUS

½ cup golden raisins

1 cup apple juice

2 tablespoons pomegranate molasses

2 cauliflowers, cut up into small florets

2 teaspoons fennel seeds

1 teaspoon minced fresh turmeric

Salt and pepper, to taste

Extra-virgin olive oil

Leaves from 1 bunch mint, coarsely chopped

Zest of 1 lemon and its juice

COD

Leaves from 1 small bunch cilantro, chopped

3 cloves garlic, minced

1½ tablespoons baharat

2 teaspoons fresh minced turmeric or ½ teaspoon ground turmeric

2 teaspoons fresh minced ginger

Zest of 1 lemon

Juice of ½ lemon

1 teaspoon sea salt

8 (6-ounce) cod fillets, skin-on

Vegetable oil or olive oil, for cooking

Unsalted butter, for cooking

Anna's pantry is indeed modern, if by modern, we mean fresh, vibrant, bold, and sourced from far and wide. Her food revives a tired palate with twists of spice and turns of texture. Born in Canada and raised in New Zealand, Anna is a classically trained chef who cut her chops under Fergus Henderson at his first restaurant, the French House Dining Room. With Peter Gordon, she then opened the Providores in Marylebone. But the Modern Pantry is unique. I still remember the first time I was handed a menu—moromi miso relish, pickled shimeji mushrooms, morcilla braised leeks, cassava chips, calamansi lime cream—the words leapt off the paper. Her imagination was humbling, as was her reach.

I love both these recipes, particularly paired together, as Anna serves them. The cod is spiced with baharat, a Middle Eastern spice mix that just happens to contain many of my favorites—allspice, cardamom, cloves, nutmeg, and cinnamon. She offsets the inherent sweetness of these spices with a hefty dose of fresh turmeric, ginger, and lemon zest. The "couscous" contains no couscous, but rather features cauliflower that has been roasted and chopped to resemble Israeli couscous. Again, it is beautifully spiced and given a sweet note with raisins that have been plumped up in apple juice and pomegranate molasses. It is hands down the most fabulous way to serve cauliflower. Even vegetable-averse children will gobble it up, if you don't get to it first.

To make the cauliflower, preheat the oven to 400°F.

Combine the raisins, apple juice, and pomegranate molasses in a small saucepan and gently bring to a simmer over medium heat. Set aside to cool.

Toss the cauliflower, fennel seeds, turmeric, and olive oil in a bowl. Season with salt and pepper. Roast for 10 to 15 minutes, until the cauliflower starts to turn golden but is still al dente. This is important! If the cauliflower is overcooked, the "couscous" will end up a mush. Remove from the oven and let cool.

Continued

Continued

GINGER- AND CILANTRO-SPICED COD
WITH CAULIFLOWER "COUSCOUS"

Tip the cooled cauliflower into a food processor and pulse until the cauliflower resembles couscous. Be careful not to over process. Drain the raisins, discarding the soaking liquid. Tip the cauliflower into a bowl and stir together with extra-virgin olive oil to coat, mint, lemon zest, lemon juice, and raisins. Adjust the seasoning. The cauliflower may be made several hours in advance and brought to room temperature just before serving.

To make the cod, stir together the chopped cilantro, garlic, baharat, turmeric, ginger, lemon zest and juice, and salt in a baking dish large enough to fit the cod in a single layer. Place the cod in the dish, turn to coat and cover with plastic wrap. Marinate for at least 2 hours and up to 4 in the fridge.

Preheat the oven to 350°F.

Warm a little vegetable oil and a decent knob of butter in a large skillet over high heat. In batches, place the fish in the pan, skin-side down, and cook until the skin is golden. Turn the fish over and transfer to a baking sheet pan. Once you have browned all of the fish, transfer the pan to the oven and bake for 4 minutes or so, until the fish is just cooked though and the flesh looks translucent.

Serve immediately on the cauliflower couscous.

SEA BASS WITH HOT PAPRIKA VINAIGRETTE

SERVES 4

POACHING STOCK

8 cups fish stock

1 cup white wine

2 teaspoons olive oil

1 yellow onion, quartered

1 bunch flat-leaf parsley

2 bay leaves, preferably fresh

5 cloves garlic, peeled

5 peppercorns

Salt, if needed

VINAIGRETTE

½ cup extra-virgin olive oil

4 cloves garlic, sliced

3 tablespoons good red
wine vinegar

1 tablespoon sweet paprika,
preferably smoked

2 teaspoons hot paprika,
preferably smoked

Salt and pepper, to taste

4 fillets Chilean sea bass,
sea bass, or black cod, about
6 ounces each

A handful of fresh herbs,
finely chopped, such as
parsley, cilantro, and chives

4 slices warm toasted or
grilled crusty bread,
for serving

The fish here is poached in a rather classic mix of wine and stock. What makes the recipe sing is the hot paprika vinaigrette. It couldn't be easier to make, but a generous drizzle of it gives a delicate fillet of fish spice, heat, and a heady infusion of garlic. It also adds a trail of striking, burnished red. At the restaurant, this fish is served with spinach and grilled bread. At home, I often replace with bread with couscous, which I also drizzle with the paprika vinaigrette.

Chilean sea bass, is not technically a bass, but a Patagonian toothfish. (It is rumored that when given the arguably more chic name of *Chilean sea bass*, Patagonia toothfish tripled in both price and popularity.) It has since become over-fished. That said, you might easily substitute black sea bass, striped bass, or even black cod (also known as sablefish) with equally delicious results—these choices are not only more reasonable in cost, but also, at present, more ecologically sound.

I crave this recipe after a few nights of rich food. It is simple, healthy, and vivid in flavor. Serve over cooked chard, if you like.

To make the poaching stock, pour the fish stock into a wide braising pot, a fish poacher, or a roasting pan. Pour in the wine and olive oil and toss in onion, parsley, bay leaves, garlic, and peppercorns. If the stock is unsalted, add a spoonful or two of salt. Bring to a boil and then turn down the heat and simmer for about 40 minutes, until the flavors meld. You can, of course, do this a few hours ahead of time. The taste will only improve if left to sit a while. Do make sure you have enough liquid to submerge the fish. Add a bit more stock or water as needed—the amount will depend on the size of the pan.

While the stock is simmering, make the vinaigrette. Warm the olive oil in a saucepan over medium heat until hot but not smoking. Add the garlic and sauté until just golden. Turn off the heat and move the pan to another, cooler burner. Pour in the vinegar, with caution as it will spit and spatter. Keeping the pan off the heat, stir in the paprikas and watch as they dissolve, turning the oil a burnished red. Add a few pinches of sea salt and grinds of pepper. Return the pan to the still-warm burner, keeping the heat off and letting it sit as you poach the fish.

Continued

Continued

SEA BASS WITH HOT PAPRIKA VINAIGRETTE

Bring the poaching stock to a lazy simmer and gently lower the fish fillets into the liquid. Poach the fish until it just starts to flake when nudged with a fork—this may take as little as 7 or 8 minutes or as long as 11 or 12, depending on the thickness of the fillet. A center-cut piece may have twice the girth of one closer to the tail.

Remove the fish to a platter or plates. Heat up the vinaigrette for a few seconds and give it a last stir.

Spoon a tablespoon or two of the poaching liquid over each fillet, followed by a generous drizzle of the paprika vinaigrette. Sprinkle with chopped parsley, cilantro, or chives to add further color.

Serve with thick slices of warm toasted or grilled crusty bread, also drizzled with vinaigrette.

HALIBUT WITH SPINACH, CHILE, AND PRESERVED LEMON DRESSING

SERVES 4

DRESSING

2 preserved lemons

Juice of ½ lemon, or to taste

1 cup crème fraiche

1 pound baby spinach

1 fresh red chile

3 tablespoons olive oil

4 halibut or wild sea bass fillets, about 6 ounces each

Salt and pepper, to taste

2 lemons, halved, for garnish

After an exquisite lunch at Spring, I asked Skye not only for this recipe, but also for the name of the wallpaper used in the main dining room and the shade of paint used in the ladies' room. She was not surprised. The restaurant is grand in an airy, feminine, restrained way that is immensely appealing. The design itself seems to set beauty and grace above ambition, but don't be mistaken, Spring is a very serious and very ambitious restaurant.

Skye is much talked about in London. The heiress to an Australian media fortune, she came to France to cook, then moved to London. A beauty, an addict, a Michelin-starred chef (at Petersham Nurseries), she found herself in the unrelenting glare of the spotlight and, perhaps wisely, disappeared from public view for several years. When she returned to the restaurant world in 2014 with Spring, her first solo venture, it was as a sober, poised grown-up. A taste of her cooking and it's hard not to imagine that her rapt attention to nature's beauty was, quite literally, a saving grace. That attention is everywhere in her cooking, and eating at Spring is a reminder, if you will forgive the cliché, to stop and smell the roses.

Skye's recipes are not complicated, but they are predicated on outstanding ingredients. They are a return to the virtues of simplicity with, thankfully, no expectation of austerity. (Note the crème fraîche.) That said, this recipe is almost spa-like in its purity and is most welcome the night after a rich feast or when the weather is warm and the windows open.

Preheat the oven to 350°F.

To make the dressing, cut the preserved lemons into quarters, scoop out the flesh, and discard. Rinse the lemon peel well under cold running water, pat dry with paper towels, and place in a food processor. Add the lemon juice and crème fraîche and purée until smooth. Set aside in a cool place.

Continued

Continued

SEA BASS WITH SPINACH, CHILE, AND PRESERVED LEMON DRESSING

Wash the spinach really well under cold running water. Drain but do not dry. Find a pan large enough to hold all of the spinach and warm over medium heat. Add the spinach, with a bit of water still clinging to the leaves, and cook, tossing, until it has just wilted. Remove from the heat, drain, and let cool. When it is cool enough to handle, squeeze out any excess liquid.

Slice the chile lengthwise, scrape out the seeds, and finely slice. Warm a little olive oil in a saucepan over low heat. Add the chile, followed by the spinach and a pinch of salt, and toss to combine. Cook for 2 minutes, until it's piping hot. Set aside in a warm place while you cook the fish.

Season the fish with salt and a little pepper. Warm a cast-iron pan over a high heat and add the oil. When the oil is hot, lay the fish, skin-side down, and cook without turning for 2 minutes, until the skin should be golden brown. Transfer the pan to the oven (still with the skin-side down) and cook for 4 to 6 minutes, until it just begins to flake easily.

Place the fish on warmed plates. Lay the spinach and a dollop of sauce alongside the fish. Serve with half of a lemon.

FOWL

CHICKEN SCALOPPINE WITH MUSHROOMS AND MARSALA

SERVES 3

3 boneless, skinless
chicken breasts

Salt and pepper, to taste

2 tablespoons
all-purpose flour

2 tablespoons olive oil

8 ounces mushrooms
(such as cremini,
chanterelles, or porcini),
stemmed and sliced

2 tablespoons
unsalted butter

½ cup dry Marsala,
white wine, or dry to
medium sherry

1 tablespoon chopped
flat-leaf parsley

Jacob says it perfectly: "Comfort food often verges on bland, whilst exciting flavors are sometimes demanding or divisive. This is a rare dish as soothing as it is zingy."

Keep a bottle of Marsala stashed in the back of the cupboard and you will find yourself returning to this speedy recipe every few weeks, never growing weary of it. Jacob likes it with creamy mashed potatoes, and though I'm always loathe to argue with creamy mash as an accompaniment, there are also egg noodles, orzo, mushroom ravioli, gnocchi—the choices are many. If I'm in the mood for extra sauce, I simply use more mushrooms and another splash or two of Marsala. Make it as you want to eat it—never a bad rule to cook by.

You can ask your butcher to cut the chicken breasts into scaloppine, or you can do it yourself. It's really quite easy.

To cut the chicken into scaloppine, lay a chicken breast on a cutting board, Hold a sharp knife parallel to the cutting board and cut the chicken into slices that are ¼ inch thick.

Preheat the oven to its lowest setting.

Season the scaloppine with salt and pepper, then lightly dust with flour. Warm the oil in a wide pan over high heat. Working in batches, add the scaloppine and fry, turning once, until nicely browned on both sides. Transfer to a baking sheet and keep warm in the oven, as you cook the remaining scaloppini and the mushroom sauce.

Once all of the scaloppine has been cooked and is in the oven you can begin making the mushroom sauce. Add the mushrooms and butter to the hot pan and cook over high heat until the mushrooms are nicely browned.

Return the chicken to the pan and carefully add the Marsala away from the heat. Cook over high heat until the sauce has thickened. Season with salt and pepper, add the parsley for a touch of color, and serve immediately.

GRILLED CHICKEN TACOS WITH CHARRED SPRING ONION MAYONNAISE

SERVES 4

MARINADE

2 pasilla de Oaxaca or meca chiles

2 cups water

¾ cup vegetable oil

3 cloves garlic, minced

8 chicken thighs, preferably boneless, skinless

MAYONNAISE

1 bunch scallions, topped and tailed

2 cloves garlic, unpeeled

1 jalapeño

1 cup mayonnaise

Juice of 1 lime

Pinch of sugar

Salt and pepper

ACCOMPANIMENTS

8 corn tortillas

Lime wedges, for serving

Good salsa, for serving

Little gem lettuce, sliced, for serving

Avocado, peeled, pitted, and chopped, for serving

True story: The night before the 2005 final competition on *MasterChef*, Tommi (Thomasina) came home to the apartment she was sharing with Joseph Trivelli (a hugely gifted protégé of Ruthie Rogers now one of the head chefs at the River Cafe), and Stevie Parle (now chef-owner of Dock Kitchen), convinced she was going to lose the popular television competition. Despite training at the Ballymaloe Cookery School in Ireland and under Skye Gyngell at Petersham Nurseries, a gap remained in her culinary education and, because of it, she found herself at a serious disadvantage. The final competition, you see, was to be handmade ravioli, something she'd never even tackled let alone mastered. And then the key turned in the front door and in walked Joseph, exhausted from a night cooking at the River Cafe. An espresso or two later, sleeves rolled back up, he taught Tommi how to make the most delicate ravioli she'd ever eaten. She, of course, won the series and is the first to credit Joseph with her success.

After a stint traveling in Mexico, Tommi returned to London and opened Wahaca, a restaurant serving Mexican street food. An instant success, it spawned a chain. But in this rare case, expansion has not diminished the quality of the food, and so I'm breaking my no-chain rule to include these excellent chicken tacos.

To make the marinade, combine the chiles and 2 cups of water in a saucepan and simmer for 30 minutes, until soft. Remove the chiles, discarding all but a few tablespoons of the soaking liquid. When the chiles are cool enough to handle, stem and seed them. Place the chiles with a few tablespoons of the soaking liquid, the oil, and the garlic into a small food processor and blitz until almost smooth. Marinate the chicken in the chile mixture for a few hours or overnight.

Preheat the oven to 350°F.

To make the mayonnaise, preheat a gas or charcoal grill or warm a dry skillet. Scald the scallions, garlic, and jalapeño until charred on all sides. The scallions will take the longest, about ten minutes. Cook them with a watchful eye, turning them as soon as one side starts to blacken. When the jalapeño is cool enough to handle, stem and seed it. Place the jalapeño, scallions, garlic, mayonnaise, lime juice, and sugar in a food processor or blender and puree. Season with salt and pepper.

Warm an ovenproof grill pan or skillet and cook the chicken, skin-side down, for 3 minutes, until the skin is golden. Flip and cook the other side for a minute or two. Transfer the pan to the oven and bake for 10 to 15 minutes, until the juices run clear and the chicken is no longer pink in the middle. Remove from the oven and slice the chicken into strips. Warm the tortillas, one at a time, in a dry frying pan over medium-high heat. Fill the tortillas with strips of chicken and a dollop of mayonnaise. Serve with lime wedges, salsa, little gem lettuce, and avacado.

INDIAN CHICKEN AND PUMPKIN CURRY

SERVES 2 TO 4

2 skin-on chicken breasts

2 skin-on chicken legs

Sea salt

¼ cup ghee or clarified butter

1 teaspoon cumin seeds

1 teaspoon ground cumin

1 teaspoon ground turmeric

1 teaspoon sweet paprika

1 teaspoon fenugreek seeds

1 teaspoon mustard seeds

1 cinnamon stick

Seeds from 4 black
cardamom pods

Good pinch of curry powder
or a few fresh curry leaves

Good pinch of saffron
threads

1 clove

1 large yellow onion,
finely chopped

3 cloves garlic, crushed

1 (2-inch) knob fresh ginger,
peeled and grated

1 small fresh red chile,
finely chopped, seeds
removed if you prefer
a milder dish, left in, if
you prefer a hot dish

1 teaspoon tomato paste

4 cups chicken stock

7 ounces pumpkin or
butternut squash, peeled
and cut into 1½-inch cubes

2 tablespoons chopped
fresh cilantro

It wasn't more than forty-five seconds after meeting Mark Hix that I found myself perched on a barstool in his office above Tramshed. He'd had various plates sent upstairs, and his private cocktail bar was exceedingly well equipped. The office was more or less what you might expect from the owner of a converted tram shed in Shoreditch that features, as its centerpiece, a huge Damien Hirst vitrine encasing a cow with a chicken standing on its back—all preserved in formaldehyde. The menu—can't you guess? Steak and roast chicken.

In other words, his office was a sort of hip bad-boy bat cave, only bright, immaculately clean, and featuring a kitchen rather than a Batmobile. And then there was Mark. He did have the look of someone who has seen and caused quite a bit of trouble, and he was, of course, wearing the requisite black T-shirt and black jeans. But the bad-boy image ended there. For one thing, Mark was no longer a kid. With nine restaurants, a dozen books, a hotel, his own wine label, a column at *the Independent*, and three daughters, he has proved himself more responsible than perhaps he'd like to admit. (And I haven't even mentioned the many years he oversaw the Ivy, Le Caprice, J. Sheekey, and Scott's.)

When Mark talks about food, his demeanor changes. Normally a bit awkward, even reticent (and I don't believe it's all attitude), he suddenly brims with ideas and boyish delight, his love of food writ large on his face. And with this wonderful excitement comes a deep well of generosity—he was one of the first chefs to offer recipes, encouragement, and introductions to me when I started researching this book.

Mark is a man who is most clearly in his element in the kitchen. This is doubly true of his kitchen in Dorset. Those who know him in Dorset know a man kicking about in Wellies on the docks or setting off in his fishing boat. And I believe it's safe to say that while Mark may own some of the coolest joints in London, at heart, he is what every good restaurateur needs to be—a generous soul who loves to feed people and look after them as if they were his dearest friends.

This simple curry is a weeknight staple of mine. Serve it with basmati rice, chutney, and some green peas for good measure. Mark uses only chicken legs, but I add breast meat because the variety pleases me. Either or both is fine. So, too, is using butternut squash instead of pumpkin. This is an autumn or winter dish, offering warmth and comfort and, from the pumpkin, a welcome hint of sweetness.

Combine all of the spices in a small bowl.

Season the chicken with salt. Warm the ghee in a heavy skillet over a medium-low heat until hot, but not smoking. Add the spices, onions, garlic, ginger, chile, cumin, turmeric, paprika, and fenugreek and cook, stirring, for a couple of minutes to release the aroma. Raise the heat to medium-high, add the chicken (skin-side down) and the tomato paste. Being careful not to burn the spices, cook until the chicken is golden. This shouldn't take more than 5 minutes.

Pour in the chicken stock, bring almost to a boil, and then immediately turn down the heat and gently simmer for 30 minutes. Add the pumpkin or butternut squash and simmer for 15 minutes longer, until tender. Adjust the seasoning. Serve piping hot with a shower of cilantro.

TANDOORI BBQ CHICKEN

SERVES 4

4 boneless, skinless
chicken breasts

1 tablespoon vegetable oil

2 tablespoons malt vinegar

2 tablespoons ginger and
garlic paste (it is sold in jars)

1 teaspoon salt

1 teaspoon cumin seeds

1 cup full-fat Greek yogurt

3 tablespoons roasted
unsalted peanuts,
lightly crushed

2 fresh hot green chiles,
finely chopped, seeds
removed

2 scant teaspoons amchoor
(dried mango powder)

1 tablespoon vegetable oil

2 tablespoons finely
chopped fresh cilantro

½ lemon

NOTE Naan, basmati rice,
chutney, and raita are all
good accompaniments.

This easy recipe is chameleon-like in its ability to adapt. In the restaurant, it is cooked in a tandoor oven. At home, Vivek suggests a combination of a hot oven and a few minutes under the broiler. In warm weather, it is fantastic cooked over a grill, and for the truly outdoors type, perhaps even over a campfire. If you are fed up with chicken, try it with guinea fowl, partridge, or rabbit.

Although inspired by the nomadic tribes in the northwest of India, this dish is quite modern in Vivek's reinterpretation. It's so healthy that I can imagine eating it at a spa (albeit a very good one, and perhaps not served with steaming basmati and sweet chutney, both of which I recommend keeping). It is excellent picnic fare, as it is equally good whether slightly chilled or at room temperature.

The hardest part of this recipe is stocking the spices. Here Vivek, in an unusual move, uses dried mango not only for acidity, but as a tenderizer that breaks through the protein of the meat. It is through this alchemy that boneless, skinless chicken breasts emerge as perfectly tender, juicy nuggets. As there are so many variables to grilling times, I give you, here, the oven version.

Enough said. The recipe is speedy and so, then, shall I try to be.

Preheat the oven to 425°F.

Cut the chicken into 1½-inch cubes. Soak eight wooden skewers in water while you prepare the chicken. (It's also possible to make this chicken leaving each breast intact.) Lightly oil a baking pan.

Whisk together the vinegar, ginger and garlic paste, and salt in a large bowl. Add the chicken and toss until well coated. Let marinate for a few minutes.

Meanwhile, warm a frying pan over medium-low heat. When hot, add the cumin seeds; toast until they give off their aroma. Lightly crush them and then place in a small bowl and whisk together with the yogurt, peanuts, chiles, and dried mango. Stir in the cilantro. Spread this second marinade over the chicken and set aside to marinate at room temperature for 30 minutes.

Remove the chicken, allowing the excess marinade to drip off before proceeding. Thread the chicken pieces onto the soaked wooden skewers and place on the prepared baking pan. Bake for 6 to 8 minutes, until almost cooked. (If using whole breasts, cook for closer to half an hour.) Turn the oven to broil and place the baking pan close enough to the flame to char the chicken a bit, but do not burn it. And do make sure the wooden skewers aren't poking up into the flame! Broil for about 3 minutes, flip the skewers, and broil the second side another minute or two. Give the chicken a squeeze of lemon and serve immediately.

If I have naan on hand, I like to serve it here, warm. If not, basmati rice, chutney, and raita are the classic choice.

CHICKEN BERRY BRITANNIA

SERVES 5

Grapeseed oil, for cooking

2 yellow onions, sliced

1 clove garlic, minced

2 teaspoons deggi mirch or
1½ teaspoons chile powder

2 teaspoons ground cumin

⅔ cup full-fat yogurt

1 bunch fresh cilantro,
leaves chopped

1 fresh green chile, seeded
and sliced

1 (2-inch) knob fresh ginger,
peeled and grated

¼ cup dried barberries or
cranberries, plus more
for garnish

Salt

1¼ pounds boneless chicken
thighs, sliced into 2-inch strips

1¼ pounds basmati rice

1 or 2 pinches of
saffron threads

½ cup heavy cream

Chopped fresh mint,
for serving

Chopped fresh cilantro,
for serving

Dishoom is not old, but the archival photographs, Art Deco sconces, and lamps fashioned from antique film projectors gently fold you into the past, shutting out the very modern world of Shoreditch. The food must be explained. First, know that it is delicious. Second, know that it harks back to the Parsi cooking once found in Bombay's Irani cafés. In particular, it is an ode to Bombay's Britannia, the most revered of the Irani cafés, for which this Parsi biryani is named.

At Dishoom, the biryani is cooked in the traditional *dum pukht* style, in a pot sealed with pastry to retain all the moisture and flavor, but a heavy-lidded Le Creuset or Staub Dutch oven works just as well. What you miss is that dramatic moment in which you break the pastry open at the table and the aroma of the spices suddenly bursts forth. Whether you lift off the lid with a grand flourish or quietly remove it and watch the smell work its magic, rest assured that the tastes to follow are a lovely balance of spice and comfort.

In a heavy skillet, warm a touch of grapeseed oil. Add the onions and cook on medium-heat until soft and colored. Add the garlic, deggi mirch and cumin and cook another few minutes. Transfer to a mixing bowl and combine with the yogurt, cilantro, chiles, ginger, and barberries. Season with salt.

Add the chicken and toss until well coated. Let marinate for 2 hours.

Cook the basmati rice in ample water until it is nearly cooked, but still has a bite. Drain. Preheat the oven to 400°F.

In a heavy-lidded pot, layer the chicken and its marinade with the partially cooked rice. In a small bowl, stir the saffron into the cream and then drizzle it over the surface of the chicken and rice.

Cover the pot. If your pot's lid is not heavy and tight-fitting, use a round of parchment paper or aluminum foil to first cover the chicken, then cover with the lid so that no air or moisture can escape. The restaurant uses a strip of dough to seal the lid.

Bake for 45 minutes, until the chicken is cooked.

Sprinkled with mint, cilantro, and barberries and serve immediately.

BUTTERMILK FRIED CHICKEN IN PINE SALT

SERVES 4

PINE SALT

1½ ounces freshly plucked pine needles, plus a few pine branches for decoration

1 teaspoon sea salt

CHICKEN

6 boneless, skinless chicken thighs

1½ cups buttermilk, preferably full-fat and artisanal

1 clove garlic, crushed

2½ cups instant (quick-cooking) polenta

1¼ cups tapioca starch

⅓ cup rice flour

12 cups safflower, canola or sunflower oil, for frying

Pine needles, for decoration

Isaac McHale is, without question, one of the most talented young chefs in London. Look around the Clove Club almost any night, and you'll find a handful of chefs from near and far feasting and taking notes. It is considered an essential landmark on the London's culinary map. When Isaac cooks, he seems to have a stock of every imaginable spice and ingredient at his fingertips. His palate knows no boundaries or constraints. He is nimble. And while his menu may look very post-Noma (where he did, in fact, work), the flavors themselves taste inevitable—that is, after you ask yourself why, say, people haven't been pairing pine needles with fried chicken for years, centuries even.

When I asked Isaac about sourcing the pine needles for the pine salt in this dish, he laughed and told me that everywhere he has cooked this dish (and he has now cooked it at festivals around the world), he's managed to find a pine tree within a mile of his hotel. In other words, take a stroll through the nearest park and discreetly pluck a few needles off the nearest Douglas fir. Isaac, himself, collects his pine needles from various parks in East London. After years of mourning discarded Christmas trees, I now eye them with a purpose, sniffing to see that their needles are still fresh and fragrant with an almost citrusy note.

If you have leftover pine salt, save it to sprinkle on sweet potato fries and roasted butternut squash. Remember that the pine salt is best made about five days in advance and that the chicken needs to marinate for a day, so a bit of planning is in order. If you can source good, old-fashioned full-fat buttermilk, do so! The difference between thick, tangy, luscious artisanal buttermilk and the thin, sour low-fat supermarket variety is huge. And, really, nothing with the word *butter* in it should ever be low fat.

To make the pine salt, grind the pine needles in a spice grinder or clean coffee grinder. When reduced to small fibers, add the salt and pulse to combine. Store in a jar and refrigerate for at least 5 days.

To make the chicken, trim any gristle, then cut into bite-size nuggets, about 8 to 10 per thigh.

Continued

Continued

BUTTERMILK FRIED CHICKEN IN PINE SALT

Shake the buttermilk, then stir together with the garlic and salt in a large bowl. Add the chicken, turn to coat with the buttermilk mixture, and let marinate in the fridge overnight.

The next day, remove the chicken from the fridge 1 hour before frying the chicken and let it come to room temperature. Drain and discard the buttermilk marinade.

In deep fryer or high-sided saucepan, heat the safflower oil to 340°F. Combine the polenta, tapioca starch, and rice flour in a bowl and give it a little whisk to thoroughly combine the ingredients. Dredge the chicken in the flour mixture and shake off the excess. Working in batches, fry the chicken nuggets, 10 or so pieces at a time, for 2 minutes, or until golden brown. Drain the nuggets on paper towels. Transfer the nuggets to a serving bowl and liberally season with the pine salt, shaking the bowl so that the salt sticks to the chicken.

Serve over a decorative bed of pine needles.

BRAISED DUCK LEG, SPICED RED CABBAGE, AND QUINCE

SERVES 4

DUCK

Grapeseed oil, as needed

4 duck legs, trimmed of excess fat

Salt

½ cup red wine

¼ cup good sherry vinegar

¼ cup sugar

2 sprigs rosemary

A small handful of chopped, fresh flat-leaf parsley

CABBAGE

1 red cabbage, thinly sliced

½ cup red wine

¼ cup good sherry vinegar

¼ cup sugar

1 teaspoon caraway seeds

1 teaspoon whole allspice (wrapped in a tied cheesecloth bundle)

QUINCE

2 quince or ½ cup quince jelly

½ cup water

½ cup sugar

Zest and juice of 2 lemons

This is a beautiful recipe and one of the most elegant I came across as I tasted my way through London. Jago opened in Shoreditch not long ago. Louis had been the head chef at the Ottolenghi on Ledbury, a Notting Hill favorite of mine. His food mixes Southern European, Middle Eastern, and Ashkenazi influences, with those of his own East London Jewish roots.

The name Jago is a playful allusion to Arthur Morrison's novel *A Child of the Jago*; Jago being the area stretching from Shoreditch High Street to Spitalfields and known in the late nineteenth century as a den of gin palaces, thieves, and prostitutes. Shoreditch today has gone the way of Tribeca, what with its renovated lofts and chic restaurants, but despite—or because of—the high real estate prices, residents seem rather determined to remind you, however ironically, of the neighborhood's seedy past. That said, Jago is situated in Second Home, an office building that bills itself as a cultural hub and looks like it could be the first home of a Silicon Valley start-up. It is, in other words, about as seedy as the Apple Store.

Now, about this recipe. I find it too good to make only during the limited season of the quince. My solution is to use a quarter cup of quince jelly and decrease the amount of added sugar. Instead of poaching the fruit, I simply bring the jelly, water, sugar, and lemon juice to a boil and then stir and reduce until it is smooth and a bit syrupy. It's delicious. My only other advice is to slice the cabbage on a mandoline. It's fast and will yield a very pretty finish. In fact, the cooked cabbage emerges a gorgeous deep dark red, making this dish perfect for a dinner party. I serve it with polenta that I cook in milk. It's a mild counterpoint to the sweet and spice of the duck.

Continued

Continued

BRAISED DUCK LEG, SPICED RED CABBAGE, AND QUINCE

Preheat the oven to 325°F. Arrange your oven racks so that you can fit both the duck and cabbage in the oven at the same time.

To cook the duck, warm the grapeseed oil in a frying pan. Season the duck with salt and cook it, skin-side down, until lightly browned. Flip and brown the other side. Discard the oil.

Place the duck, wine, vinegar, sugar, and rosemary in a braising pot and cover. Bake for 2 hours.

To cook the cabbage, combine the cabbage, wine, vinegar, sugar, caraway, and allspice in another braising pot or Dutch oven, cover, and bake for 2 hours, until luxuriously tender.

Meanwhile, cook the quinces. Quarter them and discard their seeds. Cut them into slices. Combine the water, sugar, and lemon zest and juice in a saucepan. Add the quince slices and bring to a simmer. Poach for about 8 minutes, until the quince slices are tender. Set aside to cool for a few minutes. Discard the lemon peel. Puree the quince and poaching liquid until smooth and pass through a fine-mesh sieve set over a bowl, discarding the solids.

After 2 hours, remove the cabbage from the oven, discard the allspice pouch, and set the cabbage aside, covered. Uncover the duck. Raise the heat to 400°F, and cook for 10 minutes longer.

Transfer the duck to a plate and discard the rosemary. Pour the juices from the pot into a fat separator, if you have one, and pour off the fat. Otherwise, spoon off as much of the fat as you can from the surface.

Combine the quince mixture with the duck juices in a small saucepan and bring to a boil. Turn down the heat and simmer until the liquid has thickened enough to coat the back of a spoon.

Warm a frying pan. Glaze the duck legs in the reduced syrupy quince goodness and cook over a lively heat for 3 minutes.

To serve, place the cabbage onto warmed plates and place the duck legs atop the cabbage. Generously drizzle the sauce over the top and sprinkle with parsley.

HONEY-GLAZED DUCK BREAST WITH ROASTED PLUMS AND BOK CHOY

SERVES 4

DUCK

4 boneless duck breasts, about 8 ounces each

Salt

2 tablespoons honey

¾ cup port

⅓ cup veal stock

1 tablespoon unsalted butter

2 tablespoons olive oil

1 tablespoon chopped garlic

1 tablespoon chopped fresh ginger

4 heads bok choy, leaves separated

Pepper

PLUMS

8 large red plums, halved

1 tablespoon sugar

2 pinches of ground cinnamon

Clos Maggiore is one of the prettiest restaurants in London and one of the most romantic, particularly if you eat in the conservatory, an indoor-outdoor room festooned with apple blossoms and topped with a glass roof that opens on warm summer days. It is in the heart of Covent Garden, and while Marcellin's inspiration is firmly in Provence and sometimes Tuscany, his ingredients hail almost entirely from the United Kingdom. His lamb is Welsh, his poultry is from Lancashire, and his fruits and vegetables are from Kent. I mention this only because the restaurant is so utterly French in all the best ways. If I hadn't known that he'd embraced his new land with such enthusiasm, I would have assumed that he had a crew of little minions speedboating ingredients across the English Channel several times a day.

The French know how to cook duck, and Marcellin is no exception. A hint of ginger in the bok choy should ease any concern you have about the sweetness of this dish. The port may suggest tradition, but the balance here is rather contemporary. The savory oat biscuits are, of course, an ode to his adopted country. Together, the components produce a thoughtful mix of textures. But don't hesitate to cook the duck on its own and the oat biscuits for breakfast. I've kept each recipe separate so that you can pick and choose when and what to make.

To make the duck, preheat the oven to 350°F.

Season the duck with salt. Warm a skillet or frying pan over medium heat and place the duck, skin-side down in the pan. Sear for 10 minutes, adjusting the heat so the skin browns but does not burn. Flip the breasts over and slide the pan into the oven for 3 minutes. Remove the pan from the oven, brush the top with the honey, and return to the oven for three minutes longer, until glazed.

Transfer the duck to a plate and let sit in a warm place.

Pour off the rendered duck fat and either discard or reserve for another use. Over high heat, pour in the port and deglaze the pan, scraping up any good bits stuck to the bottom. Turn the heat down and simmer until

BISCUITS

1⅓ cups rolled oats

⅔ cup all-purpose flour

⅔ cup demerara sugar

9 tablespoons unsalted butter, at room temperature

¾ teaspoon baking soda

The finely grated zest from 1 orange

The finely grated zest from 1 lemon

the port has reduced by half. Add the stock and continue to simmer until again reduced by half. Stir in the butter.

Warm a wok or large nonstick pan over a lively heat. Add the olive oil, followed by the garlic and ginger, and then the bok choy. Cook until the bok choy has just wilted. Season with salt and pepper. Toss over high heat for a few minutes to distribute the seasoning and then remove it from the heat. Set aside and keep warm.

To make the plums, place the plums, cut side up, on a baking sheet and sprinkle with sugar and cinnamon. Bake for 15 minutes, until caramelized. Set aside in a warm place.

To make the biscuits, preheat the oven to 350°F, and line a baking sheet with parchment paper.

Place all of the ingredients in the bowl of a stand mixer with a paddle attachment. Mix until the dry ingredients are moistened. The dough will come together but should still be slightly crumbly. If you don't have a stand mixer, you can mix the dough with your fingers or—being extra gentle and using the pulse button—a food processor with a dough blade.

Place the dough on the prepared baking sheet and press it evenly until it's about ¼ inch thick. I do this with the heel of my hand in light, consistent little presses. Do not use a rolling pin, as it would only toughen this delicate dough.

Bake for 15 to 20 minutes, until the dough is set and light brown. While still hot, cut the biscuits into 2-inch squares. Let cool completely on the baking sheet. These are best eaten the day they are made, but any leftovers are good for breakfast, toasted and smeared with butter.

To serve, place the bok choy on warmed plates. Slice the duck breasts and set in the middle of the plate, with the biscuits on one side and plums on the other. Pour the lovely sauce onto the duck.

SPANISH CASSOULET WITH DUCK LEG CONFIT, SOBRASADA, GANXET, AND MIGAS

SERVES 4

CONFIT

½ cup sea salt

1 small bunch rosemary

1 small bunch thyme

4 fresh or dried bay leaves

1 teaspoon black peppercorns

4 juniper berries, lightly crushed

4 duck legs, trimmed of excess fat

2 heads garlic, crushed in their skin

6 cups duck or goose fat

BEANS

14 ounces Ganxet, Judion, or a similar buttery white bean

Sea salt

Continued

To understand the inspiration for this dish, you must first know this about Bob Cairns. He still remembers the exact moment he walked into Clarissa Dickson Wright's cookbook shop in Edinburgh, Scotland, and spotted a copy of the Moro cookbook. He was 28 years old and already working, but it was this groundbreaking book that made him the chef he is now. "I remember cycling around the delis and Middle Eastern food stores in Edinburgh looking for things like membrillo, salt cod, and tahini," he told me, "and how excited I was when I scored the elusive ingredients. Fourteen years on, I still find inspiration within its pages." The book led him to move to London to work at Moro and then on to Spain to study the food. His passion for the country's robust flavors led to this recipe. A hearty thanks, too, to restaurant owner and art dealer Andrew Edmunds, who tasted Bob's talent and had the good sense to build him a new kitchen and give him free rein.

Don't be put off by the length of this recipe. There are a few shortcuts that are easily taken when time and/or patience are in short supply: Buy the duck confit, use canned cannellini beans. Chorizo is readily available, eliminating the need to search out *sobrasada*, a spicy cured Iberian sausage. That said, do try to make this the Bob Cairns way at least once. Then do as I do and cut corners when the craving strikes and the clock is ticking. This is an easy recipe to double for a winter dinner party. It's rustic, but a tad lighter than its French cousin, as the different elements are cooked separately and only assembled together on the plate. And, given the beauty of the ingredients Bob uses, it makes sense to allow each their voice. Mongeta del Ganxet beans, for example, are a variety from Catalonia, which have a lovely creaminess and hold their shape well after cooking. He'll occasionally swap them with Judion beans, which are significantly larger, but no less creamy. *Ñora* peppers are beautifully balanced, playing sweet against heat with an earthy harmony.

Continued

Continued

SPANISH CASSOULET WITH DUCK LEG CONFIT, SOBRASADA, GANXET, AND MIGAS

SAUCE

¼ cup olive oil

1 white onion, finely diced

1 carrot, peeled and diced

2 stalks celery, diced

4 cloves garlic, finely diced

2 fresh or dried bay leaves

1 ñora pepper reconstituted in hot water, seeded and thinly sliced

1 teaspoon dried oregano, preferably Spanish

6 ounces sobrasada or 2 fresh Spanish chorizo sausages

½ cup red wine

2 cups canned tomatoes, chopped or crushed

1 cup chicken stock, preferably homemade

Salt and pepper, to taste

1 tablespoon duck fat or unsalted butter

MIGAS

6 thick slices day-old country-style white bread

¼ cup melted lardo, bacon fat, or duck fat

3 tablespoons olive oil

2 cloves garlic, crushed

2 fresh or dried bay leaves

Salt and pepper, to taste

The confit, by the way, can be made a few days in advance and refrigerated. I like to cook more than is needed, as duck legs are good to have on hand for a *salade composée* or for Daniel Doherty's Congee (page 28).

To make the duck confit, in a large bowl, stir together the salt, rosemary, thyme, bay leaves, peppercorns, and juniper berries. Add the duck legs, rubbing them all over with the salt mixture until well coated. Add the garlic and give a toss.

Transfer the duck to a dish that's large enough to hold all of the legs. Don't choose too large a dish, as the duck legs should fit in snugly, skin-side up. Cover with plastic wrap and refrigerate overnight.

The next morning, or after a good 6 hours, flip the legs so that the skin side is down and refrigerate for another 4 to 6 hours.

In a Dutch oven or braising pot, warm the duck fat over low heat until it just becomes liquid.

Remove the duck legs from the salt mixture, carefully brushing off as much of it as you can. Gently lower the duck legs into the duck fat, making sure they're submerged.

Cut out a circle of parchment paper that will just fit inside the pot. Place the parchment circle on top of the submerged duck legs. Bring to a gentle simmer and cook for 2 to 3 hours, until the meat is tender but not falling off the bone.

To prepare the beans, soak the beans overnight in plenty of water.

The next day, drain the beans, discarding the soaking water. Add the beans to a large, nonreactive pot with enough cold water to cover them by a few inches. (You may add a mirepoix of carrots and celery at this point, as well as a bouquet garni, but doing so is not essential.) Bring the water to the first hint of a simmer over high heat and immediately reduce the heat to very low. Simmer gently until tender. The timing will vary according to the freshness of the beans and their size, but count on about 90 minutes. Please refrain from adding salt until the beans are just short of tender. After the first hour of cooking, add two teaspoons of salt and stir to distribute. Let the beans cool in their cooking liquid if not using immediately. They may sit for an hour or two at room temperature while you prepare the sauce. Drain before using and discard the cooking liquid.

NOTE This dish includes an Andalusian version of *migas*—or, in other words, really good croutons. (The literal translation, "crumbs", doesn't quite do it justice.)

To make the sauce, warm the olive oil in a large saucepan over a medium-low heat. Add the onion, carrot, and celery and cook until the onion starts to soften. Add the garlic, bay leaves, *ñora* pepper, and oregano and cook, stirring frequently, for 10 minutes longer, until the onion is translucent but not colored.

Peel the skin off the sausage and discard. Either crumble or slice the sausage and add it to the onions. Sauté, stirring constantly over a lively heat, until the sausages start to color. Raise the heat to high, add the wine, and cook until the alcohol evaporates. Add the tomatoes and stock, return to a boil, then reduce the heat and let it simmer for 1½ hours.

Add the beans and cook 10 minutes longer. Season with salt and pepper. Stir in a spoonful of duck fat to give the sauce a lovely glossiness and richness. Set aside to keep warm while you prepare the *migas* and crisp the duck.

To make the *migas*, cut the crusts off the bread and tear or cut into bite-size pieces. Sprinkle lightly with cold water and wrap in a dish towel.

Warm the lardo and olive oil in a wide skillet over medium heat. Add the garlic and bay leaves and let infuse for a few minutes. Remove the garlic and bay leaves and discard.

Use the towel to squeeze out any excess water from the bread. Transfer the bread to the skillet and cook over a lively heat. Keep the bread moving constantly, shaking the pan or tossing with two wooden spoons, for 10 to 15 minutes, until the *migas* are crispy and golden. Transfer the *migas* to a paper towel–lined plate and season with salt and pepper.

To assemble the cassoulet, preheat the oven to 400°F.

Remove the duck legs from the cooking fat. Place them on a baking sheet and roast until the skin is crispy, about 20 minutes.

While the duck is cooking, reheat the beans and sauce. At the last minute, give the *migas* a little heat too, if needed.

To serve, place the duck leg skin-side up next to a generous portion of the beans and sauce. Sprinkle with the *migas*. Serve piping hot.

MEAT

KOREAN STEAK AND SHOESTRING FRIES

SERVES 4

4 cloves garlic,
coarsely chopped

1 (2-inch) knob ginger, peeled
and coarsely chopped

2 star anise pods

¼ cup soy sauce

¼ cup mirin

1 tablespoon sugar

1 tablespoon gochujang
(Korean red chile paste)

1 tablespoon doenjang
(brown Korean miso paste)

1 bunch scallions, the white
and pale green parts, sliced

2 pounds hanger steak or
flank steak

Maldon sea salt flakes

4 large potatoes, preferably
russets, peeled and julienned

Vegetable oil, for frying

Kimchi, for serving

This recipe is fabulous—sweet-hot umami! You really don't need the fries or the kimchi. All you need is a napkin and a cold beer.

It's a stroke of luck that I happened to hit Dock Kitchen the week Stevie had this on the menu, as the restaurant has an ever-shifting menu and moves seamlessly from one cuisine to another. The food might be Lebanese one week, Persian the next, and Indian, Mexican, Malaysian, or Italian in subsequent weeks. What unifies the experience is Stevie's natural affinity for bold flavors and very fresh ingredients—that and his talent, honed at Moro, the River Cafe, and Petersham Nurseries. He seems to reach for little known spices and grains with an easy familiarity, making him one of the most admired young chefs in London. Dock Kitchen, however, couldn't be more relaxed. A bit off the beaten path, Northeast of Notting Hill, it has a large outdoor terrace overlooking an urban landscape. The last time my husband and I ate there, it was midsummer and not yet dark when we arrived for dinner. As the sun set, the restaurant began to glow with that beautiful light that comes after a good London rain. And, a moment later, one of the most astonishing rainbows we'd ever seen appeared. Diners and waitstaff alike gathered on the terrace, cocktails in hand, as if at a party. When we wandered back to our table, it was to feast on this fantastic steak. I'd say we found the pot of gold.

It's hard to pinpoint exactly what makes this steak so delicious, but the answer is most definitely in the sweet heat of the marinade. The star anise, ginger, and sugar make the fiery potency of the *gochuchang*, a fermented Korean red chile paste, palatable, while the *doenjang*, an assertive Korean miso paste, vies for attention. Don't be alarmed by the smell of doenjang. Think of it the way you might a smelly ripe cheese—not exactly subtle, but well worth the momentary sensory shock. Slightly thicker than Japanese miso, it too can be added to soups and will last a good year in the fridge. Serve this steak with ice-cold beer. The thin shoestring fries take a bit of prep for something that will no doubt be consumed within minutes of landing on the table, but know that they will be consumed with that primal pleasure great fries elicit.

Continued

Continued

KOREAN STEAK AND SHOESTRING FRIES

Bash the garlic, ginger, and star anise in a mortar and pestle until it's a coarse paste. Transfer the paste to a large bowl and stir in the soy sauce, mirin, sugar, gochujang, and doenjang followed by the scallions. Add the steak and turn to coat with your hands so the meat is covered in the marinade. Cover with plastic wrap and refrigerate for at least 6 hours and up to overnight.

Preheat a gas or charcoal grill until extremely hot. Shake the excess marinade off the steak, then lightly season with salt. Grill for a couple of minutes on each side, until it is done to your preference. Stevie serves his rare. Let rest while you cook the fries.

Add oil to either a deep fryer or a saucepan with high sides and heat it to 350°F.

Working in batches, very carefully lower the fries into the hot oil and cook about 3 minutes, until golden and crisp. Transfer to a paper towel–lined plate and immediately season lightly with salt.

Cut the steak into strips and serve with the fries and a spoonful or two of kimchi on the side.

ONGLET WITH HORSERADISH

SERVES 4

2 pounds hanger steak
(onglet)

Light oil (such as safflower)

Black pepper and Maldon
sea salt flakes

Horseradish Cream
(page 163), for serving

Watercress, for garnish
(optional)

8 pickled walnuts (optional)

Continued

The first time I met Jeremy Lee, I was just off a plane from New York and in something of a postflight daze when I caught a cab to Quo Vadis, the Soho institution over which Jeremy presides. I say presides because, while he is the chef and a terrific one at that, it is his ebullient, bon vivant spirit that infuses the restaurant. I opened the door and was immediately swept into a happy embrace. That Jeremy and I had never met, that I was red-eyed and airplane bedraggled, mattered not. I was Jeremy's lunch date and was brought into his warm fold. Within minutes, we were chatting over the best chips (french fries) I'd ever eaten, and several hours later we were still chatting. His liveliness and the delicious food had entirely dispelled my jet lag.

Jeremy cooked under Simon Hopkinson in Bibendum's heyday, joined Fergus Henderson on TV in *Could You Eat an Elephant?* and was the head chef at Terence Conran's Blueprint Café for eighteen years. He has, in other words, a culinary pedigree. But it's clear that his pitch-perfect cooking comes from an innate gift. His food is neither fancy nor rustic, but simply just right, offering a nice balance of delicacy and nourishment. I would happily have asked for every recipe on the menu, but limited my request to five, all of which are here in this book. And then I begged him to write his own cookbook, which he is now doing, replete with the fabulous illustrations by John Broadley that make Quo Vadis menus collector's items. I will be the first to buy it.

Onglet, or hanger steak, runs deep in flavor. It's not an expensive cut and is available in most every bistro in Paris. What it lacks in tenderness, it more than makes up for in flavor. Jeremy's recipe makes for a very rare steak. If you prefer yours pink instead of bloody, simply pop the pan into a preheated oven (say 375°F) for an additional three to six minutes of cooking time, remembering that it will continue to cook off the heat as it rests. And rest it should, for the flavors to settle in and deepen in repose.

The pickled walnuts are a good, if entirely unnecessary, garnish. As they are hard to source in the United States, I omit them. And, in fact, Jeremy sometimes serves this with an onion marmalade instead of the walnuts.

Continued

Continued

ONGLET WITH HORSERADISH

HORSERADISH CREAM

MAKES ABOUT 3 CUPS

1½ cups grated fresh
horseradish root

¼ cup sugar

¼ cup very good cider vinegar

1¼ cups crème fraiche

There's more than enough horseradish cream here for a small crowd, but I like to keep a bit on hand for sandwiches. To make it thicker or milder, simply add an extra dollop of crème fraîche. If horseradish is what separates the boys from the men, Jeremy is most certainly in the men's camp. This is the strong stuff. But the sugar is the touch of brilliance here. I like to grate fresh horseradish on a microplane, as it makes for a light and fluffy texture and easy work. But the root can be hard to find, and Jeremy isn't averse to taking a shortcut here: "A most satisfying accompaniment to make. Should, however, fresh horseradish be elusive, then explore the shelves of a merchant or two for a jar of the very good stuff. There is no shirking with the good stuff."

Trim any excess fat and sinew from the steak. Cut away half of the steak from the thick sinew running through the meat. Remove the sinew from the other half. Lightly oil the steak and season well with pepper and salt.

Heat a cast-iron frying pan or other heavy skillet over high heat and pour a light film of oil on the bottom. Lay the meat gently within. Let the meat cook undisturbed to form a gorgeous crust, 4 to 5 minutes, moving the pan, not the meat, and lowering the heat if the meat seems to be cooking too quickly. Flip the meat and cook for 30 seconds. Remove the pan from the heat and let it sit for at least 15 minutes.

Slice the steak and lay on a handsome plate along with a generous spoonful of horseradish cream. Add a posy of watercress to each plate and place a couple of pickled walnuts by its side. Pour over any juices remaining in the bottom of the pan. Take to table and take a bow.

HORSERADISH CREAM

For the horseradish cream, put the grated horseradish in a bowl and pour over the sugar and vinegar, stir together, and leave to sit for 10 minutes. Stir in the crème fraiche and cover until ready to serve.

FILET OF BEEF STROGANOFF

SERVES 4

BEEF

2 tablespoons kosher salt

1 teaspoon sweet
Hungarian paprika

½ teaspoon hot
Hungarian paprika

1½ pounds beef tenderloin

3 tablespoons vegetable oil,
plus more as needed

SAUCE

Vegetable oil, as needed

1 shallot, diced

1 clove garlic, minced

½ teaspoon hot
Hungarian paprika

½ teaspoon sweet
Hungarian paprika

1 pound cremini mushrooms,
stemmed and sliced

¼ cup brandy

1 tablespoon freshly
squeezed lemon juice

2 cups heavy cream

⅔ cup sour cream

⅓ cup veal stock

Basmati rice, for serving

A small handful of finely
chopped flat-leaf parsley

This is a decidedly refined, not to mention rich, take on a classic. With its silken, brandied sauce, it is a taste of luxury and a taste of old. I imagine it bears little resemblance to most anyone's idea of beef stroganoff, a dish that has sadly lost its reputation, having appeared, too often and never well, on one too many cafeteria lines and airplane trays. This recipe will do away with preconceived ideas and unpleasant memories. Of that, I have no doubt. Serve it with a mound of basmati rice, the better to soak up the fabulous sauce. And, speaking of sauce, there's no reason to stick to the ratio here of hot to sweet paprika. Play to your taste. The measurements I offer will produce a dish that edges toward hot without crossing that line. It is, however, important to buy Hungarian paprika, both the sweet and hot varieties. Spanish paprika, or pimentón, while deliciously smoky, will impart the wrong flavor.

To make the beef, stir together the salt and paprikas in a small bowl and then rub into the beef. If you have the time, set aside for 15 minutes to let the flavors infuse.

Warm the vegetable oil in a large sauté pan and sear the beef on all sides until it has formed a crust. Transfer to a plate and set aside.

To make the sauce, pour in more vegetable oil if necessary to the same pan and sauté the shallot and garlic until the shallots are soft and translucent. Add the paprikas, stirring to coat the shallots.

Add the mushrooms and cook, stirring frequently, about 10 minutes, until they have released their moisture and softened.

Over high heat, deglaze the pan with the brandy and then the lemon juice, scraping up any good bits stuck to the bottom.

Lower the heat and then stir in the cream, sour cream, and veal stock. Simmer until the sauce is just thick enough to coat the back of a spoon. Do not boil the cream. Return the beef to the pan, cover, and cook until it reaches desired doneness. If you like your beef rare, this will take about 5 minutes. If you prefer it pink, 10. To be safe, use a meat thermometer. A reading of 120°F to 125°F indicates rare beef, 125°F to 130°F, medium-rare. I find 125°F to be the golden ticket. Let the meat sit for 10 minutes, then slice.

Serve on top of a generous helping of basmati rice and shower with a touch of parsley.

SHORT RIBS WITH CHICKPEAS AND CHARD

SERVES 4

1 tablespoon sea salt

1 tablespoon ground cumin

1 tablespoon ground caraway

1 tablespoon ground coriander

1 tablespoon smoked paprika

4 pounds bone-in beef short ribs, one big meaty one per person

3 tablespoons vegetable oil

2 yellow onions, thinly sliced

6 cloves garlic, peeled and halved

1 bunch Swiss chard, stems removed, leaves coarsely chopped

2 cups cooked chickpeas

6 cups chicken or beef stock, preferably homemade, or water

Salt and pepper, to taste

2 lemons

1 cup labneh or full-fat Greek yogurt

2 tablespoons olive oil (optional)

Sarit and Itamar opened Honey and Co. at the height of Yotam Ottolenghi's popularity. Both had cooked for him and had witnessed firsthand how the flavors of Israel, Palestine, and the Middle East had taken London by storm. Their timing was fortuitous, but what really drew people to Honey and Co. is the atmosphere of jovial generosity that fills this small, unassuming restaurant. And the food is terrific too.

This recipe epitomizes what I love best about Sarit and Itamar's cooking. It's nourishing, humble, and smartly spiced. It's also quite simple to prepare. For years, the only short rib recipe I used was Daniel Boulud's. His is a stellar recipe but calls for copious amounts of red wine and homemade beef stock—in other words, not an everyday affair. This recipe is its polar opposite. Dry-brined overnight, the meat then simmers unattended for a few hours the following day. Swiss chard and chickpeas give it a healthy boost, as does a dollop of labneh or Greek yogurt. I tend to serve it with no more than a loaf of crusty bread, but farro, Israeli couscous, or barley would provide even more sustenance.

Combine the salt, cumin, caraway, coriander, and paprika. Sprinkle half of the spice mixture over the ribs. Cover loosely with plastic wrap and refrigerate overnight.

The next day, pat the ribs dry with paper towels. Heat the oil in a large sauté pan. Add the ribs and cook for 2 to 3 minutes on each side, until golden brown. If your pan is on the small side, work in batches so as not to overcrowd the pan. Transfer the ribs to a plate, leaving the oil behind.

Add the onions to the pan and sauté over a medium-low heat until they are soft and nearly translucent. Stir in the garlic followed by the chard and the remaining spice mixture. Stir and cook for 5 minutes longer.

Add the short ribs and chickpeas, pour in the stock, and bring to a boil. Skim any foam that floats to the surface and then lower the heat, partially cover, and simmer for 2 to 3 hours, basting occasionally. The ribs are done when the sauce has thickened and the meat pulls away from the bone.

Season with salt and pepper and the juice of 1 lemon.

If you have labneh, use it. Otherwise, vigorously whip the yogurt and olive oil together with a fork. Season to taste. Serve the stew with a dollop of labneh and a wedge of lemon.

VEAL CHEEK GOULASH

SERVES 4

1 teaspoon fennel seeds

1 teaspoon coriander seeds

1 teaspoon cumin seeds

Olive oil, as needed

Leaves from 2 sprigs thyme

4 cloves garlic, chopped

1 red bell pepper, thinly sliced

1 red onion, thinly sliced

2 tablespoons sugar

2 tablespoons sherry vinegar

1 tablespoon tomato paste

⅓ cup white wine

1 cup Madeira

1 cup veal demi-glace

16 ounces canned tomatoes, drained and chopped

Salt and pepper, to taste

½ cup all-purpose flour

1 teaspoon smoked paprika

4 veal cheeks

Don't turn the page! I realize not all of you will jump at the chance to make goulash, let alone with veal cheeks. I understand. I coerced my mother into testing this recipe the first time around (the brazen sense of entitlement of an only child). I showed up just before dinner (did I mention entitlement?) and was greeted with the scent of fennel, coriander, and cumin, with the sweet sharp notes of sherry vinegar and the fresh biting aroma of green harissa. My mother, by far the best cook I know, had added a cup of Madeira and a cup of veal demi-glace to the recipe. Having now tested the recipe with and without, I am firmly in her camp—the additional liquid and layers of flavor impart a luxurious richness to the dish. The veal cheeks were a revelation. So common in England, yet rarely eaten in the States, they resemble incredibly tender steaks of filet mignon. The green harissa here brightens the goulash with a burst of fresh cilantro, lemon and chile. Save a little and add it to tomorrow's sandwich or steak.

A bit of trivia: goulash, I've learned, was cooked and then dried out in the sun so that it could be transported and reconstituted with water by traveling Hungarian shepherds in the ninth century. Consider it one of the first packaged to go meals.

To make the goulash, preheat the oven to 325°F.

Toast the fennel, coriander, and cumin seeds in a dry frying pan over a gentle heat. Add 2 to 3 tablespoons of olive oil, thyme, smoked paprika, and chopped garlic.

Add the pepper and onion. Cover the pan and sweat the pepper and onion for 5 minutes, until soft. Add the sugar and cook until a bit caramelized.

Add the vinegar, raise the heat to high, and cook until the liquid evaporates. Stir in the tomato paste and cook a minute or so. Add the white wine and cook until reduced by a third. Add the Madeira and cook until reduced by a third. Add the veal demi-glace and cook until it, too, has reduced by a third. Add the tomatoes, season with salt and pepper, and simmer for 20 minutes over a low heat.

GREEN HARISSA

Zest and juice of 1 lemon

½ bunch flat-leaf parsley

½ bunch cilantro

1 fresh green chile

4 tablespoons extra-virgin olive oil

Cooked polenta, orzo, dumplings, or spätzle, for serving

Sour cream, for serving

Smoked paprika, for serving

Stir together the flour and paprika in a shallow bowl. Dredge the veal cheeks in the flour mixture and shake off the excess. Warm a tablespoon or two of olive oil in a skillet or braising pot. Add the veal cheeks and sear on both sides until nicely colored.

Add the veal cheeks to the sauce or the sauce to the veal cheeks and transfer to the oven. Bake for 3 hours, until the veal cheeks are so tender they nearly fall apart.

Meanwhile, to make the green harissa, zest and juice the lemon, pluck and coarsely chop the parsley and cilantro leaves, and seed the chile, if you like, and transfer to a mini food processor or powerful blender. Add the olive oil and blitz until you have a smooth paste.

To serve, spoon some polenta on a plate and top with the goulash. Add a dollop of sour cream and a spoonful of the harissa and lightly sprinkle with smoked paprika.

KAKUNI (JAPANESE BRAISED PORK BELLY)

SERVES 4

6 to 7 pounds pork belly

Short-grained rice, for
serving (optional)

Scallions, julienned,
as garnish

KOYA BRAISING LIQUID

4¼ cups water

2½ cups stout, preferably
dark Belgian

1¼ cup honey

1 bunch green onions, white
and pale green parts,
thinly sliced

1 (2-inch) knob fresh ginger,
peeled and sliced

KOYA BAR BRAISING LIQUID

4¼ cups water

2½ cups hard apple cider

1 cup sake

1 cup soy sauce

1 cup mirin

½ cup sugar

1 bunch green onions, white
and pale green, thinly sliced

1 (2-inch) knob fresh ginger,
peeled and sliced

This is bittersweet. Koya has closed, but this superb recipe provides
some consolation. So, too, does Koya Bar, which is open and thriving.
Until recently, you might have asked a London chef where they liked
to eat, and nine times out of ten, Koya would have been the answer. It
was Jamie Oliver's answer when I asked him, and Giorgio Locatelli and
Yotam Ottolenghi said the same. Every cook at the River Cafe burst out
with the name "Koya" the morning I spent in the restaurant's kitchen
scribbling notes. The refrain, at different octaves and decibels, sounded
rather like an a cappella group during rehearsal.

Koya was really nothing but a small udon canteen in the heart of Soho:
a simple menu; a crowd of serious slurpers; an inexpensive tab. But it
was good—very, very good. And by good, I mean perfect.

The wise young man behind Koya and Koya Bar is actually Irish and a
former businessman. John Devitt spent eight years trading financial
derivatives before leaving the City of London to train under Giorgio
Locatelli. He worked his way through each station of the kitchen with
a mind to starting his own restaurant. But it was only on what he calls
a pilgrimage to Japan's Shikoku Island that he tasted the famous Sanuki
udon noodles. Then and there, he decided to open Koya upon his return
to London.

Meanwhile, a young man by the name of Junya Yamasaki, had left
Tokyo for Paris to study art but soon found himself mastering not the
art of painting, but the art of the udon noodle at the Paris restaurant
Kunitoraya under the tutelage of master Nomoto Masafumi. Some years
later, John enticed Junya across the English Channel and Koya was born.
When the space next door opened up, John brought in the immensely
talented chef Shuko Oda to open Koya Bar.

My favorite dish at both Koya and Koya Bar has always been the Kakuni,
a braised pork belly. At Koya, it was rich and dark and cooked in stout
and honey. At Koya Bar, it has a startlingly delicate balance of flavors,
a bit sweet, a bit salty, a bit rich, but not too rich. It's terrifically easy to
make and can be adjusted to serve a crowd, as the ratio of ingredients
need not change.

Continued

Continued

KAKUNI (JAPANESE BRAISED PORK BELLY)

Despite Koya's enormous success, Junya missed working as a visual artist and has returned to Japan and to his art career. John wisely decided that without Junya, Koya would not be the same, and he closed its doors. How lucky we are to still have Koya Bar—and this delicious kakuni recipe to make at home. A word of warning: pork belly shrinks dramatically when cooked, as it sheds its fat, so I use a whopping 6 to 7 pounds for four people. This yields leftovers and, in fact, this dish only improves overnight. Simply remove the layer of fat that will have formed on the surface. Your flavor will be all the more concentrated. In the restaurant, the kakuni is served in small bowls with hot mustard to pass at the table. At home, I like to serve it over rice as a main course. And, if I'm making it for my son, I simply swap the hard cider for sweet cider. No grown-up has ever refused its comforting flavor.

Cut the pork belly into 3 by 5 inch brick-sized pieces, leaving the thick fatty skin on, but scoring it with a sharp knife.

Heat a large heavy skillet. Working in batches, sear the pork, starting fat side down, for a solid ten minutes. Place the pork in a stockpot and add enough water to cover it. Bring to a boil over high heat and cook at a rolling boil for 90 minutes. This will get rid of much of the fat and leave most of the collagen. Let the pork cool to room temperature in the cooking liquid.

Discard the cooking liquid. Cut the pork into 2½-inch chunks. Combine the ingredients in your choice of braising liquid. Place the meat and braising liquid in a large covered braising pot or Dutch oven. Bring to a simmer, cover, and cook over low heat for 2 to 3 hours until unctuous and tender.

Transfer half of the braising liquid to a saucepan and bring it to a boil. Cook until it has thickened and reduced by two-thirds. It will be deliriously silky. Warm the pork through and serve with a few generous spoonfuls of the reduced sauce. The julienned green onions scattered on top add a touch of color. Serve with or without rice.

PORK BELLY WITH APPLE AND YUZU PUREE AND BLACK BEAN SAUCE

SERVES 4

4 pounds pork belly

A few sprigs lemon thyme

1 (5-inch) knob fresh ginger, unpeeled and thinly sliced

1 head garlic, halved crosswise and broken roughly by hand

1 small lemon, halved

5 tablespoons coarse sea salt

3½ cups dry white wine

1 cup water

PUREE

2 tablespoons vegetable oil

2 Bramley or Granny Smith apples, peeled and cut into 1-inch cubes

4 tablespoons unsalted butter, at room temperature

1 tablespoon light brown sugar

1½ tablespoons yuzu juice

¾ teaspoon salt

Continued

Londoners have a fondness for crackling, that crisp layer of roasted pork skin that is best described as savory grown-up candy. I've seen ordinarily civilized and restrained Brits turn into predators when faced with a sole remaining piece of this fatty, crispy rind. Here, Yotam provides the crackling by cooking the pork at a high heat, which he then wisely lowers to produce a meltingly tender meat. Further riffing on traditional pork roasts, he serves his pork belly with the ubiquitous applesauce but adds a splash of yuzu juice to keep it lively. The black bean sauce references the ginger in the pork and the yuzu in the apple, bringing the meal firmly into Asian territory with Shaoxing wine, soy sauce, sesame oil, and a goodly amount of additional ginger. I wish I could find the Bramley apples Yotam likes in the United States. Tart, sour, sharp, and full of flavor, they are an ideal cooking apple. The best alternative is a Granny Smith, but the Northern Spy is also exceptional.

Sunday lunch remains a sacrosanct tradition in London, even among twenty-somethings. Every good pub is full Sunday afternoon and empty at dinnertime, when the city is still bellyful. Roast beef, Yorkshire pudding, and horseradish cream reign supreme, as they should—there are few more satisfying combinations. But more and more, the roasts are being spiced and seasoned with Asian and Middle Eastern notes, and pork often replaces the costly rib roasts of beef or legs of lamb of yore. Whenever I make this recipe, I wish I had the obstinacy to insist on a weekly Sunday lunch. The smell of this cooking alone is enough to draw friends and family from miles around. Now, if only we could all agree to leave our work to Monday and our devices hidden away.

To cook the pork, preheat the oven to 475°F.

Pat the pork belly dry with paper towels. Spread out the lemon thyme, ginger, and garlic in a large high-sided roasting tray and place the pork belly, skin-side up, on top. Rub the lemon halves all over the skin, squeezing as you rub until all of the juice has been squeezed out. Sprinkle 2½ tablespoons of the salt evenly over the skin.

Continued

Continued

PORK BELLY WITH APPLE AND YUZU PUREE AND BLACK BEAN SAUCE

BLACK BEAN SAUCE

1½ tablespoons peanut oil

1 (3-inch) knob fresh ginger, peeled and julienned

4 cloves garlic, thinly sliced

2 small fresh red chiles, seeded and julienned

¼ cup light brown sugar

½ cup Shaoxing wine

½ cup Chinkiang vinegar

⅓ cup light soy sauce

1½ teaspoons sesame oil

1¼ cup water

1 tablespoon cornstarch

12 shiitake mushrooms, stemmed, caps thinly sliced

¾ cup canned black beans, rinsed and drained

2 spring onions, the white and pale green parts, thinly sliced

Roast for 45 to 60 minutes, rotating the roasting pan halfway through cooking and gently piercing any bubbles on the skin if they form. Remove from the oven. Scrape off and discard the salt and then sprinkle evenly with the remaining 2½ tablespoons salt. You need to add more salt as the first batch will have stopped absorbing moisture.

Roast for 30 minutes longer, until the skin is crisp and golden brown. Turn down the oven to 350°F and carefully pour the white wine and 1 cup water around the pork, avoiding the skin. Roast for 45 minutes and then turn the oven to 200°F and cook for 45 minutes longer, until the meat is completely tender. Remove from the oven and set aside, covering the pan with aluminum foil so that the pork stays warm.

While the pork is cooking, make the puree. Warm the vegetable oil in a large saucepan over medium-high heat. Once the oil is smoking hot, add the apples and fry for 3 minutes, stirring constantly, until golden brown. Add 1½ tablespoons of the butter and cook for 1 minute, basting the apples with the butter once it has melted. Add the sugar and cook for 1 minute, until the apples start to caramelize. Add the yuzu juice, and cook for 1 minute, until the apples are soft. Remove from the heat. Transfer the apple mixture, the remaining 2½ tablespoons butter, and the salt to a food processor and blitz until you have a smooth puree. Set aside somewhere warm until ready to serve.

To make the black bean sauce, warm the peanut oil in a skillet over high heat. Once the oil is smoking hot, add the ginger, garlic, and chiles and fry for 2 minutes, stirring constantly, until the garlic is golden brown. Add the sugar and cook for 30 to 60 seconds and then add the Shaoxing wine, Chinkiang vinegar, soy sauce, sesame oil, and 1 cup of the water. Bring to a boil, then simmer for 8 minutes.

Place the cornstarch in a small bowl with the remaining ¼ cup water and stir to form a paste. Add the cornstarch paste to the pan along with the mushrooms and black beans. Cook for 1 minute, until thickened. Remove from the heat and stir in the green onions. Set aside somewhere warm until ready to serve.

To serve, lift the pork out of the roasting pan and discard the lemon thyme, ginger, and garlic. Trim the edges off the pork belly and cut crosswise into 4 equal rectangles. Divide the warm puree among the plates and lay the pork belly on top. Spoon the black beans on the side. Serve immediately.

PORK WITH SOUTH INDIAN SPICES

SERVES 2

SAUCE

2 tablespoons coconut oil

1 (13.5-ounce) can
coconut milk

½ cup Curry Paste (page 179),
plus more to taste

¼ cup full-fat yogurt

3 tablespoons freshly
squeezed lime juice

Sea salt, if needed

2 thick pork chops, cooked
as you choose, or a pork
tenderloin, roasted

Cooked basmati rice,
for serving

Wilted baby spinach,
for serving

1 lime, cut into wedges,
for serving

Fresh cilantro leaves,
for serving

Spice Salt (page 179),
for serving (optional)

This is a threefold recipe, yielding enough curry paste to serve a crowd or to stash in the fridge for future curries. I say this up front because making curry paste is oddly time-consuming, not terribly so, just annoyingly so. I wish I could tell you that it is therapeutic in the way stirring risotto or watching over a simmering stew can be. But the satisfaction of setting a jar aside for later use and the knowledge that your industry is to be doubly or triply rewarded more than compensates. So, too, does the taste, which is worlds better than even the best store-bought variety. This one is good enough to eat on its own with a spoon. And, yes, I have thoroughly vetted that for you.

When Isaac cooks this at the Clove Club—and he does so often; there would be riots if he didn't—he uses an entire suckling pig from a farm in North Yorkshire. "We do a lot of work ," he told me, "to break the pig down and cook the different bits at different temperatures—confit ears and tails, deboned and rolled pig's head, trotters made into crubeens, French-trimmed racks cooked to order, slow-cooked shoulders, scrag end cooked overnight, legs slowly roasted." In other words, it's the epitome of nose-to-tail cooking. But as the curry sauce is so good, there's no reason not to serve it over a thick dry-aged pork chop or even a pork tenderloin, easily roasted in less than a half hour. And then there's always the option of using chicken. Isaac serves his pork with potatoes and wilted spinach, but I find a bowl of basmati rice is the best way to soak up the sauce, and that is what everyone will most want to do.

Quite a few notes follow on the ingredients, which you may skip if you are familiar with South Indian cuisine. Both curry leaves and makrut lime leaves are far more aromatic fresh than dried. They do, thankfully, freeze well, so buy them when you happen to find them, and you'll save yourself some last-minute dashing about. Isaac calls for cilantro root here, but if you can't find it, use the stems and leaves and you will achieve a close approximation. Cilantro root is just what it sounds like—the small bulbous root at the bottom of the stem. Assess it by eye and use what looks most appealing. The first inch or so of the green stem added as well. Wash thoroughly and finely chop, as you might a green onion. Save the leaves for garnish, as they add color and freshness. Preparing lemongrass is rather similar in technique. Use the white base, wash, and slice finely. Isaac uses fresh turmeric, which is becoming widely available. In a pinch, use dried. For the chiles, choose according to your threshold and desire. I use fresh cayenne chiles whenever I can find them. Thankfully, fresh chiles also freeze well. I don't know who came up with the foul word *desiccated* as a description for dried coconut. I only use it because it is writ bold on most packages.

The spice salt here is a wonderful, if unnecessary, addition. It calls for deep-fried fresh curry leaves, which is rather less than convenient. They are, however, delicious, so do try making them at least once. If time is against you, dried curry leaves may be used. I keep the spice salt on hand and find myself sprinkling it on roast vegetables, particularly pumpkin and winter squash. I've therefore left the quantity generous.

Isaac and I scaled this recipe down to serve two. To serve four, simply double the sauce. To serve six, triple it. There is enough curry paste here to serve around ten people, so consider the sauce recipe more of a ratio than an absolute. Once you've made the curry paste, the sauce and pork are an easy weeknight affair.

Enough said! Go to it and enjoy.

To make the sauce, melt the coconut oil and ¼ cup of the coconut milk in a saucepan over high heat. Boil until the coconut milk "cracks"—that is, until the fat splits out and the milk solids start frying in the coconut oil—then add the Curry Paste and cook, stirring, over medium heat for 2 minutes. Add the remaining coconut milk and bring it to a boil. Turn down the heat and simmer for 10 minutes. Remove from the heat.

Stir in the yogurt and lime juice, tasting a few times to keep the flavors balanced. If you are serving the pork with the Spice Salt, you may want to go easy on seasoning the sauce. If you aren't, now is the time to add a bit of salt.

Continued

Continued

PORK WITH SOUTH INDIAN SPICES

CURRY PASTE

2 pounds white onions, finely chopped

Sea salt

Butter, for cooking (optional)

4 cloves garlic, thinly sliced

1 (1-inch) knob fresh ginger, peeled and minced

1 ounce fresh turmeric

1 fresh green chile, with seeds

1 fresh red chile, with seeds

2 stalks lemongrass, prepped

1 bunch cilantro, with roots

¼ cup fresh curry leaves

¼ cup fresh makrut lime leaves

½ cup coriander seeds

1 tablespoon ground black cardamom

2 tablespoons ground green cardamom

2 tablespoons ground black pepper

2 cups shredded, desiccated coconut

¼ cup coconut oil

SPICE SALT

2 tablespoons fennel seeds

2 tablespoons green cardamom pods

2 whole cloves

½ cup Maldon sea salt flakes

3 tablespoons ground cinnamon

I like to serve generous dollops of this sauce atop pork chops or slices of roasted pork tenderloin. Serve with a bounty of rice and the wilted spinach. Because the sauce is so good, I tend to add a dollop to the rice as well. A sprinkle of the spice salt finishes the dish, but do be sure to pass around a little bowl with additional spice salt.

CURRY PASTE

To make the curry paste, place the onions, a spoonful or two of water and a pinch of salt in a wide skillet, cover, and sweat until soft and tender but not colored. You'll need to take your time doing this, using the lowest heat setting on your stove. If you need to, add another spoonful or two or water and a pad of butter. Add the coriander seeds, black and green cardamon, and pepper and cook another minute or two to release their aromas.

While the onions are cooking, combine the garlic, ginger, turmeric, chiles, lemongrass, cilantro, curry and lime leaves and coconut.

Isaac combines all of these ingredients with the cooked onions in a large mortar and pestle and pounds them with great vigor to make a coarse paste. He says the effort is worth it and he is right, but a food processor can do wonders.

Melt the coconut oil in a skillet over medium heat. Add the paste and gently fry, stirring occasionally for about 6 minutes, until the flavors have melded together. Turn off the heat and set aside. Once cool, this can be stored in the fridge for several days or frozen for two months.

SPICE SALT

To make the spice salt, grind the fennel seeds, green cardamom pods and cloves, in a spice grinder or clean coffee grinder. Transfer to a bowl and stir in the salt and cinnamon. This mix is easily stored in tightly lidded jar for up to two months.

IBERIAN RIB STEW

SERVES 4

Sea salt

3 pounds meaty baby
back ribs

Olive oil, for cooking

2 yellow onions, finely sliced

6 carrots, peeled and cut
into ½-inch slices

3 leeks, white parts only,
cut into ½-inch slices

6 stalks celery, cut into
½-inch slices

8 plum tomatoes, halved

3 bay leaves, preferably fresh

4 cups homemade
chicken stock

1 cup good balsamic vinegar

¼ cup honey

Most American rib recipes assume you will pick up and gnaw on the meat, making sauce not only superfluous but extremely messy. This recipe is more of a stew that is, as it happens, wonderful over a bed of rice or grains. And, yes, utensils are in order. With onions, honey, and balsamic, the sauce is sweet and sour and definitely hearty.

Nieves sources true Iberian pork, I make these with meaty baby back ribs and find them equally delicious. A few small pointers for you: Do use a good balsamic or the sauce will suffer. Sherry vinegar may be substituted; the result will be a tad less sweet but rather more Spanish in flavor. Nieves uses Pedro Ximénez balsamic sherry vinegar, which has been aged in oak barrels and is decidedly sweeter than most sherry vinegars. If you can't find good tomatoes, use canned ones. The ribs can sit in a low oven an hour or so longer or be cooked a day in advance. This dish is rustic, so if you'd like it to be more refined, simply pass the sauce through a fine-mesh sieve at the end, discarding the solids and reducing the sauce until it has a silken quality.

Preheat the oven to 325°F.

Generously salt the ribs. Warm 1 to 2 tablespoons of olive oil over medium-high heat in a large skillet. Working in batches, sear the ribs until they form a golden brown crust. Be careful not to overcrowd the pan, which can steam rather than brown the ribs. Place the ribs in a Dutch oven to keep warm.

Add the onions to the hot skillet, adding more olive oil if needed, and cook until truly translucent. Transfer the onions to the Dutch oven. Add the carrots and sauté until softened. Transfer the carrots to the Dutch oven. Sauté the leeks, followed by the celery, in the same manner, transferring each to the Dutch oven once soft. Raise the heat to high and place the tomatoes cut side down in the skillet so that they start to caramelize. Leave for a minute before lowering the heat and cooking 2 or 3 minutes longer to further soften the tomatoes. Transfer the tomatoes and the ribs to the Dutch oven and add the bay leaves, chicken stock, vinegar, and honey. The ribs should fit, submerged in liquid. Bring them to a simmer, move to the oven and bake for 2 hours.

Slice the ribs into four servings and serve in warmed shallow plates with plenty of sauce and rice or grains to soak up the good flavors.

TREACLE-CURED PORK BELLY

Treacle is made during the refining process of sugar or, more accurately, it's the leftover syrup—a mere by-product that's rich as sin. Light treacle is most often called golden syrup. Black treacle has a more pronounced flavor with a bittersweet edge. Tins of Lyle's Golden Syrup and Lyle's Black Treacle abound in the United Kingdom, the company design iconic, the quality unmatched. Both syrups are now easy to order online. Blackstrap molasses is the American version of treacle and works perfectly in this recipe. (A small aside: Try using Lyle's Golden Syrup in recipes calling for corn syrup. It's far better in pecan pie.)

And now a warning: this recipe is addictive, particularly if you find yourself unobserved in proximity to the carving board. The pork belly is brined for 24 hours in a mixture of herbs, spices, salt, treacle, and citrus zest and then slow-roasted in a further dose of treacle. It's terrific served warm as is, or roasted and then grilled, as they do at Pitt Cue Co. Leftovers—and these are essential, so prepare to make extra—are terrific for pulled pork sandwiches. Just be sure never to serve the pork cold. Pork belly simply has too much fat, even after most of it has rendered. Definitely serve this with something to cut the richness, perhaps bitter greens, a squeeze of lemon, and to drink, bourbon, straight up.

SERVES 6, OR 4 WITH LEFTOVERS

3 cups kosher salt

Zest of 1 orange

Zest of 1 lemon

10 sprigs thyme

1 sprig rosemary

½ cup coriander seeds

12 juniper berries

6 cloves garlic, peeled

6 bay leaves, preferably fresh

4 whole star anise

1½ cups dark treacle or blackstrap molasses

6 pounds pork belly

Combine the salt, citrus zests, thyme, rosemary, coriander seeds, juniper berries, garlic, bay leaves, and star anise in a large stockpot or pasta pot and add enough water to fill the pot.

Bring the water to a boil and stir until the salt has dissolved. Whisk in 1 cup of the treacle and then remove from the heat. Let cool completely.

Place the pork in a nonreactive roasting pan and pour in the cooled brine, making sure the pork is submerged . Reserve any extra brine for a week in the fridge, as it is also excellent with pork chops. Cover loosely with aluminum foil or plastic wrap and refrigerate overnight.

Early the next day, preheat the oven to 250°F. Rinse the pork under cold water for 10 minutes to remove any excess salt. Pat dry with paper towels.

Discard the brine and wash and dry the roasting pan. Return the rinsed and dried pork to the pan. Rub the pork meat with the remaining ½ cup of treacle and lightly score the fat. Set the pork, fat side up, in the pan.

Bake the pork belly for 5 or 6 hours, until it starts to soften. It should be tender and yielding. Discard the liquid fat that has accumulated on the bottom of the roasting pan. The pork belly can rest covered in aluminum foil for an hour before serving.

Serve the pork warm, as is, or let it cool completely and then slice and grill it for hot, sticky, smoky goodness.

SPICED LAMB, CHICKPEAS, AND LABNEH

SERVES 6

2 cups full-fat Greek yogurt

Sea salt

Olive oil, as needed

Minced parsley, optional

Cilantro, optional

Minced garlic, optional

1 pound dried chickpeas

1 bone-in lamb shoulder,
about 6 to 7 pounds

½ cup olive oil

1 tablespoon unsalted butter

2 tablespoons cumin seeds

2 tablespoons black
mustard seeds

2 tablespoons Isot chile
powder

3½ ounces fresh curry leaves
or a handful of dried
curry leaves

4 yellow onions,
coarsely chopped

6 cloves garlic, thinly sliced

1 (5-inch) knob fresh ginger,
peeled and thinly sliced

2 tablespoons ground
turmeric

5 cups homemade chicken or
vegetable stock, or water

32 ounces chopped
canned tomatoes

1½ cups pitted dates, halved

There are certain restaurants you try because the people inside look interesting. And so it was that one busy day in Soho, when I paused outside Ducksoup and peered in. It wasn't much to look at—a little distressed, perhaps on purpose, perhaps not—but it was filled with a serious young crowd, including a few filmmakers and journalists I knew. People were eating hungrily, loving their food, their conversation, and the easy vibe of the place. It was hip, but not posh, at least not visibly so. It had the confidence to be low key. A few hours later, I was still at the bar, finishing lunch with two of the friends I'd spotted through the window. I'd found a new haunt.

The food at Ducksoup is London in a nutshell, its myriad cultures reflected in every dish. This lamb is slow-cooked food at its best. A bit fierce, a bit sweet, rather bold, always warming, it is complex in taste and simple to prepare. Chef Tom Hill has borrowed liberally from India, the Middle East, and North Africa to create a recipe that feels not new, but old, age-old.

A few notes for you: Isot chile is recognizable for its dark, almost aubergine color. It is sometimes simply called Isot pepper and sometimes Urfa Biber, after the Urfa region of Turkey, where it is grown. It is not a particularly hot chile but prized for its depth of flavor. If you can't find it easily, you may substitute equal parts Aleppo pepper and smoked paprika. The result will be different, but no less delicious. I've used both bone-in and boneless lamb shoulders for this recipe with equal success, but I do make sure to use broth, not water, if using a boneless shoulder. As this is quite saucy, do serve it with crusty bread or a bowl of couscous. It is at its best if made a day in advance, the fat skimmed off the surface, and the dish reheated until piping hot.

Continued

Continued

SPICED LAMB, CHICKPEAS, AND LABNEH

Whisk together the yogurt and 1 teaspoon salt. Wrap the yogurt mixture in cheesecloth and suspend it over a bowl. Let the yogurt drain overnight in the fridge.

Once drained, discard the liquid and transfer the drained yogurt to another bowl. Whip with a fork or whisk to lighten it up. Don't hesitate to add a drizzle of olive oil, minced fresh parsley or cilantro, and minced garlic, but remember, it's meant to counter the spice of the meat with a smooth mellow tang. Set your labneh aside.

Place the chickpeas in a large nonreactive bowl and cover with several inches of water. Leave to soak overnight.

Simmer the soaked chickpeas in abundant water for 90 minutes, until tender. The key to cooking most any bean is to keep the water at a lazy simmer. Boiling water will only toughen them, as will adding salt before they are tender.

Preheat the oven to 325°F.

Put the lamb into a deep roasting pan or a large Dutch oven with a lid and rub generously with salt. Warm the olive oil in a large skillet over medium-low heat. Add the cumin, black mustard seeds, Isot chile, and curry leaves and cook for about 5 minutes, until the seeds start to pop. Add the onions. Cook over a gentle heat until soft and translucent. Add the garlic, ginger, and turmeric, followed by the stock, tomatoes, and dates. Bring to a boil, and then pour the stock mixture over the lamb. Cover the roasting pan with a double layer of aluminum foil, or cover the pot with a lid.

Roast for 4 hours, until the lamb is falling off the bone. A little more cooking time won't hurt and, in fact, you can keep the meat in a warm oven for another hour or so. Stir in the chickpeas.

At this point, I like to take a few ladlefuls of the cooking liquid, including some dates, onions, and chickpeas, and blitz it all in a food processor or blender. Return this thick goodness to the pot, stirring well to combine. If you prefer a brothier sauce, leave it as is. It is delicious both ways.

To serve, it is easiest to remove the lamb and break the meat into large chunks using two forks. Discard the bones. Return the lamb meat to the pot. Ladle the stew into warmed shallow bowls and top with a dollop of labneh.

SLOW-COOKED AND GRILLED LAMB RIBS, BARBECUED CUCUMBER, AND POTATO SALAD

SERVES 2 OR 3

LAMB

4 pounds lamb ribs, cut into individual ribs

Sea salt

1¼ cups lamb or chicken stock, preferably homemade

½ cup grapeseed oil

A few sprigs thyme

8 cloves garlic, crushed

4 black peppercorns

SALAD

8 ounces small red potatoes

Sea salt

1 large cucumber, unpeeled

Grapeseed oil, for cooking

½ cup plain full-fat yogurt

Leaves from 1 bunch mint, finely chopped

1 clove garlic, grated or minced

Juice from 1 lemon

Here, Tomos has taken standards—grilled lamb and potato salad—and given them unexpected dimension in the simplest of ways. The lamb is both slow-cooked and grilled. The slow cooking gives it incomparable tenderness, and the grilling creates that barbecued exterior we all love. The smokiness and bitterness of the charred potato and cucumber skins combined with the bright freshness of the mint and lemon give the salad a double edge that I think you'll like.

Tomos uses lamb ribs from the breast, which resemble spare ribs. Sometimes they are called riblets, which accurately suggests that their size is small and that you will need a good quantity of them. Alternatively, grill your favorite cut of lamb for this recipe.

To make the lamb, preheat the oven to 325°F.

Season the ribs with sea salt and place in a roasting pan with all of the other ingredients. Tightly cover the pan with foil and roast in the oven for 1½ hours, turning the ribs every 30 minutes. Once the ribs are tender, remove them from the roasting pan. Discard any accumulated liquid. Preheat a gas or charcoal grill or a griddle to high. Grill or griddle the lamb for 5 minutes, turning once, until the outside is charred and crisp.

To make the salad, cook the new potatoes in boiling salted water for about until just tender. Drain, let cool, and peel.

Season the whole cucumber with sea salt and drizzle with a bit of oil. Place the cucumber on the grill and cook, turning every 3 or 4 minutes, until blackened all over. Remove when the cucumber has just softened slightly, but not too much. It needs to remain quite firm. Remove the cucumber from the grill. Set aside to cool.

Meanwhile, stir together the yogurt, mint, and garlic. Stir in the lemon juice and season with salt.

Lightly crush and oil the cooked new potatoes. Place the potatoes on the grill and cook, turning them a couple of times, until the skins are nicely charred. Set aside to cool for a few minutes.

Cut the cucumber into small cubes and toss, in a large bowl, with the mint yogurt, and charred potatoes.

DESSERTS

CHOCOLATE NEMESIS

This is the River Cafe's most famous dessert, and there are copies of it—never as good—all over London and, by now, really, all over the world. Some copycats credit the River Cafe, others have simply stolen the name Nemesis, and still others call it something of their own making. There are also an abundance of recipes for this cake online. Ignore them all. Most have fatal flaws. This is the real thing, carefully refined after a morning spent in the kitchen at the River Cafe observing and taking notes.

The Nemesis is a nine-inch circle of perfection. It is at once dense and mousselike, with a consistency that seems ideal for deep chocolate appreciation, so use the absolute best chocolate you can find. In fact, use really good butter and farm eggs too. The restaurant uses dark chocolate with a ratio of 70 percent cocoa, but I've sunk into the 60s with equally delicious results. Do keep to a bittersweet rather than a semisweet chocolate. Valrhona Guanaja (70 percent) or Valrhona Caraïbe (66 percent) are excellent choices. The restaurant serves the cake with a dollop of crème fraîche. Its tanginess provides a good counterpoint to the richness of the chocolate. I prefer a mixture of crème fraîche and heavy cream, whipped together. The choice, of course, is yours.

What you must know: This is a simple cake and requires no expertise, but do not take any shortcuts. The eggs and sugar must really be whipped until they've quadrupled in size, and the cake really must cool in its bain-marie for at least 2 hours, or you will end up with glop when you unmold it. Do not be alarmed. This recipe will enter your repertoire as a loyal answer to almost every demand and many a fantasy.

Preheat the oven to 250°F.

Generously butter a 9-inch cake pan (not a springform) and line the bottom with a circle of parchment paper. Butter that too.

Set a kettle of water to boil for the bain-marie. Fold a clean towel and set it at the bottom of a baking pan larger than your cake pan. The dish towel will keep the pan from moving and will reduce the impact of heat touching the bottom of the cake.

SERVES 8

12 ounces 70 percent bittersweet chocolate, chopped

1 cup (16 tablespoons) unsalted butter, cut into pieces

1½ cups granulated sugar

5 eggs

1 cup heavy cream

1 cup crème fraîche

1 teaspoon confectioners' sugar

Melt the chocolate and butter in a double boiler over just simmering water. Stir until both have melted and married and then remove from the heat.

Combine 1 cup of the granulated sugar with about ⅓ cup of water in a small saucepan and cook over a lively heat until the sugar has dissolved into a light syrup. Let it boil away for 2 minutes to thicken but not color. Pour the hot syrup into the melted chocolate, stir well, and set aside for 5 minutes to cool slightly.

This is important: In a stand mixer or using electric beaters and a large bowl, beat the eggs and the remaining ½ cup of the granulated sugar, until the volume quadruples.

Keeping the mixer running, pour the chocolate mixture into the eggs, and continue to beat until the mixture is thoroughly combined. Pour the batter into the cake pan. Rap the pan on the counter a few times to dispel any air pockets.

Place the pan onto the folded dish towel and pour enough hot water into the bain-marie to come three-quarters of the way up the side of the cake pan.

Bake in the oven for 50 to 60 minutes, until set. You want to remove the cake when it has just set and the edges can be pulled away from the side of the pan. It will look moist but not wet.

Leave the cake to cool in the water for at least 2 hours. Do not remove the cake until it has really cooled. The water of the bain-marie should now be cool to the touch as should the base of the cake pan as well. If your kitchen is warm, this may take 3 to 4 hours.

Gently transfer the cake to a cake plate. If wobbly, place it in the fridge for 15 minutes to firm up a bit. If serving later in the day, leave the cake in the fridge until about 30 minutes before serving. It is best chilled but not cold.

Whip the heavy cream with the crème fraîche and confectioners' sugar until it forms soft, cloudlike billows. Cut the cake with a sharp knife into relatively small slices, as it is rich. Serve with a dollop of cream.

RAS EL HANOUT AND BUTTERMILK LOAF

MAKES I LOAF

LOAF

1 cup (16 tablespoons) unsalted butter

¼ cup treacle or blackstrap molasses

¼ cup golden syrup, preferably Lyle's

⅓ cup dark muscovado sugar

2 cups all-purpose flour

1½ teaspoons ras el hanout (page 194), or 1 teaspoon ras el hanout and ½ teaspoon ground cinnamon, plus more for sprinkling

1 teaspoon ground ginger

½ teaspoon baking soda

¼ teaspoon sel de Guérande or other fleur de sel

⅔ cup buttermilk, preferably full-fat and artisanal

2 eggs, lightly beaten

GLACÉ

¾ cup confectioners' sugar, sifted

1 teaspoon ginger syrup from a jar of stem ginger, or bottled ginger syrup

Stemmed ginger, for garnish (optional)

Continued

Before I came along to make such adventures impractical, my parents—an anthropologist and a journalist—spent two years in Meknès, in northern Morocco. It was the kind of carefree, romantic time that children never successfully imagine their parents having. They lived a stone's throw from the Medina, wrote by day, and cooked by night—a simple existence and all the more intensely lived for being so. It was there that my mother learned to mix her own *ras el hanout*. Translated roughly as "best of the shop," ras el hanout is the very personal, highly nuanced blend of spices that gives much Moroccan cooking its aroma and depth. One cook might include upward of thirty spices, another no more than five or six. No two will ever taste the same.

By the time I was born, my parents had returned to New York. My father had published *Tuhami*, a portrait of a Moroccan man who believed himself married to a she-demon, and my mother had published *Honor to the Bride*, an account of a teenage girl whose virginity must be restored before her wedding day. Their couscoussière was moved to the top cupboard in the kitchen, only to come down a few days a year. But oh those days . . . . I'd smell the butter melting, and then the ras el hanout, as my mother swirled it into the foaming butter. The marriage of spices was exotic, earthy, and sweet, and a passion for cardamom and ginger grabbed hold of my senses and never left.

Jump ahead a few decades, and I am just off the plane and walking through Soho in desperate need of a caffeine fix before heading into a meeting with a film producer. I stop at Fernandez and Wells and order a coffee and the last slice I see of what I assume is gingerbread. And then I bite into it. A rush of spices, both mellow and heady, hits me with the force of a core childhood memory. The cake is neither too sweet nor too savory. It is the ideal afternoon pick-me-up. The spices offer just enough heat to wake the palate from its midday lull, and the crumb is tender, while not so crumbly that it can't be eaten out of hand while hurrying to my meeting.

There are two secrets to making this quick bread. One is fresh ras el hanout. The spices must be at their most vibrant. Jansal Valley and

Williams-Sonoma both make good versions that are easy to find. And I'm including my own recipe here. Taste it before using it. You may want to add more cinnamon, ginger, or cloves for this loaf, or more coriander and turmeric if, say, making chicken. The other secret to this quick bread is the use of a full-fat artisanal buttermilk. The good, old-fashioned deal bears little to no resemblance to the thin supermarket variety. Dee tells me this cake improves with age, but it has never lasted long enough in my house for me to confirm this. I can imagine, however, that it would be lovely toasted in the morning with a spread of cool butter.

Continued

Continued

RAS EL HANOUT AND BUTTERMILK LOAF

RAS EL HANOUT

MAKES ABOUT ¼ CUP

2 teaspoons freshly
grated nutmeg

1½ teaspoons freshly ground
black pepper

2 teaspoons ground
cinnamon

1 teaspoon ground allspice

1½ teaspoons freshly ground
cardamom

10 saffron threads (optional),
rubbed between your fingers
until powdery

1 teaspoon ground mace

1 teaspoon ground turmeric

¼ teaspoon ground cloves

¼ teaspoon cayenne pepper

1 teaspoon ground coriander

Preheat the oven to 350°F. If using a convection oven, preheat the oven
to 325°F. Butter an 8 by 4 by 3-inch loaf pan and line the bottom with
parchment paper.

In a small pot, warm the butter, treacle, golden syrup, and muscovado
sugar over low heat until the butter is just melted. Stir to combine.

Sift the flour, ras el hanout, ginger, baking soda, and sel de Guérande into
a large bowl.

Stir the molasses mixture into the flour mixture until just combined.

Fold in the buttermilk and eggs. The ingredients must be well combined,
but don't overwork the dough. A light touch is best.

Pour the dough into the prepared pan. Bake for 35 to 40 minutes, until
the center is set and springs back when pressed gently.

Dee suggests letting the loaf cool to room temperature and wrapping it
tightly in parchment paper for 2 days. This will make it nice and sticky.
Or give way to temptation and eat it straightaway. The flavors will be less
concentrated, but the smell of it cooking makes waiting hard.

When ready to serve, make the glacé. Place the confectioners' sugar in a
bowl and whisk the boiling water into the sugar, using just enough to get
your desired consistency. Stir in the ginger syrup. Pour the glacé over
the cake. If you have stemmed ginger, chop some and use as a garnish
with a light shower of ras el hanout. Candied or crystallized ginger
would also be a lovely option.

RAS EL HANOUT

Combine all the spices. Leftover ras el hanout keeps in a tightly sealed jar
for two months.

CLAFOUTIS AUX PÊCHES

SERVES 6

3 large ripe peaches

1⅔ cups sugar

4 eggs, at room temperature

1 tablespoon all-purpose flour, sifted

1¼ cups heavy cream

2 tablespoons crème de framboise

Crème fraîche, for serving

Despite having spent a fabulous chunk of my childhood in Paris, I have rarely enjoyed and even less rarely sought out a clafoutis. This may have something to do with the leaden ones served in my school cafeteria there. But then a few years ago, I whipped up a rich chocolate and pear version as a last-minute dessert and finally understood the fuss made over this simple dessert, which falls somewhere between a pancake and a soufflé. My favorite version is that made by the legendary Pierre Koffmann, a chef who has been at the culinary heart of London for almost forty years and whose techniques are widely regarded as almost biblical, and certainly definitive. What I love about this clafoutis is that it is a particularly eggy concoction. And then there is the beauty of a perfect peach at the height of its season. Here, the peaches are ever so briefly poached. The batter holds a splash of crème de framboise, just as a good crepe batter will often contain a bit of alcohol. I consider this alchemy because I am not a scientist. For a formal affair, serve this with a raspberry coulis. But a clafoutis is really meant to be brought to the table in its earthenware cooking vessel and eaten *en famille*.

Preheat the oven to 350°F.

Find a pot large enough to hold the peaches and fill it with water. Add 1 cup of the sugar. Bring to a boil, stirring, and cook for 5 minutes. Using a slotted spoon, lower the peaches into the boiling syrup. Return to a boil and cook for no more than 3 minutes. Remove the peaches with the slotted spoon and, once cool enough to handle, peel, halve, and pit. Set the peaches aside.

Generously butter an ovenproof dish. (I use a tarte Tatin dish, a pie plate, or a gratin dish.) Place the peach halves, cut side down, in the dish.

Using an electric beater, whisk together the eggs and remaining ⅔ cup of sugar on high speed until frothy. Add the flour, then the cream, and then the crème de framboise, beating well after each addition. Pour the batter over the peaches.

Bake for 30 minutes, until set. Remove from the oven, let sit 10 minutes before serving. Pass a bowl of crème fraîche at the table for the super indulgent!

APPLE TARTE NORMANDE WITH CALVADOS AND CARAMEL SAUCE

MAKES ONE 11-INCH TART

4 to 6 apples, depending on their size, peeled and cored

1 tablespoon grapeseed oil

6 tablespoons unsalted butter, as needed

2 tablespoons dark brown sugar

1 cup heavy cream

½ cup loosely packed light brown sugar

3 egg yolks

2 teaspoons cornstarch

1½ teaspoons pure vanilla extract

1 prebaked tart shell

1 cup granulated sugar

1¼ cups heavy cream

¼ cup Calvados

Crème fraîche, for serving

Bruno Loubet has earned his popularity. In 1982, he crossed the English Channel to work for Pierre Koffmann at La Tante Claire, arguably the best French restaurant in London in that high-rolling decade. He went on to become the head chef at Raymond Blanc's superlative Le Manoir Aux Quat'Saisons in Oxfordshire—then the best anywhere in the United Kingdom. Upon returning to London after an eight-year jaunt to Australia, he opened Bistrot Bruno Loubet at the Zetter Hotel in 2010, and he was in fine form. Australia had lightened his touch, but it had certainly not taken the French out of the Frenchman. Having said that, let me now tell you that this tart is not light.

The recipe hails from Normandy, where the cream is as rich as the apples are abundant. The home of Calvados and crème d'Isigny, a cream even thicker than crème fraîche, the region is known for, among other caloric beauties, its glorious butter. Walk into a *fromagerie* or *laiterie* in Normandy and you may find a selection of more than a dozen varieties of butter, from *beurre pâtissier*, with a fat content of no less than 99.8 percent, to butters holding their own AOC (Appellation d'Origine Contrôllée), to the lovingly named *beurre tendre*, a butter that is whipped to tender perfection. This tart is, as you might by now have imagined, very, very rich. But there are times to indulge, and this is the dessert for those occasions.

Choose a good baking apple, neither too tart nor too sweet, that will hold its shape. Don't be afraid to really brown your butter and your apples. *Beurre noisette*, or butter that has melted to a lovely brown, provides an irresistible nuttiness. Browning the apples ensures a caramelized edge to your fruit. (Do sauté a few extra for a nibble.) There's some flexibility here in size. I like to make this tart in an 11-inch porcelain quiche dish, but a simple 9-inch tart pan will work too. Simply use less filling. Pour the excess in a ramekin, pop it in the oven, and serve to anyone who has just run the marathon or scaled a high peak.

Preheat the oven to 350°F.

If your apples are on the large side, cut each into 8 equal wedges. If they are small, quartering them will do.

Warm the grapeseed oil and 1½ tablespoons of the butter in a wide heavy skillet over medium heat. When hot but not smoking, add the apples and cook for 6 minutes, until they are well browned, not burnt, of course, but a lovely dark gold. Be brave: the color comes from the apple sugars caramelizing and is therefore much to be desired.

Add the dark brown sugar and cook for 3 minutes, stirring to coat the apples with the melting sugar. Remove from the heat and set aside to cool.

In a small frying pan over medium heat, brown the remaining 4½ tablespoons of butter. The solids should brown, but not burnt. Set aside to cool for 5 minutes.

In a stand mixer or using electric beaters and a large bowl, beat the cream, light brown sugar, egg yolks, cornstarch, and vanilla, to combine well. With the mixer running, pour in the brown butter.

Arrange the apples inside the tart shell in a pretty circular pattern and pour the cream-sugar mixture over the apples.

Set the tart on a baking sheet to catch spills and place in the oven. Bake for about 40 minutes, or until the center is set and no longer jiggles. A deeper or larger tart might require an extra 5 or 10 minutes. It's better, in this particular instance, to err on the side of caution and bake this tart an extra 5 minutes if you are unsure whether it is entirely set.

Transfer to a wire rack to cool while you prepare the sauce.

Place the granulated sugar in a stockpot over medium heat, stirring constantly with a wooden spoon for 10 minutes, until the sugar dissolves.

Remove from the heat and—carefully!—pour the cream into the caramel very, very slowly, stirring constantly. The caramel will sputter and splatter and burn something awful if you let it get on your skin. Wear gloves! Avert your face!

Return the pot to low heat. Stir in the Calvados, whisking until well combined. Pour into a pitcher and serve immediately.

Cut the tart into slices, dollop with crème fraiche, and generously drizzle with sauce.

MUSCOVADO CUSTARD

SERVES 6

3¼ cups heavy cream

⅔ cup granulated sugar

7 egg yolks

¼ cup muscovado sugar, either light or dark

Flaky sea salt, such as Maldon

I first had this custard as the filling of a tart. That tart was served most extravagantly with a black-sesame crumble and a scoop of crème fraîche sorbet. Elegant in texture, with an exceptional depth of flavor, the filling needed neither the crust, I decided, nor the other embellishments. Most chefs believe that no plate is complete without contrasting textures and flavors to excite the palate. In theory, I agree. But there are moments when you want to close your eyes and just have that perfect bite of pudding, uninterrupted. Forgive me, Jason and Cary for running amok with your beautifully composed dessert.

Do try to find a very rich, nonhomogenized heavy cream; in New York, where I live, the one produced by Ronnybrook is an excellent option. The final result will be, well, creamier than a pudding made with the ultrapasteurized variety. A garnish of flaky Maldon sea salt adds intrigue, but keep it sparse. The choice between light and dark muscovado sugar is yours. I use dark, as I like its stronger hint of molasses; at the restaurant, they use light. In a pinch, dark brown sugar may be substituted.

I've prepared this dessert in deep pie plates and shallower tart dishes. It also works in individual ramekins or even ovenproof teacups. For festive meals, when proper pies and tarts are in order, you may, of course, do as Cary does at Little Social and pour it into a parbaked sweet pastry crust. But then don't forget to take at least one bite, eyes closed, of just the delicious filling.

Preheat the oven to 275°F.

Warm half of the cream in a small saucepan over medium heat. Turn off the heat just before it comes to a full simmer. Set aside.

Place half of the granulated sugar in a tall heavy pot (I use a pasta pot) and set it over high heat. As the sugar starts to melt around the edges, swirl the pan to dissolve the sugar evenly. The caramel should take on a deep golden brown, but do not let it burn. You'll know its done by the color. Remove immediately from heat.

Stand back as you pour in the warm cream, as the caramel will splatter.

Continued

Continued

MUSCOVADO CUSTARD

(Few kitchen burns are worse than one inflicted by molten sugar—be careful!) Using a mittened hand, stir over medium heat to mix and melt any hardened bits. Once the sauce is smooth, remove from heat and stir in the remaining cream.

Beat the egg yolks with the muscovado sugar and the remaining granulated sugar, then slowly stir into the caramel sauce. Strain through a fine-mesh sieve into a pouring jug or heatproof liquid measuring cup.

Place a 9-inch deep-dish pie pan or a 10- or 11-inch porcelain quiche dish on a baking sheet. Carefully pour the caramel filling into the dish. Bake for 1 hour, until the edges are set and the top just a bit wobbly. Let cool on a rack to firm up a bit, then pop it in the fridge until ready to serve. It can be made several hours in advance. Remove it from the fridge twenty minutes before serving time.

Just before serving, sprinkle it with a bit of flaky sea salt.

ORANGE, MINT, AND ROSE PETAL CAKE

MAKES ONE 9-INCH CAKE

CAKE

1 cup unsalted butter, at room temperature

1 cup packed light brown sugar

4 eggs

1½ cups self-rising flour

⅓ cup almond flour

½ teaspoon baking powder

½ cup whole milk

1 cup loosely packed fresh mint

Zest of 1 orange

ICING

½ cup unsalted butter, at room temperature

2 cups confectioners' sugar, sifted

1 teaspoon rose water

Dried rose petals, for garnish (optional)

1 strip orange zest, for garnish (optional)

Thin shreds of fresh mint, for garnish (optional)

Confectioners' sugar, for dusting (optional)

This is one of the most enticing cakes imaginable. Almonds, milk, orange, mint, rose water—the list of ingredients alone seduces. The cake itself is strewn with dried rose petals to further snare any who haven't already been lured by its aroma. Dee is one of my favorite bakers in London. For years, I'd pop into Fernandez and Wells in Soho and grow indecisive in the face of her Moroccan Honey Cake and her Greek Orange Almond Semolina Cake, until, that is, I tasted this beauty and never looked back. When I asked to speak to the baker, I was told that if I hurried I'd catch her around the corner—Jorge Fernandez and Rick Wells have several cafés, each unique, including one on Beak Street and one a few paces away on Lexington Street. I dashed after her with a fury, and minutes later we were seated in a back courtyard talking recipes. We were still there an hour later.

When Dee heard that my parents had lived in Morocco, she told me the story of traveling there with her husband, a Moroccan, to meet his mother. Dee had thought herself a decent baker, but seeing her mother-in-law crouch by the side of a sandy road one day and, with little more than honey, olive oil, and almonds, produce a cake with a delicate, moist crumb and lingering perfume—well, it was a revelation. Dee's cakes now carry the flavors of North Africa, Greece, Turkey, and the Middle East, and Fernandez and Wells has garnered a fanatical following among foodies searching for a bit more than a classic scone and clotted cream. For those who've had their sweet tooth pulled, the cured meats, farmhouses cheeses, sourdough bread, and fierce coffee will make you a regular.

Preheat the oven to 375°F. Butter a 9-inch cake pan and line the bottom with parchment paper.

In a stand mixer or using electric beaters and a large bowl, cream the butter and brown sugar until the color is light and the texture is fluffy. Add the eggs one at a time, beating well after each addition.

Continued

Continued

ORANGE, MINT, AND ROSE PETAL CAKE

In a separate bowl, combine the flour, almond flour, and baking powder. Add this to the butter mixture in three batches, alternating with the milk, and beating to combine. Very finely chop the mint and stir into the batter, along with the orange zest.

Pour the batter into the prepared cake pan. Bake for 45 to 60 minutes, until a knife inserted into the middle of the cake comes out clean.

To make the icing, in a stand mixer or using electric beaters, cream the butter on low speed. Slowly pour in the confectioners' sugar while beating. Once combined, raise the speed to medium and beat until the mixture is light and fluffy. Sprinkle with the rose water and beat for another minute.

Let the cake cool completely before icing the top of the cake.

Rose petals make the prettiest garnish. But if you haven't any on hand, the zest of an orange and the thinnest shreds of mint will give color and a hint of what's to come. A light dusting of confectioners' sugar only adds to the feminine beauty of this cake.

DOUBLE-DECKER TART

MAKES ONE 9-INCH TART

BASE

½ cup white chocolate

2 cups Coco Pops, Cocoa Krispies, or most any other chocolate cereal

FILLING

⅓ cup honey

½ cup sugar

1 tablespoon water

2 teaspoons liquid glucose, light corn syrup, or golden syrup

1 egg white

1 cup lightly toasted almond flakes

¼ cup lightly toasted pistachios, coarsely chopped

⅓ cup smooth peanut butter

CHOCOLATE GANACHE

½ cup heavy cream

3½ ounces 70 percent bittersweet chocolate

1 tablespoon unsalted butter

Pinch of salt

NOTE If you happen to have a tart pan that is square or rectangular in shape, use it and cut each slice to look like a candy bar. Serve with lots of napkins, but you'll still want to lick your fingers clean.

This double-decker is actually a quadruple-decker. It is a grown-up candy bar disguised as a tart. It is good. You will crave it. You will feel like a kid eating it. You will imagine there is a golden ticket hidden in the wrapper, even though you know for a fact that it did not come in a wrapper because you made it yourself. So let loose your inner Willy Wonka and dig in!

To make the base, melt the white chocolate in a double boiler over just simmering water. Stir in the chocolate cereal. Pour the chocolate mixture into the bottom of a 9-inch springform pan or deep tart pan and press. Refrigerate while preparing the rest of the layers.

To make the filling, in a small saucepan, warm the honey until it reaches 250°F. Alternatively, microwave the honey for 90 seconds.

In a separate saucepan, warm the sugar, water, and glucose until it reaches 300°F.

In a standing mixer or using electric beaters and a large metal bowl, whisk the egg white on low speed until soft peaks form. When the honey comes to temperature, slowly pour it down the side of the bowl and into the egg white with the mixer on medium speed. Repeat this with the sugar mixture, when it comes to the proper temperature. Keep mixing until the bowl no longer feels hot (it does not need to be cool, but it should be about room temperature). Stir in the almond flakes and pistachios. Pour the filling onto the chocolate cereal base, smoothing the top if necessary. Refrigerate until firm and set, about 1 hour.

Once set, remove from the fridge and cover with a smooth layer of peanut butter. Refrigerate for another half hour, until cold and firm.

To make the chocolate ganache, in a third small saucepan, warm the cream until it reaches 175°F. Add the chocolate, butter, and salt and whisk until smooth. Pour the ganache immediately over the filling and rock the pan until it levels out. Refrigerate for an hour until the chocolate sets, up to 8 hours.

Remove from the fridge 30 to 45 minutes before serving and let the tart come to room temperature.

THREE POACHED FRUIT RECIPES

These are three of my favorite poached fruit recipes. Use them as you wish. They work wonderfully well with the Orange Blossom and Milk Pudding (page 263), on ice cream or yogurt, or simply on their own. Bob serves his blood oranges over a buttermilk panna cotta; Skye serves her kumquats over chocolate sorbet; Sarit and Itamar serve their jasmine apricots over cardamom pudding. Each serves 4.

Andrew Edmunds O Bob Cairns

POACHED BLOOD ORANGES WITH ORANGE BLOSSOM AND ALMONDS

1 cup water

¾ cup sugar

Squeeze of lemon juice

1 teaspoon orange blossom water

2 blood oranges, preferably Moro, peeled and cut into segments

½ cup sliced almonds, toasted

Combine the water, sugar, and lemon juice in a saucepan and bring to a boil. Turn the heat to low and simmer for 10 minutes, until the liquid thickens to a syrupy consistency. Remove from the heat. Add the orange blossom water and the orange segments, gently stirring to coat the fruit. Pour into a bowl and refrigerate for at least 2 hours and up to 8. After 1 hour in the fridge, cover with plastic wrap. Serve at room temperature with scattered almonds.

Honey & Co. ○ Sarit Packer and Itamar Srulovich

JASMINE CARDAMOM APRICOTS

1 jasmine tea bag or
1 teaspoon loose-leaf
jasmine tea

1 cup boiling water

2 green cardamom pods,
crushed

½ vanilla bean

2 tablespoons honey

½ cup dried apricots

Make a strong cup of jasmine tea using 1 cup of boiling water. While it
is steeping, combine the cardamom, vanilla, honey, and apricots. Pour
in the hot tea and allow the compote to infuse for at least 2 hours, or
overnight. Serve at room temperature.

Spring ○ Skye Gyngell

POACHED KUMQUATS

2 pounds kumquats

1 cup sugar

1 cup water

Cut the kumquats in half lengthwise. Tip the sugar into a saucepan,
add the water, and cook over low heat, without stirring, until the sugar
dissolves. Turn the heat to medium and cook until the syrup starts to
thicken but not color. Add the kumquats, turn the heat to low, and cook
for 10 minutes. By now, the fruit will have softened considerably and
will be wonderfully glossy. Remove from the heat and let cool. Serve
at room temperature. When poached, as they are here, kumquats need
not be peeled.

SANTIAGO TART

MAKES TWO 10-INCH TARTS

PASTRY SHELL

2½ cups all-purpose flour

1 cup confectioners' sugar

2 tablespoons almond flour

1 egg plus 1 yolk

1 vanilla bean, split lengthwise, with the seeds scraped out

Pinch of salt

1 cup (16 tablespoons) unsalted butter, at room temperature

ALMOND FILLING

3 cups whole blanched almonds

1¼ cup (20 tablespoons) unsalted butter

1 cup confectioners' sugar

2 eggs plus 3 yolks

⅓ cup Amaretto

Zest and juice of 2 lemons

Zest and juice of 3 oranges

QUINCE FILLING

¼ cup quince jelly

1 tablespoon water

Squeeze of lemon juice

Confectioners' sugar, for dusting

This almond tart never leaves the menu at either of the Barrafina locations. Nieves, however, would improve upon it, changing it ever so slightly from year to year. Ask Nieves or owners Sam and Eddie Hart about this tart, and they will compare the virtues of the 2011 to the 2015 with all the reverence usually reserved for the great Bordeaux years. Nieves believed she had finally hit upon perfection this year and sent me the recipe. A few weeks later, I received a second email with a few modifications to the recipe and an assurance that this was it—the final, the best, the one to set to ink. I couldn't agree more.

Santiago tarts date back to the Middle Ages, and their origin is easily traced to Galicia, home of the Cathedral of Santiago de Compostela, where the relics of the apostle Saint James are said to be buried. It is the Cross of the Order of Santiago, also referred to as the Cross of Saint James, that appears on its face. This is easily accomplished by creating a parchment paper stencil and dusting confectioners' sugar around it. Pilgrims who traveled, some walking a thousand miles from Le Puy, in the Massif Central area of southwest France, to Galicia, would find the antidote to their hunger in the many pastry shops surrounding the cathedral. To this day, the windows of these shops display rows and rows of Santiago tarts, and while the recipes may be unique to each baker, the imprint of the cross has not changed in five centuries, nor, fundamentally, have the ingredients.

The tart is made with ground almonds, laced with citrus zest, and spiked with sweet wine or brandy. In 2010, the Santiago tart was given Protected Geographical Indication (PGI) status within the European Union, a move that will protect its legacy and its future. Serve it at room temperature with an espresso or a glass of dessert wine. It is a dessert, but I think it is best in the afternoon with a coffee. Poke your head into Barrafina any afternoon, and you will find many happy people who think so too. But don't be shocked if the tart's latest incarnation has subtle differences from this beautiful vintage 2016.

Continued

Continued

SANTIAGO TART

Preheat the oven to 325°F. Butter two 10-inch tart tins.

To make the pastry shell, combine the flour, confectioners' sugar, almond flour, egg and yolk, vanilla, and salt in the bowl of a stand mixer fitted with a paddle attachment or in a food processor fitted with a dough attachment. Mix on medium speed just to combine. With the mixer on low speed, add the butter a tablespoon or two at a time, mixing well after each addition. Continue to mix until the dough comes together as a homogenous mass. Remove and shape very gently into 2 balls, press each lightly to flatten a bit, then wrap in plastic wrap and chill in the fridge for 40 minutes.

Remove the plastic wrap and, on a cool and well-floured surface, roll out each ball of pastry to a thickness of about ⅛ inch. Try to work as quickly as possible so that the pastry does not warm up.

Line the prepared tart tins with the rolled out pastry, making sure to press the dough into the edges. Trim off any excess. Cover the pastry with parchment paper or aluminum foil and weight down with pie weights or dried beans. Bake for 15 minutes. Remove the pie weights.

To make the almond filling, toast the almonds until golden brown and let cool completely. Use a food processor to finely grind the almonds, but stop short of turning them into flour.

In a stand mixer or using electric beaters, cream the butter and sugar together until light and fluffy. Add the eggs and yolks one at a time, beating well after each addition. By hand, stir in the toasted almonds, Amaretto, and the lemon and orange zest and juice, scraping the sides and bottom of the bowl once or twice to ensure all of the ingredients are incorporated. Set aside.

To make the quince layer, in a small saucepan, warm the quince jelly, water, and the lemon juice, stirring over medium heat, until it liquifies.

To assemble and bake the tarts, pour the quince mixture into the tart shells and spread evenly over the bottom. Divide the almond filling between each of the tart shells and smooth evenly to the edges.

Bake for 40 to 45 minutes, until the filling is set. Let the tarts cool to room temperature. Draw a cross on a sheet of parchment paper and cut it out. Place the paper stencil in the center of the tart. Dust confectioners' sugar over the tart. Carefully remove the stencil, by lifting it up and away so as to avoid spilling any accumulated sugar. Serve both tarts at room temperature or freeze one for up to a month.

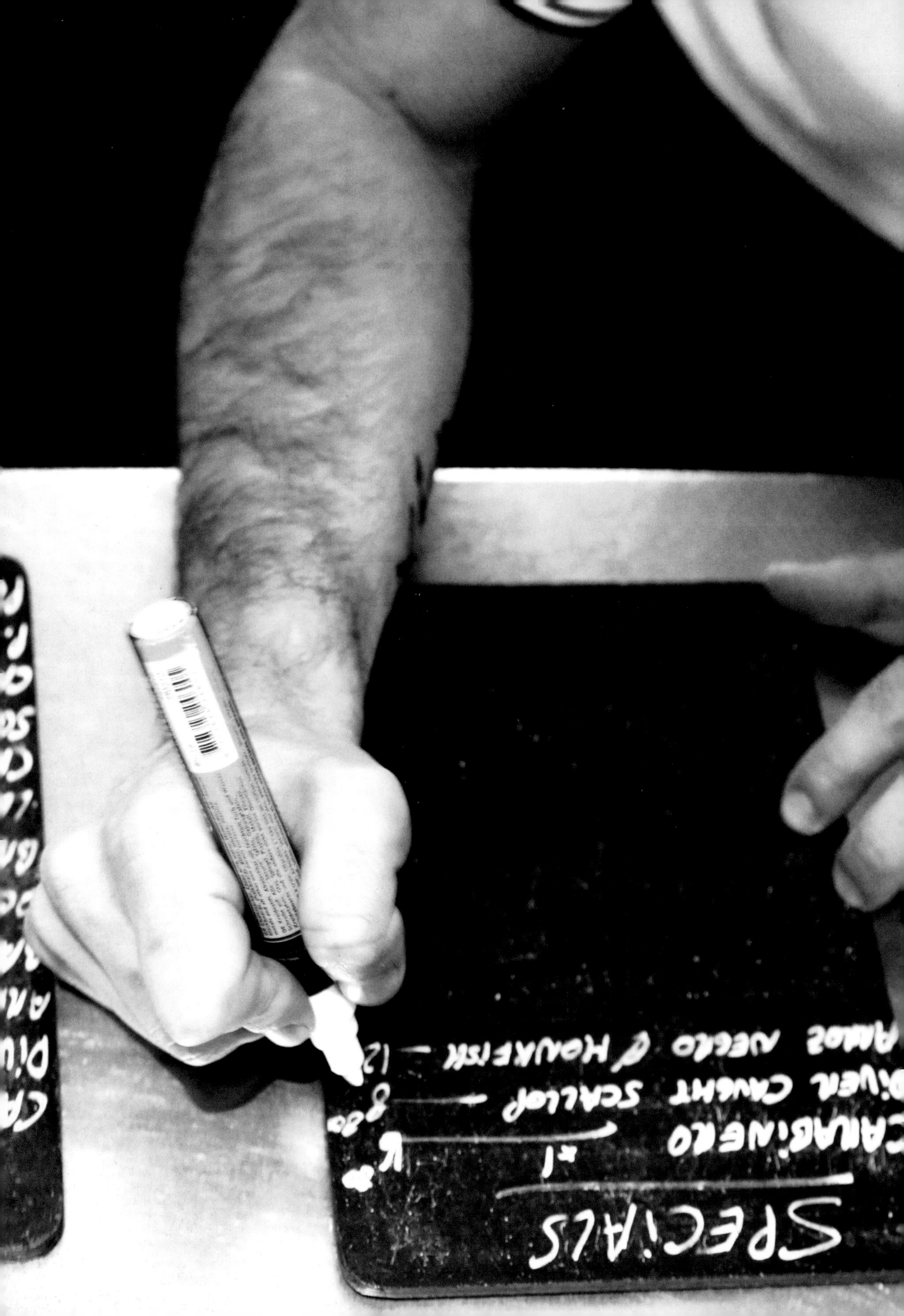
SPECIALS
CALABINERO
DIVER CAUGHT SCALLOP

barrafina

MEAT

Chickpeas, Ropa Vieja ?

Chorizo, Potato and
Watercress 7.5

Morcilla Ibérica, Quail Eggs ?

Grilled Quail with Alioli 8.6

Solomillo de Ternera 16

Chicken Thigh with
Romesco Sauce ?

Milk Fed Lamb

Pluma Ibérica with
Confit Potatoes

VEGETABLES

Baby Gem Salad wi
and Smoked Pancet

Beetroot Salad

Green Salad

Chips with Brava Sa

Fennel, Radish and C
Tomato Salad

APPLE AND CALVADOS CAKE

SERVES 6 IN FERGUS PORTIONS, WHICH ARE ALWAYS GENEROUS

2 cups sugar

3 eggs

1½ cups vegetable oil

¼ cup Calvados

3¼ cups all-purpose flour

2 teaspoons ground cinnamon

1 teaspoon baking soda

Pinch of salt

Pinch of ground cloves

3 or 4 baking apples, peeled and chopped, preferably Bramley or Granny Smith

1 cup walnuts, chopped

Crème fraîche, for serving

When Fergus sent me this recipe, he wrote me this note at the top of the page: "A very fine cake. What is not fine with a little Calvados!" How right he is, on both counts. I'm mad for this cake. The Calvados seems to ambulate in the background, like a haunting. The chopped apples and walnuts provide texture. The oil would keep it moist for days, were it not certain to be devoured within hours. The cinnamon offers comfort, the clove intrigue. The whole is like a perfectly conceived short story, with a dollop of crème fraîche as the final punctuation mark.

Preheat the oven to 350°F.

Butter a 9-inch springform pan or a 10-inch cake pan.

Whisk the sugar and eggs together either by hand, in a stand mixer, or with electric beaters. Add the vegetable oil as you would to make mayonnaise—in a thin stream as you continue to whisk until emulsified.

Add the Calvados, while continuing to whisk. Add the flour, cinnamon, baking soda, salt, and cloves and whisk to incorporate.

Fold in the apples and walnuts. Pour the batter into the prepared pan and smooth the top.

Bake for 90 minutes, until a sharp knife inserted in the center of the cake comes out clean. Serve at room temperature with a generous bowl of crème fraîche.

BAKEWELL TART

MAKES ONE 9-INCH

PASTRY SHELL

2½ cups all-purpose flour

⅔ cup (11 tablespoons) cold unsalted butter, diced

½ cup sugar

Good pinch of salt

2 eggs, beaten

FRANGIPANE

¾ cup sugar

6 tablespoons unsalted butter, at room temperature

2 eggs

1⅓ cup almond flour

1 tablespoon rum

2 tablespoons sifted all-purpose flour

6 tablespoons raspberry jam

A handful of sliced almonds

Clotted cream or crème fraîche, for serving

However jaded I sometimes worry I've become, I still get a frisson of excitement sitting in the very restaurant Charles Dickens, William Thackeray, H. G. Wells, and Graham Greene frequented. If that doesn't do it for you, Buster Keaton, Clark Gable, Charlie Chaplin, and Laurence Olivier might. Or perhaps it is knowing that the restaurant opened the same year that Napoleon began his campaign in Egypt. No one was really surprised to hear Lady Mary call it her favorite London restaurant in an episode of *Downton Abbey*, nor to see that the restaurant didn't need a set change. But if you live in London today, you favor Rules not only for its storied past, but for the impeccable food.

At first appearance, Rules would seem to be serving the same food it did when Thomas Rule opened it in 1798, but this thankfully is not the case. The brilliance of its owners has been to preserve tradition, while ever so subtlety moving the preparation of the classics into the modern era. A piecrust might be a tad lighter, the vegetables crisper, the sauces lighter—making the thought of the Steamed Steak and Kidney Suet Pudding with Oysters or the Rump of Venison with Roast Pear, Stilton, and Port surprisingly appealing, particularly after a Black Velvet (Champagne and Guinness) or simply because the wine-red velvet banquettes have lulled you into a languorous state of contentment. And then you will take a bite of your food, and it will be so seamlessly perfect you may forget to notice how really good it is. And it will be really good, thanks to David Stafford, a young chef who honed his skills at the River Cafe and the legendary Café Anglais. David was a smart choice for Rules. Professional, affable, energetic, he is both humble and immensely talented. He seems to carry the weight of history effortlessly, knowing how to improve without jarring the loyalists. Or should I say royalists?

I think this Bakewell Tart is the best in London. The frangipane filling is light and not too sweet. The flaked almonds on top add a bit of crunch, and the layer of raspberry jam is wisely thin. David makes his own raspberry jam, but Rules has a country estate from which to source game, wild mushrooms, and presumably berries. A good jam from the market is just fine. This pudding dates back to only 1846, making it something of an upstart. But I, for one, am glad it slipped in unnoticed.

To make the pastry shell, pulse the flour, butter, sugar, and salt together in a food processor until they reach the consistency of bread crumbs. Add the eggs and mix with the flour mixture until the pastry comes together as a homogenous mass. Remove the dough from the food processor and shape very gently into a ball, pressing lightly to flatten. Cover in plastic wrap and refrigerate for 40 minutes.

Remove the plastic wrap. On a cool and lightly floured surface, roll out the pastry until it's about ⅛ inch thick. Try to work as quickly as possible so that the pastry does not warm up. Line a 9-inch tart tin with the rolled-out pastry, making sure to press the dough into the edges. Trim off any excess and refrigerate again.

At this point, you have two choices. You can proceed or you can parbake the pastry. David does not parbake. I do, because parbaking results in a crisper crust, which I like.

To parbake the crust, preheat the oven to 375°F. Cover the pastry with parchment paper or aluminum foil and weight down with pie weights or dried beans. Bake for 15 minutes, until it has started to dry. Remove the pie weights and parchment paper and bake 5 minutes longer. Remove from the oven and set aside for 20 minutes, until cooled to room temperature. Reduce the oven to 325°F.

To make the frangipane, set up a stand mixer if you have one or electric beaters and a large mixing bowl. Cream the sugar and butter together on high speed until pale and fluffy. Slow the speed down and add the eggs one at a time, beating well, after each addition. Add the almond flour and continue beating for 30 seconds. Add the rum, followed by the flour, beating well, after each addition.

To assemble and bake the tart, evenly spread the raspberry jam over the bottom of the tart shell. With an offset rubber spatula, create an even layer of frangipane that is the same height as the tart shell.

Sprinkle the top with almonds and bake for 35 to 40 minutes. The tart is done when the interior has risen a bit and the top is a lovely pale gold.

Serve slightly warm with a dollop of clotted cream or crème fraîche.

CHOCOLATE SQUARES

MAKES 16 SMALL SQUARES

1¼ cup (20 tablespoons) unsalted butter

1 cup cocoa powder

¾ cup all-purpose flour

Pinch of salt

3 eggs

1½ cups granulated sugar

1 cup semi-sweet chocolate chips

Despite possessing clean-cut, rather preppy good looks, James is at the red-hot center of London's hip, young culinary universe. He was, as it happens, on track to be a commercial airline pilot when a meal at the Fat Duck set him on a new course. After a notable rise cooking for Fergus Henderson—he became head chef at St. John Bread and Wine at twenty-six—he partnered with chef friends Isaac McHale and Ben Greeno and, in the spirit of swaggering revolutionaries, the trio dubbed themselves the Young Turks. A borrowed, thumb-in-the-eye nomenclature indeed, and yet their credo was a simple, pure one. Cook sustainably and locally, reclaim forgotten ingredients and lost recipes, and let the ingredients take center stage. Ben Greeno left to cook for Momofuku's David Chang, but Isaac and James took over the floor above the Ten Bells Pub in Spitalfields and, for six months, wowed London. Although Isaac then started the Clove Club and James started Lyle's, their philosophy has changed little and their food continues to wow.

Lyle's is open all day and, with its white-on-white simple design, oversize windows, and airy calm, it is a lovely place to read, work, and feast. It is housed in what was once the Lyle's Tea factory, but the aroma today is rather more barista than *chai walla*. Come evening, however, a seriousness pervades—the food reflects James's tenure at Heston Blumenthal's ode to molecular gastronomy, the Fat Duck, even as it captures the easy spirit of St. John. In other words, it is highly refined and without pretension, as James himself appears to be. His talent is huge. The recipe I include here is perhaps his simplest. It is served at the restaurant, with a burnt pear sorbet, which is markedly more complicated. This cake is really a brownie—a very, very good brownie. And if you make it with Valrhona cocoa, it becomes a brownie for the ages.

Preheat the oven to 350°F. Butter an 8-inch square cake pan and line with parchment paper, using enough so that it hangs over the sides of the pan, making it easier to remove the cake.

Melt the butter in a small saucepan over low heat. Remove from the heat. Stir together the cocoa powder, flour, and salt in a bowl, then pour it into the melted butter and stir until combined.

Whisk or beat the eggs and sugar together in a large bowl. Add the flour-butter mixture and whisk or beat together, making sure to scrape the sides and bottom of the bowl to ensure all of the ingredients are incorporated. Fold in the chocolate chips.

Pour the batter into the prepared pan. Bake for 25 or 30 minutes, until the center is set and the edges have just begun to pull away from the pan.

Let the cake cool for 15 minutes in the pan. Using the parchment paper, lift the cake out of the pan and let it cool completely. Cut into squares and serve.

MOLASSES CAKE WITH GARAM MASALA ICE CREAM AND MULLED AUTUMN FRUITS

SERVES 6 OR MAKES 10 MUFFINS

MOLASSES CAKE

6 tablespoons unsalted butter

½ cup molasses

½ cup firmly packed light brown sugar

¼ cup granulated sugar

1¼ cups plus 2 tablespoons all-purpose flour

1¼ teaspoons baking soda

1 teaspoon ground ginger

¼ teaspoon ground cinnamon

¼ teaspoon salt

¾ cup whole milk

1 egg

½ teaspoon pure vanilla extract

NOTE You may also bake the batter in a 10-cup muffin tin for 15 to 20 minutes.

Anna's restaurant isn't small, but it somehow feels like a home. It is, in fact, a substantial brick building on quiet St. John's Square in Clerkenwell. From the casual café downstairs, which opens onto the square in good weather, to the rambling array of dining rooms upstairs, the effect is one of a house party—neither too raucous nor too staid. Imagine, then, that you are served this warm molasses cake and a pot of tea. You are in a serene, pale gray room with stripped wood floors and tall windows that fill the room with light. You don't hear a single car. You might forget you are in London and think yourself in the countryside. And then you take a spoonful of the garam masala ice cream and you are in London, in the hands of a master. There are few chefs who have as great a command of foreign ingredients as Anna does. Here, the use of Indian spices is subtle, but it moves this most traditional of British desserts into something memorable and distinct. Anna's food never fails to excite, never fails to stretch your imagination. But, at its heart, it's intended to nourish and comfort, and it does so generously.

Consider this recipe as three that you may make in any combination. Double the mulled fruit so you have some for breakfast for the next few mornings. The ice cream, of course, keeps a good month. The molasses cakes are not so sweet that they can't be considered a snack or even made as muffins. I've even reduced the poaching stock to a syrup, chilling it and drinking it topped with Champagne. Do note that you may need to special order the licorice juice stick to make the mulling wine. I order mine, imported from Italy, on Amazon. If you've never cooked with licorice before, you're in for a treat, so buy a few extras. They can be dissolved in boiling water to make a potent, somewhat medicinal tea. These sticks, you see, may look like candy, but they are pure, almost pharmaceutical grade. Toto, you're not in Twizzler land anymore—this is the real, dark, bitter deal. Pucker up. Or better yet, stick with Anna's mulling wisdom and temper the truth with port and muscovado sugar.

ICE CREAM

1 cup sugar

6 egg yolks

2 cups heavy cream

1 cup whole milk

1 teaspoon garam masala

MULLED FRUIT

3 whole cloves

1 star anise pod

1 cinnamon stick

4 black peppercorns, crushed

1¾ cups red wine

½ cup port

½ cup plus 2 tablespoons muscovado sugar

¼ licorice juice stick

Zest and juice of ½ orange

Zest and juice of ½ lemon

¼ dried red chile, sliced lengthwise

Sliced pears and plums and whole blackberries

NOTE The cake or muffins are done when a knife inserted into the center comes out clean. Serve while still warm.

To make the cake, preheat the oven to 350°F or 325°F if using a convection oven. Butter an 8-inch square or 9-inch round cake pan.

In a small saucepan over low heat, melt the butter, molasses, and sugars, until the sugars have dissolved. Transfer to a mixing bowl and set aside to cool.

Meanwhile, stir together the flour, baking soda, ginger, cinnamon, and salt in a bowl. Whisk together the milk, egg, and vanilla in a separate bowl. Whisk the egg into the cooled sugar mixture and then whisk in the flour mixture. Make sure there are no lumps.

Pour the batter into the prepared cake pan and bake for 25 to 35 minutes.

To make the ice cream, whisk together the sugar and egg yolks in a small bowl and set aside.

In a medium saucepan, combine the cream, milk, and garam masala. Set this over low heat, whisking occasionally until it just begins to simmer. Slowly pour about a third of the hot cream mixture into the eggs, while whisking constantly. This is to gently raise the temperature of the eggs. Then pour the combined mixture back into the saucepan and continue to whisk. Return it to a simmer.

Strain the custard through a fine-mesh sieve into a clean bowl, set in an ice bath, and whisk occasionally until chilled. Churn in an ice-cream maker and freeze for at least 2 hours before serving.

To mull the fruit, lightly toast the spices in a frying pan to release their fragrance.

Combine the red wine, port, muscovado sugar, licorice, orange and lemon zests and juices, and the chile in a medium saucepan. Stir in the toasted spices. Bring to a boil and cook until reduced to a thin syrup. Strain through a fine-mesh sieve and discard the solids.

Return the liquid to the saucepan and bring to a simmer over low heat. Add the pears and plums and poach for 5 to 10 minutes, or until tender. Remove from the heat and add the blackberries. Set aside to cool to room temperature.

To serve, place a slice of warm molasses cake in a wide bowl and top with a generous spoonful of the mulled fruits and a scoop or two of the ice cream. Serve immediately.

WALNUT CHERRY CAKE

MAKES ONE 8-INCH CAKE

BATTER

9 tablespoons unsalted butter

1 star anise pod

1 cup walnuts

¼ cup slivered almonds

2 cups confectioners' sugar

⅔ cup all-purpose flour

½ teaspoon baking powder

¼ teaspoon salt

¼ teaspoon ground cinnamon

7 egg whites

TOPPING

2 cups fresh cherries or 1 (12-ounce) bag frozen cherries

2 to 4 tablespoons sugar

1 tablespoons cornstarch

Pinch of ground star anise or ground cinnamon

Confectioners' sugar, for serving

Whipped cream or crème fraîche, for serving (optional)

NOTE Alternatively, you may make 8 muffins. The baking time will be approximately 25 minutes.

This lovely sweet reminds me of what the French call Le Weekend Cake. It is terrific with whipped cream for Friday night's dessert, Saturday breakfast with a cup of strong coffee, on a picnic, at tea, and, of course, again at dinner. It works as well in a lunch box as graced with a shower of confectioners' sugar and served on Wedgwood china. In winter, I make it with frozen pitted cherries, in the summer, with fresh cherries or blackberries, and in late summer, with juicy ripe plums.

This recipe is classic Honey & Co., by which I mean that it is a warm, generous dessert, comforting in appearance and yet, quietly, rather a revelation. It is made with little more than confectioners' sugar, ground nuts, and egg whites. The runny batter seems a mistake until the cake is baked and springs to perfection. You may depend upon it, your affection growing by the year, the pleasure it offers never waning.

To make the batter, brown the butter in a frying pan over a lively heat with the star anise. The butter should foam lightly, then turn a golden brown. Remove it from the heat before it starts to blacken, and let it cool a bit while you make the batter.

Finely grind the walnuts and almonds in a food processor. Add the dry ingredients, including the ground nuts, into a large bowl. Stir in the egg whites. Here, I like to use a stand mixer or an electric beater and a large bowl, but it is not necessary to do so. Just make sure to fully incorporate the whites into the dry ingredients. Discard the star anise and pour the brown butter into the batter. Don't forget to scrape out all the burnt pieces on the bottom of the pan, as they hold the most flavor. Refrigerate the batter for 1 hour.

Preheat the oven to 350°F. Line an 8-inch square cake pan with parchment paper.

To make the topping, combine all of the ingredients in a large bowl, gently tossing the fruit with your hands to coat it with the cornstarch and sugar.

Pour the batter into the cake pan and sprinkle with the topping. Bake for 20 minutes. Rotate the pan and bake for 20 minutes longer, until a knife inserted into the center comes out clean. Let the cake cool a good 10 minutes before inverting it onto a plate and then flipping it again so the topping is—you guessed it—on top. Shower with confectioners' sugar.

PEAR HAZELNUT TART

MAKES ONE 10- OR 11-INCH TART

PASTRY

1 cup (16 tablespoons) unsalted butter, cold

4 cups all-purpose flour

3 tablespoons sugar

2 eggs, plus 2 yolks

FILLING

2 cups hazelnuts

18 tablespoons unsalted butter, at room temperature

1¼ cups sugar

1 teaspoon pure vanilla extract

Zest of 1 lemon

2 eggs

6 ripe pears, preferably Comice, at room temperature

1 cup crème fraîche, to serve

1 to 2 teaspoons freshly ground espresso beans, to serve

Spring's pastry chef Sarah Johnson uses my favorite variety of pear for this frangipane tart. Comice pears are delicate, bruise easily, exude juice when they are ripe (eat over a sink!), and never hide their pink blush. They are rarely baked, presumably because they are anything but hardy. Here, however, they stand up with quiet assurance and their sweet perfume provides a delicate counterpoint to the rich nuttiness of the hazelnut "frangipane."

One taste of this tart and it will come as no surprise that Sarah worked with Alice Waters at Chez Panisse in Berkeley, California, before joining like-minded Skye Gyngell in London. The tart lovingly pays homage to its ingredients, drawing out the essence of their flavors with little distraction and no unnecessary embellishment.

The tart can be made in a standard metal tart pan with a removable bottom. There's ample filling here for a 10- or 11-inch pan. But I prefer to make it in a slightly deeper ceramic quiche dish. If you have only a 9-inch pan, simply fill it with less frangipane and fewer pears. Either way, do set the pan on a baking sheet, as any sugary spills will otherwise cause your oven to smoke. The tart is best served still warm from baking, within an hour or so of removing it from the oven. This tart is a natural fit with rich and tangy crème fraîche. Sarah gives each plated slice a light shower of finely ground espresso.

To make the pastry, take your butter out of the fridge just before using it, as you want it to be cold. Dice or slice it into about 20 pieces. Combine the flour, sugar, and butter in a food processor and blitz, using short pulses, until the butter starts to break up. Add the eggs and yolks, one at a time, pulsing between additions.

Once the pastry starts coming together, transfer it to a lightly floured work surface. A cool countertop or marble pastry board works best. Gently knead the dough together and shape it into a ball. Flatten the ball with the heel of your palm to form a disk. Cover it tightly with plastic wrap and refrigerate for at least 2 hours or, preferably, overnight.

Remove the plastic wrap. On a cool floured surface, roll out the pastry with a floured rolling pin, turning the pastry as you go to ensure an even thickness. Roll until the dough is a mere ⅜-inch thick. Try to work as quickly as possible so that the pastry does not warm up. Carefully drape the pastry into the tart pan. Using the tips of your fingers, lightly press it into the sides of the pan, trimming off any excess. Refrigerate for 20 to 30 minutes.

Preheat oven to 350°F. Remove the pan from the fridge. Cover the pastry with parchment paper or aluminum foil and weigh down with pie weights of dried beans. Pop it in the oven for 15 minutes, or until it is no longer tacky and is starting to dry.

Remove the pie weights and parchment paper and bake 10 or so minutes longer, until the pastry is golden. Remove from the oven and set aside to cool. Leave the oven on.

To make the filling, roast the hazelnuts until they turn a light golden color. Set aside to cool to room temperature wrapped in a clean dish towel. After 15 minutes, rub the dish towel vigorously over the hazelnuts to remove their skins. Blitz the nuts in a food processor until they are coarsely ground. You're not trying to make a flour here, nor anything too coarse and chunky, but rather a textured grind, closer to fine sand than powdery flour.

Cream the butter in a stand mixer or using electric beaters. Add the sugar and continue to beat until pale, light, and fluffy. Add the vanilla and lemon zest and beat to combine. Add the eggs, one by one, beating well, after each addition. Gently fold in the hazelnuts by hand.

To assemble the tart, pour the filling into the bottom of the cooled tart shell. (You may have a bit left over.)

Peel the pears, if you so choose. (I do; the restaurant does not.) Slice each pear into six wedges. Gently press the pears into the filling in a pinwheel pattern.

Place the tart on a baking sheet. Bake at 350°F with, if you have it, the convection fan running, for 50 to 60 minutes, until the surface is golden brown and firm to the touch. The pears should be soft and the center set but still quite moist. At the restaurant, where the ovens have powerful convection fans, the tart only takes 40 minutes. In a home oven, it takes closer to an hour. Start checking it at 45 minutes, but do wait to remove it until the center is set.

Transfer to a wire rack to cool slightly. Cut into wedges and serve with a dollop of crème fraîche and sprinkle with the finely ground espresso.

STEAMING PUDDING AND MAKING CUSTARD

Forgive me if you are already a master at making steamed puddings. Or better yet, skip ahead. For those of you who, like me, approach the steaming of puddings with a long list of questions, read on for some of the answers.

Steamed puddings are essentially moist cakes that cook in a covered bain-marie. They are classically served with custard. Please note that failure to do so will rouse rage in many a Brit. They are hardly light fare, but when made properly, they are delicate and fine. Banish all thoughts of leaden puddings; the recipes to follow are elegant in texture and surprising in flavor.

What you need to know: Should you become a steamed pudding aficionado, there are a multitude of pudding basins (dishes) on the market. A high-sided porcelain soufflé dish is my vessel of choice. Look for a model that has a sealing top. On occasion, I've used a Bundt pan, probably because I wasn't alive in the 1950s and so never learned to loathe them as a symbol of prefeminist enslavement. And I think the shapes are pretty.

In the words of Jeremy Lee of Quo Vadis: "It is vital that not a whisper of steam be permitted egress to the pudding within." Therefore cover the pudding in two layers. (Unless of course, you have purchased that nifty model with the sealing top.) The first layer should be parchment paper, the second aluminum foil. Lay each sheet on your countertop and fold a pleat down the middle. Do this with both the parchment and the foil. The pleat will billow up as the pudding rises.

Butter the side of the parchment that will lie atop the pudding, cover the pudding with the pleated parchment and tie a string around the side of the dish to secure the parchment. Repeat with the foil. If you are good at knots, which I am not, you may also make a string handle.

Cut off any excess paper and foil.

To steam the pudding, I use a Le Creuset Dutch oven or a pasta pot. Place a metal trivet, rack, a scrunched up and flattened piece of foil, an overturned ramekin, or a tuna can with top and bottom removed in the bottom of your pot. If your pasta pot has a colander, use it. This will protect your pudding from direct heat. Place the covered pudding on top of the trivet. Pour boiling water into the pot. You want roughly half of the pudding to be submerged. Cover the pot. Your pudding is now ready to cook. This can either be done in an oven or on the stove, per recipe instructions. A caution: Steam burns are painful. Be careful. If I am certain the pudding is done, I will stab little slits in the paper and foil to let some of the steam escape before attempting to untie my ill-formed knots.

JEREMY LEE'S CUSTARD

SERVES 4 TO 6

2 cups whole milk

1 vanilla bean, split lengthwise

6 egg yolks

1 tablespoon granulated or light brown sugar

⅓ cup heavy cream

"Custard is a wonder that cannot be denied," Jeremy tells me with a certain ferocity, and most of the United Kingdom would agree. But when I asked him for his recipe, he did a double take, as that is a bit like asking for the Nestle Toll House Chocolate Chip Cookie recipe—it is set to memory by age ten. And yet Jeremy simply does things better, and so I asked again and he obliged.

Warm the milk and vanilla bean in a medium saucepan over low gentle heat until you see stirrings of a simmer. Remove from the heat and let infuse for at least 10 minutes. Discard the vanilla.

In a mixing bowl, stir the egg yolks with the sugar until mixed, but not frothing. Slowly pour the warm milk over the yolks, stirring all the time until smooth, and then return to the saucepan and place over low heat.

Cook, stirring the sauce gently, until it thickens to the consistency of cream. Remove from the heat. Pour the cream into the custard, stirring to combine.

Pour the custard through a fine-mesh sieve into a bowl and cover with plastic wrap. With the tip of a very sharp knife, make holes in the plastic 4 or 5 times to let any steam whisper through. Place the bowl over a pan of warm water and set aside. Come the moment, warm through over a very low heat (taking care not to let the custard get too hot or it will split) and stir gently before serving.

GINGER SPICE STEAMED PUDDINGS
WITH RUM SYRUP

SERVES 10

⅔ cup Lyle's black treacle or blackstrap molasses

1⅔ cups Lyle's golden syrup

2 cups all-purpose flour

1½ cups fresh white bread crumbs

1 cup almond flour

14 tablespoons minced suet or frozen unsalted butter

2 teaspoons ground ginger

1 teaspoon baking powder

1 teaspoon ground Mixed Spice, plus more for serving (page 230)

½ teaspoon ground cinnamon

Pinch of ground cloves

1 large baking apple

1 (4-inch) knob fresh ginger, unpeeled

4 pieces stem ginger in syrup

3 large eggs

⅓ cup milk

⅔ cup dark rum, plus more for serving

Vanilla ice-cream, crème fraîche, custard, or heavy cream, for serving

Continued

Imagine the most comforting of desserts, boldly spiced and generously spiked, perhaps even sitting in a puddle of cream, the warm pudding meeting the cool cream in each bite. Hungry yet? This pudding is everything I love about British desserts. Steamed puddings are never too fancy, never too refined. Somehow, through the centuries, pudding was spared the propriety that existed in almost every other aspect of daily life. Voluminous skirts, powdered wigs, corseted waists, top-hatted gentlemen, and gold livery might have been de rigueur, but pudding reminded everyone to have a little fun. It may have been served on the finest bone china and spooned from the heaviest of silver, but the easy delight it afforded was sacrosanct and not open to discussion . Even in the decades of tough mutton and gray vegetables that once, sadly, defined British cuisine, good baking was an art, however common.

If I could import one pantry item from the UK, it would be stem ginger in syrup (in particular, the version made by Fortnum and Mason). I'm convinced that one day soon it will suddenly pop up in every American market, but, in the meantime, it is easily ordered online. Buy several jars right away. It keeps, if you can resist it long enough to store it. Or you can make it yourself by simmering thrice-blanched pieces of ginger root in simple syrup for 20 minutes. Preserved this way, the ginger retains its heat without its bite. It is softer, as well, making it easy to use. The syrup is addictive and best described as liquid candy. Many bakers spoon a bit of it into the base of the pudding dish or ramekin before adding the batter. Mixed with rum, it makes a mean hot toddy. Spooned over vanilla ice cream, or better yet, swirled into vanilla ice cream, it adds spice, intrigue, and warmth.

Justin is widely known in London for having created the beloved cream-filled doughnuts and bread at St. John Bread and Wine. In his words, "Fergus Henderson showed me the ways of the Jedi." Apparently, Fergus also taught him the ways of baking. Recently, Justin started his own bakery at Borough Market. Beware the queue! This recipe is a family favorite of his, and now of mine.

Continued

Continued

GINGER SPICE STEAMED PUDDINGS
WITH RUM SYRUP

MIXED SPICE

1 tablespoon ground allspice

1 tablespoon ground
cinnamon

1 tablespoon ground nutmeg

2 teaspoons ground mace

1 teaspoon ground cloves

1 teaspoon ground coriander

1 teaspoon ground ginger

—————————

NOTE It's best to make the
bread crumbs in a food
processor. The ones Justin
calls for are meant to be
neither as fine as store-
bought, nor as light as panko.
In place of suet, which can be
hard to source, I grate frozen
sticks of butter on a box
grater. The flavor is a touch
mellower, which I happen to
find preferable. Stem ginger
may be ordered online.

Preheat the oven to 300°F.

Combine the treacle and ⅔ cup of the golden syrup in a small saucepan
and cook over low heat for a few minutes, until they melt together.
Remove from the heat just before they come to a boil.

In a large bowl, stir together the flour, bread crumbs, almond flour, suet,
ground ginger, baking powder, mixed spice, cinnamon, and cloves.

Peel and core the apple, cut it into small dice, and place it in a small
bowl. Peel the fresh ginger, grate it on the largest holes of a box grater,
and add to the bowl with the apple. Dice the stem ginger and add as well.

Lightly beat the eggs with a fork in a small bowl. Stir in the milk.

Add the warmed treacle mixture to the flour mixture and stir together
until well incorporated. Stir in the apple and gingers. Add the eggs and
milk and stir until well incorporated. Pour the batter into an 8- or 10-cup
pudding dish or other such vessel.

Cover the pudding with a round of pleated parchment paper and, then
a round of pleated aluminum foil. Tie a string around the dish to secure
the paper and foil.

Bring a teakettle of water to a boil. Place the pudding atop a trivet in a
deep roasting pan or Dutch oven to create a bain-marie. Fill the pan with
boiling water until water reaches halfway up the sides of the pudding
dish. Cover the pan with a layer of aluminum foil or the Dutch oven with
its lid. Bake for 90 minutes, until set throughout. Check the water level
regularly, topping it up with more boiling water as necessary to keep the
dish halfway submerged. The pudding is done when a knife inserted in
its center comes out clean and the pudding springs back when touched.
Do be careful checking on it as steam can burn quite badly.

While the pudding is baking, prepare the syrup. Combine the remaining
1 cup of golden syrup and the rum in a small saucepan and bring to a boil.
Lower the heat and simmer until thickened into an unctuous syrup.

Remove the pudding carefully from the bain-marie and transfer to a rack
for a couple of minutes before unwrapping, unmolding, and inverting it
onto a pretty serving plate. Pour the syrup over the puddings and then
generously splash rum over them as well, if you're in the mood to do so.
Or give them the faintest dusting of mixed spice.

Serve warm with vanilla ice cream, crème fraîche, custard, or a pitcher
of cream.

OLIVE OIL CAKE

SERVES 6

2 cups all-purpose flour

1 tablespoon baking powder

1¼ cups sugar

3 eggs

¾ cup great extra-virgin olive oil

¾ cup whole milk

1 to 2 teaspoons grated orange zest

Juice of 1 juicy orange

If you find yourself, in the hours before a dinner party, in an anxious or insecure frame of mind, make this cake. The very afternoon Lori sent me this recipe, I made it for a party of my own, and it was so good that I cooked it two more times that very week. Like Ruthie and Rose's Chocolate Nemesis (page 190), this is a recipe that will never fail you. It's light and moist and dresses up beautifully with a dollop of crème fraîche. Save a slice for breakfast. Take it on a picnic. Put it in a lunch box.

A few notes: Lori uses one teaspoon of orange zest. I use two. One gives center stage to the olive oil; the second offers a brighter burst of citrus. The olive oil here is key, as it gives the cake a subtle complexity that is barely discernable but essential. Choose one with fruity notes and spring for the almost best you can. I say "almost best" because it need not be the supreme one you drizzle sparingly over warm burrata. I use Frantoia Barbera most of the time. While hardly meek, it is elegant and well rounded with a buttery finish. A strong, grassy, or herbaceous olive oil will overpower the delicacy of this cake. The recipe, Lori tells me, comes from the wonderful oil and wine producers of Tenuta di Capezzana in Tuscany. She secured it from Contessa Lisa Contini Bonacossi for Towpath, and I've secured it for you.

Preheat the oven to 350°F.

Butter a 9-inch springform pan and line with parchment paper. Butter and flour the parchment paper and sides of the pan.

Stir together the flour and baking powder in a small bowl.

In a stand mixer or using electric beaters and a large bowl, beat the sugar and eggs on medium speed until pale yellow.

Add the olive oil, milk, and orange zest and juice, and beat for another minute or two. Add the flour mixture and stir by hand until just blended.

Pour the batter into the prepared pan. Bake for 45 minutes, until golden brown and a knife inserted into the center comes out clean. The cake is delicious both warm and at room temperature.

GARAM MASALA CHRISTMAS PUDDING WITH NUTMEG CUSTARD

SERVES 8

¾ cup dried apricots, chopped to about the size of a raisin

¾ cup dried figs, chopped to about the size of a raisin

¾ cup dried black currants

¾ cup seedless black raisins

¾ cup golden raisins

½ cup hazelnuts, finely chopped

½ cup whole, blanched almonds, finely chopped

½ cup walnuts, finely chopped

½ cup pecans, finely chopped

⅓ cup pine nuts, finely chopped

½ cup cashews, finely chopped

2 teaspoons ground garam masala

½ teaspoon freshly grated nutmeg

For those of you who didn't eat your first bite of Christmas pudding at the age of two, as I did, this intensely flavored, very moist steamed pudding may fall under the rubric of fruitcake—in other words, something to regift to your dearest enemy. When I was little, my parents wisely—or unwisely—allowed me plenty of hard sauce as enticement to accept this favorite Christmas dessert of my father's. I'd eat the hard sauce with a silver spoon, the butter cool and smooth, the slight crunch of sugar, the illicit taste of brandy—it was thrilling. I'd let it melt in my mouth, leaving the fire of alcohol, an expanding flame. When we moved to Paris, my first bûche de Noël made up for the annual arrival of that dark, sticky mass that came in the red Fortnum and Mason box. And so for years (make that 20), my mother had the loving sense to procure both a log and a pudding. And then, sometime around the age of 30, I was suddenly seduced by the pudding's dark complexity. I consider this a moment of enlightenment, or perhaps a coming of age, since this dessert's pleasures are both mature and particular. It's no wonder, then, that I fell for this marriage of Indian spice and British tradition.

The brilliance here is that the garam masala both deepens and mellows over time, and these puddings are, in fact, meant to be stored and aged in a cool, dry place. This takes some trust in our refrigerated era. What you bite into is tender, almost falling apart, warm, comforting, and faintly exotic. The cardamom, rose petals, and fennel of the garam masala bring what Vivek calls "a hint of Delhi" while also infusing the house with lush aromas. While I'm still hard-pressed to forgo hard sauce, the delicacy of this nutmeg custard is a perfect match. The nutmeg is heady, the custard mild. I like to double the recipe and make an ice cream out of the remaining half. I make the pudding in one of my mother's stack of Fortnum and Mason porcelain bowls, in memory of Christmases past.

Place all the dry fruits, nuts, and spices into a large bowl; add the rum, brandy, and orange and lemon zests and juices. Stir together thoroughly, cover, and leave overnight at room temperature to soak in the flavors.

Preheat the oven to 350°F and butter an 8-cup pudding dish.

¾ cup dark rum

¼ cup brandy

Zest and juice of 1 orange

Zest and juice of 1 lemon

1 cup (16 tablespoons) salted butter, at room temperature

2 cups muscovado sugar

3 eggs

1 cup all-purpose flour

NUTMEG CUSTARD

2 cups heavy cream

½ cup milk

1 vanilla bean, split lengthwise

3 egg yolks

2 tablespoons sugar

4 nutmegs, grated

In a stand mixer or using electric beaters and a large bowl, cream the butter and sugar until light and fluffy. Add the eggs, one at a time, beating well, after each addition.

Add the flour, beating just until combined. Fold in the soaked fruits and nuts and whatever soaking liquid remains.

Pour the pudding into the prepared dish.

Cover the pudding with a round of pleated parchment paper and then a round of pleated aluminum foil. Tie a string around the dish to secure the paper and foil.

Bring a teakettle of water to a boil.

Place the pudding atop a trivet in a deep roasting pan or Dutch oven to create a bain-marie. Fill the pan with boiling water until water reaches halfway up the sides of the pudding dish. Cover the pan with a layer of aluminum foil or the Dutch oven with its lid. Bake for 90 minutes, until set throughout. It may take up to 2 hours, depending on the depth of your dish. Check the water level regularly, topping it up with more boiling water as necessary to keep the dish halfway submerged. The pudding is done when a knife inserted in its center comes out clean and the pudding springs back when touched. Do be careful checking on it as steam can burn quite badly.

If you're preparing weeks ahead, this Christmas pudding benefits from the flavors developing upon keeping it in a cool, dry place for a month. To reheat, steam (covered) for 20 to 30 minutes, or until completely heated through. Serve warm with custard.

To make the nutmeg custard, warm the cream, milk, and vanilla bean in a saucepan until it just comes to a boil. Remove from heat.

In a large bowl, beat the egg yolks, sugar, and nutmeg. Pour about one-third of the hot cream into the egg yolk mixture, whisking vigorously. Pour everything back into the saucepan, continuing to whisk. Bring to a simmer over low heat and cook until the mixture thickens sufficiently to coat the back of a spoon.

Strain the custard through a fine-mesh sieve. Serve warm, poured generously over the Christmas Pudding.

J. Sheekey ○ Tim Hughes

CHOCOLATE MARMALADE PUDDING

SERVES 6 TO 8

¾ cup Seville orange thick-cut marmalade

⅔ cup bittersweet chocolate

½ cup (8 tablespoons) unsalted butter, at room temperature

1 cup sugar

4 eggs, lightly beaten

1¼ cups all-purpose flour

⅓ cup cocoa powder

2 teaspoons baking powder

Zest of 2 oranges

Chocolate and orange make an adoring couple, and this recipe gives them honeymoon status. It is perfection. The rich dark chocolate is offset by bittersweet marmalade. The pudding is steamed and emerges with a deep taste, a delicate crumb, and a surprising lightness. At the restaurant, it is served with both custard and chocolate sauce. I prefer it with nothing more than a dollop of crème fraîche lightened with a bit of whipped cream. Serve it on New Year's Eve, as it pairs well with Champagne, or on Christmas for those not partial to plum pudding, or really anytime something truly grand is in order. It is extremely elegant when made in a decorative mold.

The recipe, oddly, comes from J. Sheekey, a Covent Garden fixture since the 1890s, known more for its oysters and raw bar than its desserts. But the regulars know to save room for it. Oysters and chocolate may not be an obvious match, but there are nights when roving from one indulgence to the next outweighs the need for any rules.

Custard, chocolate sauce, crème fraîche, whipped cream, heavy cream, or some combination thereof, for serving,

Butter an 8-cup pudding dish or porcelain dish, and then spread ½ cup of the marmalade over the bottom of the dish.

Break the chocolate into small pieces and place half of it into a heat-proof bowl, reserving the remaining half. Place the bowl over a pot of simmering water or use a double boiler. Melt the chocolate, stirring occasionally, until smooth. Remove the chocolate from the heat.

In a stand mixer or using electric beaters and a large bowl, cream the butter and sugar until light and fluffy. Slowly add the eggs, scraping the sides and bottom of the bowl once or twice to ensure that every bit gets incorporated.

Sift the flour, cocoa powder, and baking powder together and stir into the butter and egg mixture. Fold in the melted chocolate and orange zest.

Continued

Continued

CHOCOLATE MARMALADE PUDDING

Pour the batter into your prepared pudding basin and press the remaining pieces of chocolate into the batter. Cover the pudding with a round of pleated parchment paper and then a round of pleated aluminum foil. Tie a string around the dish to secure the paper and foil.

Bring a teakettle of water to a boil.

Place the pudding atop a trivet in a deep roasting pan or Dutch oven to create a bain-marie. Fill the pan with boiling water until water reaches halfway up the sides of the pudding dish. Cover the pan with a layer of aluminum foil or the Dutch oven with its lid. Bake for 75 to 90 minutes, until set throughout. Check the water level regularly, topping it up with more boiling water as necessary to keep the dish halfway submerged. The pudding is done when a knife inserted in its center comes out clean and the pudding springs back when touched. Do be careful checking on it as steam can burn quite badly.

Once cooked, turn the pudding out onto a warm serving plate. Heat the remaining ¼ cup marmalade with an equal amount of water and pour over the pudding. For something absurdly over the top, serve with custard and chocolate sauce. For something a bit more restrained, serve with a dollop of crème fraîche whipped with a touch of heavy cream.

ETON MESS

SERVES 4

MERINGUE

⅔ cup sugar

2 egg whites

THE WHOLE MESS

8 ounces ripe fresh
strawberries, hulled
and quartered

½ cup sugar

2 cups heavy cream

½ teaspoon pure
vanilla extract

Eton, the oldest and most venerable boarding school in the world, is known, not only for its academic excellence and aristocratic roster, but for the freezing cold showers once poured on its students' heads. It is also known for the compensatory desserts that kept many of those same young charges in sweet bliss. Eton's Mess, as this dessert is aptly named, was traditionally served at Eton's annual cricket match against Harrow—a match that was first recorded in 1805 and continues to this day.

The name says it all. It is a glorious mess of meringue, whipped cream, and strawberries, all swirled together. I love this dessert. And Mark makes my favorite version. He keeps some of the strawberries fresh and he briefly cooks the rest to intensify their flavor, producing a cross between a flash-made jam and a strawberry coulis. Brits, especially, of course, Etonians, are rather particular about their Eton Mess. There are the strict adherents and then there are the deviators who mess with raspberries and blackberries. Some add strawberry ice cream. Some don't swirl their mess, which in theory, I suppose, results in an Eton Neat.

To make the meringue, preheat the oven to 200°F (or the lowest setting) and line a baking sheet with parchment paper or a Silpat.

In a stand mixer or using electric beaters and a large bowl, beat the sugar and egg whites with increasing speed, until stiff peaks form.

Spread the meringue on the prepared baking sheet. The meringue will later be broken up, so shape is not important here. Bake overnight, 6 or 7 hours is long enough, until dry and brittle. Another option is to start baking in the morning, if serving at dinner. The meringues can sit for several hours after being baked.

To make the whole mess, place 6 ounces of strawberries in a small pot with ¼ cup of the sugar and bring to a gentle boil. Boil for 2 minutes and then remove from the heat. Let cool to room temperature. Puree in a blender until smooth. Refrigerate until chilled.

Just before serving, in a stand mixer or using electric beaters and a large bowl, beat the cream, the remaining ¼ cup of sugar, and the vanilla until stiff peaks form. Transfer to either a serving dish or individual bowls.

Break the meringue into bite-size pieces and fold these into the cream. Swirl in the strawberry puree. Top with the remaining fresh strawberries.

PEACH RASPBERRY MESS
WITH TOASTED ALMOND MERINGUE

SERVES 6

1 cup whole blanched almonds

1 tablespoon sliced almonds

5 egg whites

1½ cups sugar

½ teaspoon wine vinegar

½ teaspoon vanilla extract

2½ cups heavy cream

Confectioners' sugar, for serving

2 cups fresh raspberries

4 to 6 very ripe, perfect peaches, peeled and sliced

NOTE Some of you may like less whipped cream, others more. The same may hold true for the meringue. Create your own ratio of cream to meringue to fruit as you go. If I have frozen raspberries on hand, I'll make a quick puree in the blender with a bit of crème de framboise and a touch of confectioners' sugar. The coulis looks and tastes terrific swirled into the whipped cream. Or toss with the fresh raspberries.

There's little reason to limit your intake of mess to strawberry season. In the autumn, Jeremy Lee's Walnut Meringue, Poached Pear, and Quince Mess (page 240) banishes all thoughts of the impending winter with a joyous sense of folly. My Thanksgiving mess involves stewing cranberries in vintage port with a little sugar.. Around February, when there's a dearth of berries, I take a cue from Giorgio Locatelli and make an Amalfi lemon mess, swapping in Amalfi or Meyer lemons for the usual Eurekas when making the lemon curd on page 197. I like to add a touch of limoncello to the cream while whipping it or I might add a scoop of lemon gelato spiked with limoncello to the mess. I've never tried a key lime mess, but why not?

All to say, the possibilities are many. But a recent favorite that I must share with you is Jeremy's late summer mess of peaches and raspberries. Only make it when the peaches are perfect and the raspberries freshly picked. As with an Eton Mess, the essence of the fruit must be distinct if it is to flirt successfully with the billowing cream and the crisp meringue.

Preheat the oven to 350°F. Spread the blanched almonds out on a baking sheet and toast for 10 minutes, until fragrant and golden brown. Let cool completely before grinding them into a coarse meal. Separately, toast the sliced almonds for a few minutes, until pale gold. Set aside. Leave the oven on.

Line another baking sheet with parchment paper.

In a stand mixer or using electric beaters and a large bowl, whisk the egg whites with increasing speed. Once the egg whites start to grow in volume, add the sugar, a tablespoon or two at a time, and continue whisking until stiff peaks form. Whisk in the vinegar and vanilla just until combined. Using a spatula, gently fold in the ground almonds.

Drop big dollops of the meringue onto the prepared baking sheet.

Bake for 45 minutes, until dry and firm to the touch. Turn the oven off. Let the meringues cool completely with the oven door ajar.

Just before serving, in a stand mixer or using electric beaters and a large bowl, whip the cream until it billows. Add the confectioners' sugar to taste and whip a few seconds longer. Fold in half of the raspberries and peaches. Break the meringue into bite-size pieces and fold in as many bits as appeals to you. Any extra meringues will do well in the cookie jar for a few days.

To make your mess, spoon the cream, fruit, and meringue into bowls. Top with the remaining half of the fruit, pressing it into the cream a bit, sprinkle with the toasted sliced almonds and dust with confectioners' sugar. Serve immediately.

WALNUT MERINGUE, POACHED PEAR, AND QUINCE MESS

SERVES 8 TO 10

PEARS

6 cups water

1 bottle of good white wine

3 cups sugar

7 fresh bay leaves, preferably fresh

3 strips lemon zest

2 vanilla beans, split to reveal their aroma

12 peppercorns

20 pears, ripe but still firm

Juice of 3 lemons

QUINCES

8 quinces

1 vanilla bean

¼ cup quince or medlar jelly

Enough of the syrup from poaching the pears to cover the quince halves

MERINGUES

1½ cups very best walnuts

6 egg whites

1⅔ cups sugar

THE MESS

Vanilla ice cream, for serving

Whipped cream, for serving

Toasted walnuts, chopped, for serving

Confectioners' sugar, for dusting

This is a festive, sophisticated winter variation on the classic Eton Mess. Jeremy's poached pears are delicious on their own, so, if possible, poach more than are needed. Save a few for breakfast and a few to add to a salad of greens and Stilton. The quince here are wonderful, but not essential. Don't worry if you can't find any. The walnuts in the meringue offer that layer of depth that satisfies in the colder months.

To serve, Jeremy suggests mounding a "jolly heap" on a platter, but this mess is really no less fabulous served individually in bowls or—my son's favorite—in a tall ice cream soda glass with a long spoon. A more formal option would be to make one giant meringue and turn this into something of a pavlova. Jeremy adds ice cream to the mix, a scattering of chopped roasted walnuts, and a dusting of confectioners' sugar. All to say, more is more here because, really, that is the joyful chaos of an edible mess. As Jeremy is as terrific with language as he is with food, I've left his recipe nearly verbatim.

To prepare the pears, pour the water and wine into a heavy nonreactive pot or roasting pan. Add the sugar, bay leaves, lemon zest, vanilla beans, and peppercorns. Bring to a rapid boil over high heat and then immediately lower to a quiet simmer while you prepare the pears.

Peel the pears and roll each one in lemon juice before peeling the next, thereby preventing any unseemly discoloration. Add the pears and lemon juice to the pot.

Cut a circle of parchment paper and lay this directly on top of the pears in their poaching syrup. Place a lid or sturdy plate on top of the parchment and push down very gently until the syrup comes up over the edges and the pears are fully submerged. Bring the pot to a boil once more and let the pears cook at a gentle simmer, until tender. Poke a sharp knife into the pear toward the core. If there is no resistance, the pears are cooked. Depending on how ripe, and what variety they are for that matter, the pears may take 45 to 60 minutes. It is a pleasant business cooking pears, and the delicate perfume rising from the pot is a delight. Cool the pears and store in a jar or some such in the fridge for a week or so. Do save the poaching syrup to use when poaching the quince.

If there are a few extra pears, say 5 or 6, it is a happy thought to puree them, spooning the result over the ensuing jolly heap.

To prepare the quinces, peel and halve the quinces and remove the seeds. I was recently blessed with the obvious and sound advice that the quinces need no lemon juice as the rust color they turn is to be prized and not prevented. Place the quinces in a heavy pot. Add the vanilla bean and jelly. Ladle over enough pear syrup to cover by an inch or so. Make a circle of parchment paper (or a cartouche, as it is known), and place atop the quinces. A plate over this is good to keep the fruit submerged.

Place the pot over gentle heat and bring to a simmer and let cook for an hour or however long it takes the quince to cook through. Ripeness is a great decider on the time so patience is vital.

These will keep very well for a week or so in the fridge, improving very much with each day steeped in their own syrup.

To make the meringues, preheat the oven to 280°F. Line two baking sheets with parchment paper.

Coarsely chop the walnuts, the coarser the better.

Scrupulously clean a bowl and whisk or electric beaters. Beat the egg whites with increasing speed, until they form a stiff peak. Gently add half the sugar and then beat once more until they stiffen. Add the remaining half of the sugar and the walnuts. Fold deftly and swiftly. Place spoonfuls of the meringue, evenly spaced, on the prepared baking sheets. Place the baking sheets in the oven, turn the heat down to 250°F and bake for a few hours, until the meringues are the palest gold color and can detach easily from the parchment. The familiar plaster of Paris is not welcome here.

To make the mess, all you need now is vanilla ice cream and a big bowl of whipped cream. Some roasted and chopped walnuts are good here too.

Take a handsome serving dish, well proportioned. Liberally apply whipped cream to each meringue and start building a heap, adding great scoops of ice cream along the way, studding with large pieces of chopped quince and about half of the pears (save the rest) along with the odd spoonful of pear puree. Once the heap has consumed the lot, tumble the chopped walnuts over the heap, add a light dusting of confectioners' sugar, and spit spot to the table, serving swiftly.

CHILLED DESSERTS

BAVAROIS FRAMBOISE

SERVES 4

RASPBERRY LAYER

1 cup raspberries, fresh
or frozen

½ cup water

2 leaves sheet gelatin

½ cup sugar

CREAM LAYER

2 leaves sheet gelatin
(see note page 258)

1¼ cups heavy cream

¼ cup sugar

1 vanilla bean, split
lengthwise and seeds
removed

1 cup crème fraîche

1 tablespoon eau-de-vie
(optional)

Fresh raspberries,
for serving

Confectioners' sugar,
for serving

This is a gorgeous dessert. If served in a glass tumbler, you will see a layer of the red jelly at the base, a layer of white in the middle, and a layer of fresh red raspberries on the top, sprinkled perhaps with the lightest dusting of confectioners' sugar. The Brits like jelly—not the jarred PB&J purple sticky mass and not the neon container of Jell-O, but rather fresh gelatin-based desserts that taste like pure incarnations of their ingredients. They are light and elegant and easy to make, but do note that the jellies take time to set, so plan accordingly.

To make the raspberry layer, puree the berries and water in a blender or food processor until smooth. Strain through a fine-mesh sieve.

Soak the gelatin in a bowl containing at least 2 cups of ice-cold water for 5 to 10 minutes, until soft. Lift the sheets from the water and wring gently to remove excess water. Imagine wringing delicate lingerie, not an old dish towel.

Meanwhile, combine the raspberry purée and sugar in a small pot and bring to a boil. Once it boils, remove the pot from the heat and let cool for 20 seconds. Stir in the gelatin leaves.

Divide evenly among four glass tumblers and refrigerate for 1 hour, until set. The raspberry gelatin must be set before proceeding.

To make the cream layer, soak the gelatin in a bowl containing at least 2 cups of ice-cold water for 5 to 10 minutes, until soft. Lift the sheets from the water and wring gently to remove excess water.

Meanwhile, combine the heavy cream, sugar, and vanilla bean seeds in a small pot and bring to a boil. Once it boils, remove the pot from the heat and let cool for 20 seconds. Stir in the gelatin leaves.

In a bowl, stir together the crème fraîche and eau-de-vie. Pour the hot cream mixture over the crème fraîche, stirring to prevent any lumps from forming. Set the bowl over ice or refrigerate to set slightly, but not completely. While the cream is still pourable, pour it over the set raspberry jelly, dividing it equally among the four tumblers. Refrigerate until set, at least 1 hour and up to 4 hours.

To serve, garnish with fresh raspberries and perhaps the faintest dusting of confectioners' sugar.

SAZERAC JELLY

**SERVES 1 OR 2, DEPENDING
ON HOW MUCH YOU WANT
TO IMBIBE**

2 tablespoons sugar

5 tablespoons water

½ teaspoon agar agar flakes

3½ ounces rye whiskey

¼ teaspoon absinthe

6 dashes of Peychaud's
bitters or Fee Brother's
Whiskey Barrel-Aged bitters

Unwaxed organic lemon,
for zesting

It would not be inaccurate to call this the Devil in Disguise. It may appear at pudding time, but it is more like a very delicious poison—a strong wallop of alcohol that looks as innocent as Jell-O. Don't let the kids find this! The creator of this trouble is none other than Jamie Berger. He, too, is not what he appears. One of the owners of the best—not to mention the poshest and most coveted by connoisseurs and Soho hipsters alike—barbecue joints in London, Jamie is, in fact, an eccentric and a philosopher with a voracious appetite for mischief. There is something timeless about him—the slightly wacky, brilliant, very colorful, fabulously fun Lone Ranger of Britain's upper class. He was in fact born in Holland and partially raised on the Upper East Side of Manhattan, but his accent is preposterously perfect in most any language. He could as easily be the hero of a Fitzgerald novel as one by Dickens, and I can't say that about anyone else I know. Without further ado, here are the facts.

A life member of the University Pitt Club, Jamie read Chinese at Cambridge and sold his house upon graduation in order to back his friend Karan Bilimoria in founding Cobra Beer. After a stint dabbling in finance in the Far East, Jamie completed a Ph.D. at Harvard that involved a two-year stint as a Fulbright Scholar at Tokyo University and three years at the Collège de France in Paris. He returned to England, took an MBA, and went on to front a corporate investigations firm but was quickly reminded of why he'd fled the corporate world in the first place and fell back on his joint loves: food and drink. Having received his first cocktail shaker from his American mother at age 12, Jamie finally realized his dream of setting up a food truck when he cofounded Pitt Cue Co., in 2011, with his chef friend Tom Adams. The name is a nod and a wink to the elite University Pitt Club at Cambridge. To those unfamiliar with the club, the name may conjure an image of a barbecue pit. The double entendre is intended, and the joke is on us all, Jamie first and foremost. But Pitt also happens to be the name of the small village near Winchester where Tom grew up.

A bit of trivia: As a young American army officer in Paris during World War II, Jamie's mother's godfather invented the beloved cocktail, the sidecar.

About this recipe: The ratio of ingredients has been calculated to make a jelly as close to a liquid as possible. From Jamie: "Agar is preferable to gelatin for creating high ABV (alcohol by volume) jellies—and what we are making here is no children's pudding." And a warning: "If using a wooden utensil to stir, please make sure that it's not been used for savory dishes—there are few things worse than a faint garlicky flavor to a dessert." Peychaud's Bitters, a key component to any Sazerac, liquid or solid, are similar to the more commonly found Angostura Bitters, but hold a lovely, lighter floral aroma. For a real treat, try the Fee Brothers Whiskey Barrel Aged Bitters. Aged in oak barrels, previously used to age whiskey, these bitters have a smooth, well-rounded edge. They are not as sweet as Pechaud's but bring instead a more sophisticated complexity. They're also delicious in an Old-Fashioned.

Make a simple syrup by dissolving the sugar in 2 tablespoons of boiling water and stirring to combine.

Combine the simple syrup with 3 tablespoons of additional water in a small nonreactive saucepan. Sprinkle the agar agar flakes on top and bring the liquid to the gentlest of simmers over the lowest of heat without stirring the flakes. Once simmering, quietly stir from time to time for several minutes, until all the agar agar flakes are dissolved.

Add the rye, absinthe, and bitters to the saucepan to check that the agar agar flakes have dissolved—any flake stubbornly resisting dissolution will be much more visible in the resulting amber liquid. Continue to stir until dissolved. (Jamie: "At this point you can gently inhale the vapors coming from the saucepan as a foretaste of what's to come!")

Divide the liquid into two smallish glasses to cool. Cover the jelly with plastic wrap, lightly touching the wrap to the surface to prevent a skin from forming. After a few minutes, refrigerate the jellies for a few hours, until set.

Just before serving, slowly pull back the plastic wrap. Any skin that would have formed should lift off with the wrap. Use a sharp vegetable peeler to remove two strips of lemon peel from an unwaxed organic lemon. Twist one lemon strip over the surface of each jelly, peel side down, to express the citrus oil. Serve chilled.

SAINT CLEMENT'S POSSET

SERVES 4

2 lemons

1½ oranges

2 cups heavy cream

⅔ cup sugar

Cookie, for serving

Candied orange peel,
for serving

───────────

NOTE For a Lemon and Violet Posset, use 4 lemons and no oranges. When whisking in the lemon juice, add violet extract drop by drop until the posset tastes right to you. Garnish with edible violet flowers or crystallized violet candy. The hue will be a lovely pale purple. Do note that different makes of violet extract hold different concentrations, so until you are familiar with it, add it drop by drop. If using a concentrated extract, you may only need a few drops.

"Oranges and lemons, / Say the bells of St. Clement's." And so begins the well-known British nursery rhyme about the church bells of London. Like so many rhymes supposedly for children, this one has a gruesome end: "Here comes a candle to light you to bed, / And here comes a chopper to chop off your head! / Chip chop chip chop the last man is dead." Not the usual reference for a pudding, is it? Somehow over the centuries, St. Clement's has come to stand not for tragedy, but for the bright and cheerful fusion of orange and lemon. Thinking most decidedly of the latter, not the former, I include here Justin Gellatly's most traditional of British desserts—the posset—infused with the flavors of St. Clement's.

Possets are perhaps the easiest dessert to make apart from scooping ice cream onto a cone. They need but three elements: cream, sugar, and a note of flavor. They're made in advance and served chilled in anything from pretty teacups to the little canning jars. Sometimes they are eaten with a spoon; sometimes a wedge of shortbread serves as an edible spoon. One look at the amount of cream and you'll see that small portions are in order. Possets are irresistible, which, perhaps, accounts for the posset as Lady Macbeth's choice of temptation in poisoning Duncan's guards.

There is no particular skill in making a posset. Traditionally, the ingredients are merely stirred together. I do, however, suggest giving it a light beating or whisking, a trick Justin taught me. This, he explained, produces a slightly lighter texture. Justin, while not yet well known in the United States, is known in London for having created the cult doughnuts and much prized bread at St. John Bread and Wine. As he explains it, he went to learn about offal, but by day's end had fallen in love with baking. Recently, he left to open his own bakery and cooking school and to publish the excellent book *Bread, Cake, Doughnut, Pudding*. When I heard Justin had had his sourdough starter blessed at Southwark Cathedral, I knew this was the man for a pudding that harks back to the fifteenth century and is the stuff of literary legend. I was not wrong.

Zest 1½ lemons and 1 orange. Set aside. Juice all of the citrus into a small bowl. Pour the cream into a heavy saucepan. Add the sugar and zests and slowly bring to a boil over low heat. Immediately turn down the heat to the lightest of simmers with a watchful eye. Do not let it boil. Cook for 3 minutes. The cream will now be infused with the oils from the zest.

Pour the citrus juices through a fine-mesh sieve into a bowl. Add the cream, also through the sieve, whisking or beating with electric beaters as you pour it.

Pour the posset into four pretty teacups or small glass jars. Chill in the fridge for an hour, cover with plastic wrap, and chill for 3 hours longer or until set. This can sit in the fridge for up to 6 hours. After that, they are still delicious but not quite as firm.

BAKED ALASKA

This is a showstopper, entirely conceived to delight anyone of any age. It is a dessert that is talked about in London with the reverence usually reserved for classic British puddings and custard. It arrives at the table, a great snowy peak, in a crown of flames. Moments later, the flames subside, leaving the meringue beautifully caramelized. Take a bite, and the pleasure of cold vanilla ice cream at its center will surprise almost as much as the base of panettone.

The panettone is a brilliant addition, with its taste of Fiori di Sicilia—an extract that combines vanilla, orange, and sometimes rose. The almost Creamsicle-like flavor of this yeasty, buttery, sweet Italian Christmas bread provides just enough contrast for the mellow meringue and vanilla ice cream, while keeping this dessert firmly in the comfort zone of the familiar and childlike.

With excellent panettone and vanilla ice cream readily available, there's no need to make either from scratch, but I've included Tom's ice cream recipe for anyone with an ice cream maker and a bit of time to spare. If you make only the meringue, the recipe will prove to be a quick one. By all means, swap the vanilla for other ice cream flavors, should you feel the urge to do so. Apricot is a favorite of mine, as it is plays nicely with the panettone. So, too, is coffee or black cherry on a base of chocolate brioche. But it is hard to beat the simple pleasure of Tom's rendition.

The recipe is flexible. For two people, I like to make one Baked Alaska and share it. But there's enough of everything here to make either two large or four individual ones. Simply cut the panettone to the desired size and assemble from that foundation. This is a playful dessert and shouldn't look too perfect or it will have pretensions of grandeur. But if you are feeling fancy, use a pastry bag with a star tip to create a dramatic meringue. The final touch requires a blow torch: Caution required. Bravery rewarded.

MAKES ONE BAKED ALASKA, SERVING 2

ICE CREAM

8 egg yolks

1 cup granulated sugar

½ teaspoon salt

2 cups whole milk

1 cup heavy cream

1 vanilla bean, split lengthwise, seeds scraped out and reserved

MERINGUE

2 cups superfine sugar

1¼ cups water

2 tablespoons Lyle's golden syrup or honey

5 egg whites

1 large panettone

To make the ice cream, whisk together the egg yolks, ½ cup of the sugar, and the salt in a small bowl.

Combine the milk, cream, vanilla bean, and the remaining ½ cup sugar in a medium saucepan. Warm over low heat, whisking occasionally, until it just starts to simmer.

Slowly pour about a third of the hot cream mixture into the egg yolk mixture, whisking constantly. This is to gently raise the temperature of the eggs. Then pour the egg-milk mixture back into the saucepan and continue to whisk. Warm over low heat until it returns to a simmer.

Discard the vanilla bean. Strain the custard through a fine-mesh sieve into a metal bowl. Set the bowl in an ice bath and whisk occasionally until chilled. Churn in an ice cream maker according to the manufacturer's instructions. Transfer to an airtight container and freeze at least 2 hours.

To make the meringue, whisk together the sugar, water, and golden syrup in a small saucepan. Warm over medium heat until it reaches to 240°F on a candy thermometer.

Meanwhile, in a stand mixer or using electric beaters and a large metal bowl, beat the egg whites on low speed, increasing the speed as you continue beating until frothy and starting to expand in volume.

When the sugar mixture comes to temperature, slowly pour it into the egg whites and down the side of the bowl with the mixer on low speed.

Increase the speed and continue to whisk until the mixture cools and the bowl no longer feels hot to the touch.

Put the meringue into a pastry bag with a star tip.

To assemble the dessert, cut a ¾ inch slice off the bottom of the panettone. Place the panettone at the bottom of an ovenproof dish, such as a small cast-iron skillet. Place 3 large scoops of ice cream on panettone, with each scoop touching each other to form a triangle. Pipe the meringue evenly around the ice cream, being sure to fully cover the ice cream and panettone. Use a kitchen torch to cook the meringue until bits of it turn a golden brown, but do not darken more than about a quarter of the meringue.

Share or devour alone immediately.

DECONSTRUCTED CHEESECAKE WITH FRESH LEMON CURD

SERVES 8 TO 10

CHEESECAKE CREAM

2 cups cream cheese, at room temperature

1 cup mascarpone

¾ cup full-fat Greek yogurt

½ cup crème fraîche

Juice of 1 lemon

LEMON CURD

1 cup granulated sugar

½ cup unsalted butter

Zest and juice of 4 lemons

3 eggs plus 1 yolk

TOPPING

8 ounces digestive biscuits, graham crackers, or shortbread

¼ cup unsalted butter

Raspberries and blueberries

Were he still alive, the French philosopher Jacques Derrida would almost certainly find humor in the deconstruction of dishes that followed his revolutionary deconstruction of literary texts. Along with poststructuralism, postmodernism, and semiotics, it seems he also, however inadvertently, gave rise to a culinary trend. That chefs misappropriated his theory is really beside the point. (So did most literature professors, for that matter.) Sometimes deconstructing food works, this dessert being a fine example, and sometimes it doesn't (the ubiquitous deconstructed Caesar salad). Here a cheesecake has been reimagined as a casual dessert, more akin to a parfait than a cake.

This recipe is really a two-in-one, as the lemon curd is also terrific on scones, biscuits, and toast. The cheesecake element may be topped with fresh berries in lieu of, or in addition to, the lemon curd. In that case, I might use crumbled shortbread instead of digestive biscuits.

To make the cheesecake cream, combine all of the ingredients in the bowl of a stand mixer and beat on a medium-high speed until silky smooth and as cloud-like as you can expect of anything containing that much cream cheese and mascarpone. Cover and refrigerate.

To make the lemon curd, combine all of the ingredients and heat over a double boiler, whisking regularly, until the mixture thickens and can coat the back of a spoon.

Pour the curd through a fine-mesh sieve into a chilled bowl sitting in an ice bath. Whisk occasionally as it cools. Once truly cool, cover it with plastic wrap, lightly touching the wrap to the surface of the curd to prevent a skin from forming. Refrigerate until needed. The curd may be made a day or two in advance and refrigerated and then brought back to room temperature before serving.

To make the topping, place the biscuits, graham crackers, or shortbread in a sealed ziplock bag and coarsely crush with a rolling pin. Transfer to a bowl. Melt the butter in a saucepan over low heat and pour over the biscuits, tossing to coat thoroughly.

To construct the deconstructed cheesecake, scoop a few dollops of the cream into bowls. Swirl a generous dollop of lemon curd on top. Sprinkle with the crumb topping. Serve immediately.

BLACK SESAME PANNA COTTA

SERVES 10

6 leaves sheet gelatin

3¼ cups whole milk

2⅔ cups heavy cream

⅔ cup sugar

⅓ cup black sesame paste

UMESHU ROAST PLUMS

1 cup plum wine, Muscat de Beaumes de Venise, port, or Sauternes

½ cup demerara sugar

Juice of 1 lemon

3 star anise pods

10 plums

Continued

This intriguing panna cotta could be called the male counterpart to the floral Orange Blossom and Milk Pudding (page 263) from Ducksoup. This is by no means to suggest that women won't fall for it. I did, after all. But it has an almost smoky, men's club aroma to it, with faint echoes of tobacco and leather. I'm not sure exactly why, but it does. And once chilled, it falls into layers, one dotted black and one deep brown, making it rather more masculine in appearance than most puddings. The roasted plums and candied seeds are a brilliant addition but not necessary if you are short on time. The panna cotta is excellent served on its own, allowing you to ponder its mysterious flavor without distraction. Likewise, the extra roasted plums and candied seeds will no go to waste. Both make a fine thing of Greek yogurt at breakfast or vanilla ice cream at dinner.

Once you've got a jar of black sesame paste open in your fridge, you'll find it staring back at you with a challenging grin. I thought I'd save mine for Halloween cookies, but the temptation to try black sesame ice cream, chiffon cake, and the Cantonese sweet soup *tong sui* was too strong. If you have any trouble locating a jar, simply make a puree of roasted black sesame seeds at home.

If you're not familiar with Iranian (or Persian) limes, know that they are dried and readily available online. They are, I suppose, the opposite of preserved lemons in that they are left to dry in the sun until they are rock hard. I like to grind mine in a coffee grinder or to use them whole when making Persian stews. Yotam Ottolenghi, who sells them on his website, includes them in many of his grain-based salads. Here, they provide a sharp citrusy note to the candied seeds countering the overt sweetness of the confectioners' sugar.

Continued

Continued

BLACK SESAME PANNA COTTA

CANDIED SEEDS

½ cup confectioners' sugar

2 tablespoons fennel seeds

1 tablespoon water

2 teaspoons cumin seeds

2 teaspoons coriander seeds

2 teaspoons caraway seeds

1 dried Iranian lime, ground in a spice grinder

Decent pinch Maldon sea salt

———————

NOTE Sheet gelatin, sometimes called leaf gelatin, is often favored by pastry chefs as it produces a very clear gelatin with a pure taste. Using sheet gelatin also reduces the risk of undissolved granules.

To make the panna cotta, soak the gelatin in a large bowl containing at least 6 cups of ice-cold water for 5 to 10 minutes, until soft. Lift the sheets from the water and wring gently to remove excess water.

Combine the milk, cream, and sugar in a saucepan and bring to a boil. Immediately remove the saucepan from the heat and set aside to cool slightly.

Add the gelatin leaves to the cream mixture along with the black sesame paste. Whisk thoroughly. Set aside to cool to room temperature and then pour into ten 5-ounce ramekins.

Refrigerate the panna cottas until set, at least 3 hours or up to the better part of a day. After 1 hour in the fridge, cover the panna cottas with plastic wrap, lightly touching the wrap to the surface to prevent a skin from forming.

To roast the plums, preheat the oven to 300°F.

Combine the plum wine, sugar, lemon juice, and star anise in a pot over a lively heat and simmer for 5 minutes, until syrupy.

Meanwhile, halve the plums and remove their pits. Place them cut side up in a small roasting pan that is just big enough to fit them snugly. Pour the syrup over and around them. Roast for 15 minutes or so, until just tender, turning them over midway through cooking. Remove from the oven and let cool in their syrup. Refrigerate, covered in plastic wrap, until ready to serve. You may make the plums a day in advance.

To make the candied seeds, preheat the oven to 280°F.

Line a baking sheet with parchment paper or a Silpat mat.

Stir together all of the ingredients in a small bowl and then spread evenly on the prepared baking sheet. Bake for 10 minutes, until fragrant and golden. The candied seeds can be stored in an airtight container for up to a week.

To serve, quickly dip the ramekins in a bowl of warm water to loosen the panna cottas and invert onto plates. Arrange the plums around each panna cotta and then scatter with the candied seeds. Serve immediately.

COCONUT AND MAKRUT LIME GREEN TAPIOCA

SERVES 8

1⅓ cups small pearl
green tapioca

4 cups coconut milk

½ cup palm sugar

3 makrut (kaffir) lime leaves

¼ cup freshly squeezed
lime juice

1 cup diced fresh pineapple

Lime zest, for serving

—————

NOTE If you can find small
pearl green tapioca, use it—
it makes this dish a vivid
green! Regular tapioca, as
seen here in this photo, is
equally delicious. Makrut
lime leaves and kaffir lime
leaves are one and the same.

This tastes like a vacation, and it might just be bright enough to get you through the short, gloomy days of a landlocked February. The makrut lime leaves burst with citrus and floral vibrancy. The coconut milk and palm sugar keep it relaxed and balmy.

Soak the tapioca in lukewarm water for one hour before cooking. Drain.

Combine the coconut milk, palm sugar, and lime leaves in a pot and bring to a boil over medium-high heat. Stir in the tapioca and bring to a simmer, stirring constantly.

Lower the heat and continue to simmer for 30 minutes, until the tapioca is translucent and tender to the bite. (Tapioca varies from brand to brand, so start testing after 15 minutes.)

Remove from the heat and transfer the tapioca mixture to a metal bowl. Add 4 ice cubes and set the bowl in an ice bath to cool quickly.

Once cool, stir in the lime juice and refrigerate until set, 1 to 2 hours. If you are making the tapioca in advance—and you can make it several hours in advance—cover it with plastic wrap once set

Spoon into dessert glasses and top with the pineapple and lime zest. Serve chilled.

VANILLA CREAM POTS WITH TEQUILA ORANGES

SERVES 4

1 leaf sheet gelatin
(see note, page 258)

1⅔ cups heavy cream

1 vanilla bean, split
lengthwise

½ cup sugar

¾ cup full-fat Greek yogurt

3 oranges

6 tablespoons reposado
tequila

These little *pots de crème* are exactly what fits the bill after a Mexican feast. They are light, chilled, just sweet enough, and spiked with tequila. Tommi (Thomasina) served them at a private dinner she cooked as a guest chef at Fortnum and Mason. Topped with chopped oranges, they are at their most playful if served in *coupettes* or martini glasses. If on the wagon, simply swap the spiked oranges for poached fruit (page 206).

Soak the gelatin in a bowl containing at least 2 cups of ice-cold water for 5 to 10 minutes, until soft. Lift the sheets from the water and wring ever so gently to remove excess water.

Meanwhile, pour the cream into a deep saucepan with the split vanilla bean and place over medium-low heat. Cook gently for 5 minutes, but keep an eye on it and don't let it boil. Stir in the sugar and remove from the heat.

Stir the gelatin into the hot cream until melted. Scrape the seeds out of the vanilla bean and return to the cream. Discard the bean. Spoon in the yogurt and whisk well until smooth; then set aside to cool completely. Divide among 4 to 6 small glasses and refrigerate for 2 hours, until set. You may make the pots several hours in advance, but do then cover with plastic wrap to prevent a skin from forming on their surfaces.

Peel and segment the oranges and then chop the segments into ½ inch pieces. Place in a bowl, add the tequila, and let marinate for 30 minutes. Alternatively, let them marinate in the fridge for 2 or 3 hours.

To serve, spoon the oranges onto the *pots de crème*. Eat at once.

ORANGE BLOSSOM AND MILK PUDDING

SERVES 10

6 leaves sheet gelatin
(see note, page 258)

3 cups whole milk

¾ cup confectioners' sugar

1 cup double cream

3 tablespoons orange
blossom water

1¼ cups pistachios,
coarsely chopped

―――――――――

NOTE You may instead use
2 tablespoons of powdered
gelatin in this recipe. This
is equivalent to 2 standard
gelatin envelopes.

This is lovely with poached
fruit. You may want to use
teacups or even small glasses
or Mason jars, in which case
don't try to unmold the
pudding; simply serve it in
its cup. If serving at room
temperature, it may be better
to leave the puddings in their
cup or ramekin, as they are
more likely to lose their
shape if unmolded.

This delicate, floral pudding is a distinctly feminine recipe. While
the assumption is that men like to graze their lips over the perfumed
neck of their inamorata of the moment, the assumption is equally true
that they rarely want to eat said perfume in their pudding. Serve this
beauty at a baby shower, a bridal tea, a girl's brunch, a ladies luncheon,
a Mother's Day supper, and you will receive oohs and aahs and lots of
happy gushing. Just don't serve it during the World Cup or Super Bowl.

Soak the gelatin in a large bowl containing at least 6 cups of ice-cold
water for 5 to 10 minutes, until soft. Lift the sheets from the water and
wring ever so gently to remove excess water

Combine 1 cup of milk and the sugar in a saucepan and bring to a
gentle simmer; cook until the sugar dissolves. Turn the stove off but
leave the saucepan on the hot burner. Add the gelatin and whisk until
it dissolves. Add the remaining 2 cups of the milk, the cream, and the
orange blossom water.

Divide the mixture among ten 6-ounce porcelain ramekins or molds.
Refrigerate, uncovered, for about 2 hours, until set. Once set, you may
keep the puddings in the fridge for several more hours but first cover
them with plastic wrap. The puddings may be served cold or at room
temperature. I like to remove them about 20 minutes before serving
so that they are chilled, but not cold.

To serve, quickly dip the molds into a bowl of warm water to loosen
the pudding and invert onto a plate. Garnish with the pistachios.

BURNT ORANGE CHOCOLATE SORBET

SERVES 8

¹⁄₂ cup cocoa powder

1 cup plus 1 teaspoon sugar

2 cups water

3 tablespoons glucose syrup or pale, mild runny honey

9 ounces 70 to 74 percent bittersweet chocolate, broken into pieces

1 orange

1 teaspoon grated orange zest

Here is what Jacob wrote me when sending this recipe: "My grand-mother, Agnes, always used to make us Christmas stockings. She'd use her old (rather unattractive and brown) tights, which were very stretchy, so she could fit a lot in. There would always be clementines and toys and little books along with inexplicable dog biscuits along with the one thing I lived all year for—a chocolate orange. I'd always try and stay awake Christmas Eve till midnight so I could eat the chocolate orange there and then but would invariably fall asleep before Santa came and so had a chocolate orange for breakfast on Christmas morning every year until she and I grew too old for Christmas stockings."

I, too, loved the chocolate orange that Santa put in my stocking. I'd press the top ever so gently and watch the chocolate segments fall away like a blossom opening. Imagine now a grown-up version of that childhood favorite, with rich dark chocolate and aromatic orange zest whipped into a smooth sorbet. This is a divine recipe. In fact, I've been known to skip the ice cream maker entirely. Simply chill for an hour and eat standing at the fridge directly from the container, spoon, optional.

Combine the cocoa powder and 1 cup sugar in a small pot. Slowly add the water, stirring vigorously to try to avoid lumps. Add the glucose syrup and just bring to a boil, removing from the heat as soon as big bubbles appear. Add the chocolate and stir until it melts. Pour into a metal bowl. Set the bowl in an ice bath and whisk occasionally until chilled.

While the chocolate mixture cools, prepare the orange. Slice a ¹⁄₂-inch thick round slice from the center of the unpeeled orange and pick out any seeds. Put the orange slice in a small pan and sprinkle with the remaining 1 teaspoon sugar. Use a kitchen torch to caramelize the sugar—you can also do this under the broiler, but be sure to keep a close eye on it. Cook until the sugar is a deep and bitter caramel, the orange just starting to char. Remove before it blackens. Chop up the burnt orange slice and add it, along with the orange zest, to the cooled chocolate mixture and stir to blend well. Strain the mixture through a coarse-mesh sieve, pressing down on the orange to extract its juice.

Churn in an ice cream maker according to the manufacturer's instructions and then freeze for at least 2 hours.

MARSALA RAISIN ICE CREAM

MAKES 1 QUART

½ cup black raisins

1 cup Marsala, plus more
for soaking the raisins

12 egg yolks

¾ cup superfine sugar

2 cups heavy cream

1 cup whole milk

1 vanilla bean

Imagine a cross between rum raisin and tiramisu and you will understand the grown-up appeal of this flavor. Now marry that thought with *affogato*, the Italian "drowning" of vanilla gelato in espresso. In other words, make this ice cream and, if it suits you, pour a shot of espresso over it and give in to the pleasure of hot, cold, rich, spiked goodness. Or skip the espresso—this ice cream stands alone with distinction.

My intern, Chrissy, first tested this recipe at her parents' house and left it in the freezer while she ran a quick errand. When she returned, she found her mother at the kitchen counter finishing it. I love it when Chrissy calls me apologetically to tell me her family has devoured her latest assignment before she could so much as taste it herself. She comes from a family devoted to food. Their discerning taste is matched only by their athleticism, and their many marathons and triathlons make them ideal taste testers. A quart of ice cream counts as fuel and is burned even as it is eaten. Eat a quart of this and you, too, may well run 26.2 miles.

Place the raisins in a small bowl and cover with Marsala. Macerate for a good 24 hours.

In a stand mixer or using electric beaters and a large bowl, beat the egg yolks and sugar together until the yolks are pale and have doubled in volume. Whisk in the remaining 1 cup of Marsala.

Combine the cream, milk, and vanilla bean in a small saucepan. Bring to a boil over a lively heat and then immediately remove from the heat.

Whisk just a little of the hot milk into the eggs to prevent the eggs from scrambling. Pour the egg-milk mixture back into the pot and bring to a boil, whisking constantly. Cook the custard until it is thick enough to coat the back of a spoon. Discard the vanilla bean.

Strain the custard through a fine-mesh sieve into a metal bowl. Set the bowl in an ice bath and whisk occasionally until chilled.

Churn in an ice cream maker according to the manufacturer's instructions. Drain the raisins, discarding the soaking liquid and then fold into the churned ice cream. Transfer to an airtight container and freeze until ready to eat. This ice cream will become icy after 4 or 5 days and, while not spoiled, will no longer have a luscious consistency.

COCKTAILS

WHITE PEACH SUMMER MARTINI

MAKES 1 COCKTAIL

1¾ ounces vodka, preferably Grey Goose

1¾ ounces fresh ripe white peach puree (see recipe)

1 lemon wedge (optional)

Small bunch of fresh basil leaves, plus an extra for garnish

Dash of simple syrup (see page 273), for more sweetness (optional)

WHITE PEACH PUREE

2 or 3 ripe white peaches

A squeeze of lemon juice (optional)

Shake all of the ingredients vigorously in a cocktail shaker with ice. Strain into a chilled martini glass.

To make the puree, score the white peaches and blanch them in boiling water for a couple of minutes. Remove to an ice bath to cool. Peel the skin, cut in half, and remove the stone. Add a little bit of fresh lemon juice, if desired, and blend until you have a smooth purée.

BLOOD ORANGE WINTER MARTINI

MAKES 1 COCKTAIL

1 ounce vodka, preferably Grey Goose

½ ounce Solerno

1¾ ounces freshly squeezed blood orange juice

Dash of simple syrup (see page 273), for more sweetness (optional)

Shake all of the ingredients vigorously in a cocktail shaker with ice. Strain into a chilled martini glass.

SULLA LUNA

MAKES I COCKTAIL

1 ounce vodka, chilled

½ ounce Merlet Lune d'Abricot or other French apricot brandy

½ ounce freshly squeezed lemon juice, preferably from a Meyer lemon

1 or 2 dashes Poire Williams eau-de-vie

Chilled Prosecco, for topping off

Combine the vodka, apricot brandy, and lemon juice in a cold cocktail shaker filled with ice. Shake and strain into a chilled Champagne flute, add the Poire William's, and top off the glass with Prosecco.

LEMON THYME

MAKES I COCKTAIL

1¾ ounces apple juice, preferably freshly pressed

1⅓ ounces thyme vodka (see note)

½ ounce limoncello

½ ounce elderflower cordial

⅓ ounce freshly squeezed lemon juice

⅓ ounce simple syrup (see page 273)

Shake all of the ingredients vigorously in a cold cocktail shaker. Strain into a chilled *coupette*.

NOTE If you don't have thyme vodka or the time to infuse your own, simply make a thyme syrup and use it in place of the simple syrup. To do this, heat I cup of water and ¾ cup sugar in a small saucepan. Bring it to a boil, stir to dissolve the sugar, and remove from the heat. Add a handful of fresh thyme sprigs, preferably lemon thyme, and let stand until cool. Strain and refrigerate for up to 3 days.

MUMBAI MARTINI

MAKES 1 COCKTAIL

11 fresh curry leaves

1¾ ounces vodka

⅔ ounce freshly squeezed lemon juice

⅓ ounce simple syrup (see recipe)

1 teaspoon ginger juice (see recipe)

SIMPLE SYRUP

1 cup sugar

1 cup water

GINGER JUICE

A few inches of fresh ginger

Benares is one of the most sophisticated restaurants in London, and this martini spikes the appetite with just the right notes of curry and ginger.

Muddle 10 of the curry leaves in a cocktail shaker. Add the remaining ingredients. Shake vigorously with ice. Strain into a chilled martini glass. Garnish with the 1 remaining curry leaf.

To make simple syrup, combine the sugar and water in a small pot and bring to a boil. Boil, without stirring, for 10 minutes, until the syrup has reduced by half. Do not let it color. If it starts to brown, immediately turn down the heat. Set aside to cool to room temperature but do not refrigerate as it will crystalize.

To make ginger juice, peel and finely grate the ginger root, and then squeeze hard in a piece of muslin or cheesecloth over a bowl to catch the juice. The advantage to doing this by hand is that you avoid including any of the fibrous bits.

ETNA

MAKES 1 COCKTAIL

A sprig of oregano

½ ounce chilled Marsala

1 white sugar cube

5 dashes Angostura bitters

Chilled Champagne, for topping off

Muddle the oregano and Marsala in a chilled cocktail shaker. Place the sugar cube in a Champagne glass or large *coupette*. Pour in the strained Marsala and the bitters and top with the Champagne.

CINNAMON BELLINI

MAKES I COCKTAIL

Assam tea leaves

Cinnamon sticks

1 teaspoon cinnamon schnapps, preferably Goldschläger

½ teaspoon cinnamon syrup (see recipe)

Chilled Prosecco, for topping off

CINNAMON SYRUP

1 cup water

4 cinnamon sticks

1 cup sugar

Assam tea, Goldschläger cinnamon schnapps, a few drops of cinnamon syrup, and a few cinnamon sticks topped with a splash of Prosecco—this is a tea lover's cocktail.

To make the cinnamon tea, steep standard Assam with cinnamon sticks, one per cup. Once steeped, strain the tea leaves but leave the cinnamon stick in the tea. Let cool to room temperature and then refrigerate for a bit. Set aside ⅔ ounce.

Combine the cinnamon tea, schnapps, and cinnamon syrup in a Champagne flute and swirl or stir to mix. Top with Prosecco.

CINNAMON SYRUP

To make the cinnamon syrup, combine the water and cinnamon sticks in a small pot and bring to a boil. Lower the heat and simmer for 10 minutes. Remove the cinnamon sticks, bring the water back to a boil, add the sugar, and stir until it dissolves. Turn off the heat and set aside to cool to room temperature. Pour into a bottle and refrigerate for up to 2 weeks.

BIRCH SAP OLD-FASHIONED

MAKES 1 COCKTAIL

2 ounces bourbon, preferably Four Roses 2013 single barrel

⅓ ounce birch sap

Dash of orange bitters

Dash of Angostura bitters

1 ounce peaty single-malt whisky, preferably Ardbeg Corryvreckan

1 licorice stick, for garnish (optional)

1 orange twist, for garnish (optional)

1 maraschino cherry, for garnish (optional)

This is Ollie's favorite cocktail. It's a fixture on the menu at Oskar's Bar, which is just downstairs from Dabbous. Birch sap, which comes from white or silver birch trees, has a faint citrus note that cuts its sweetness and makes it almost refreshing. Unlike maple syrup, which has a sugar content of roughly 8 percent, birch sap is maybe 2 percent sugar at most. In a pinch, you may substitute maple syrup for the birch sap, but the drink will then be significantly sweeter. That said, you might find a sweeter drink preferable and may even want to add a touch of sugar if using birch sap.

If you can't find the limited edition Four Roses 2013 single-barrel bourbon used at the bar, do not fear. It is quite spectacular, but to my mind, it's best enjoyed straight. Ollie uses it because "the 2013 edition comes at barrel proof, which is 63.9 percent alcohol by volume. That makes this whiskey very big on flavor, and as a result, it stands up to the birch sap. The peaty whisky adds a hint of smoke that ties in with the burnt caramel and toffee notes in a harmonious finish."

Combine all the ingredients in a chilled Old Fashioned glass and add ice. Stir with a bar spoon for about 30 seconds. Garnish with a licorice stick, orange twist, and/or maraschino cherry.

QUININE SOUR

MAKES I COCKTAIL

1 (4-inch) knob fresh ginger,
peeled and thinly sliced

4 fresh curry leaves, plus
1 for garnish

1¾ ounces gin, preferably
Tanqueray

1 ounce freshly squeezed
lemon juice

1 ounce simple syrup
(see page 273)

1¾ ounces egg white

Dash of vanilla bitters

Shake all of the ingredients vigorously in a cocktail shaker without ice. Add the ice and shake for 20 seconds longer. Strain into a chilled *coupette* glass. Garnish with a floating curry leaf.

THE AVENUE

MAKES I COCKTAIL

1 ounce cider brandy, preferably
Somerset Cider Brandy

1 ounce bourbon, ideally Bulleit

1 ounce fresh or thawed frozen
passion fruit puree

½ ounce grenadine, preferably
homemade (see recipe)

Dash of orange blossom bitters

GRENADINE

2 cups pure pomegranate juice

1¾ cup sugar

Combine all of the ingredients in a cold cocktail shaker filled with ice. Shake for 20 seconds. Strain into a chilled coupe glass.

GRENADINE

To make grenadine, bring the pomegranate juice to a boil in a small pot. Reduce the heat and simmer until the juice has reduced by a third. Remove from heat and stir in the sugar while the juice is still warm. Set aside to cool to room temperature. Pour into a jar and refrigerate up to two weeks.

SAGE AND CARDAMOM GIN
WITH PINEAPPLE AND CLOVES

MAKES 1 COCKTAIL

3½ ounces infused gin
(see recipe)

1¾ ounces pineapple puree
(see recipe)

¾ ounce freshly squeezed
lemon juice

¾ ounce clove syrup
(see recipe)

PINEAPPLE PUREE

1 large pineapple, leaves
trimmed and discarded

INFUSED GIN

20 fresh sage leaves, plus
2 for garnish

4 cardamom pods, coarsely
crushed by hand or in a
mortar and pestle

1 (24-ounce) bottle London
dry gin, preferably
Tanqueray

CLOVE SYRUP

2½ cups sugar

2 cups water

4 whole cloves

Shake all of the ingredients vigorously in a cold cocktail shaker with ice for 10 to 15 seconds. Strain into a chilled martini glass. Garnish with a fresh sage leaf and serve at once.

To make the pineapple puree, preheat the oven to 350°F.

Without peeling the pineapple, wrap it in aluminum foil and roast for 3 hours. Remove from the oven and remove the foil.

When cool enough to handle, peel the pineapple and cut it, lengthwise, into four wedges. Cut out and discard the core and then place the flesh in a blender. Blitz until it's a smooth puree. Set aside. You'll have more than you need here, but you can freeze the remainder in batches for a month to be used as needed.

To make the infused gin, add the sage and cardamom to the bottle of gin and then set aside for at least 3 hours, preferably 6, swirling the bottle from time to time. Strain through a fine-mesh sieve, discard the cardamom and sage, and return the gin to the bottle. The gin will keep for months.

To make the clove syrup, combine the sugar and water in a medium saucepan and bring to a boil, stirring to dissolve the sugar, and then turn the heat to low. Add the cloves and simmer for 10 minutes, stirring from time to time. Remove and discard the cloves. Set aside to cool to room temperature. Pour into a bottle. The syrup will keep for several weeks.

SUPER BLOODY MARY

MAKES I COCKTAIL

3½ ounces Andina mix

1¼ ounce Pisco infusion

½ ounce vodka, preferably
oak smoked

1 celery stalk, cut at an angle

Lime juice, for dipping

Pinch of Peruvian black
smoked salt, plus more
for the garnish

ANDINA MIX

**MAKES 4 CUPS,
ENOUGH FOR I0 DRINKS**

1 large carrot, peeled

1 parsnip

3 inches peeled cucumber

4 ripe tomatoes

6 juicy limes

½ red bell pepper

½ beet

2 radishes

1 fresh red chile with seeds

2 sprigs rosemary

3 sprigs cilantro

PISCO INFUSION

1 bottle Pisco, preferably
Pisco Quebranta

3 stalks celery

1 teaspoon black peppercorns

3 dried aji panca chiles or
other smoked chiles

This is no simple affair, but it is nectar to those who love a strong, fresh Bloody Mary. I've always found that there is much passionate argument over the balance and ratios of ingredients among devotees of this drink. For the record, then, this version, made with pisco, is as good as it gets.

Approach making this cocktail in two parts: first is the Andina mix; second is the Pisco infusion. The restaurant uses Peruvian pisco made from quebranta grapes, known for their earthy, grassy notes. Do note that you will need to start a few days in advance to allow the flavors to sufficiently infuse. And I'm afraid you will need either a juicer or a Vitamix. Or bring your ingredients to the nearest juice bar and barter—juicing services for a Bloody Mary.

Combine the Andina mix, Pisco infusion, and vodka into a cocktail shaker with ice and roll gently for 20 seconds. Don't shake or the tomato juice will lose color. Taste and adjust for spiciness and acidity.

Strain into a tall glass that's full of ice. Garnish, if you wish, with a celery stalk dipped in lime juice and then into black salt.

ANDINA MIX

To make the the Andina mix, juice the carrot, parsnip, cucumber, tomatoes, limes, bell pepper, beet, radishes, and chile. Place the juice in a pitcher or large jar and add the rosemary and cilantro. Refrigerate for 24 hours to infuse.

PISCO INFUSION

To make the Pisco infusion, place all of the ingredients into an airtight container and set aside to infuse in the fridge for 2 days. Try to shake it a little once or twice a day. (In a rush, chop up the celery and chiles, and you can get away with infusing for only 1 day.)

ACKNOWLEDGMENTS

One day, not many months ago, as I was considering photographers for this book, I came home from a long day of errands to find my son, Garrick, on the floor of his bedroom surrounded by stacks of cookbooks. He had taken it upon his nine-year-old self to filter through a mountain of books to help find me the best photographer. With a keen eye, he'd boiled it down to three finalists and presented me with an impassioned, articulate case for each. Had I not been so interested in his arguments, I might have burst into tears. That he supported this undertaking of mine, despite the weeks I'd spent abroad doing research, the late nights copyediting, and the weekends of recipe testing, moved me to the core. Garrick is like that. He never fails to surprise, and his well of generosity never fails to replenish. His thoughtfulness is true thoughtfulness, carefully considered, imagined, and executed with love. This book is dedicated to him.

There's not a page that leaves my desk and enters the outside world without first being edited by my husband, John. In this, I am truly lucky, as not only is his editing fierce and exacting, but it affords me the confidence and fearlessness that I, for one, need in order to write. He is my favorite writer and reader, and, at heart, everything I write of my own, I write for him.

My dog, Griffin, is a Bouvier des Flandres, a soulful, wise, gentle furry noble giant, who leads me upstairs to my desk to write every morning. I simply follow his work ethic as best I can. When I doubt myself, he steadies me. When I finish, he is there to play. When I wake, he's there to set the day in motion. Thank you, my sweet Grif.

Everything I know about food I know thanks to my parents. They had the wonderful sense never to give me kid food, but rather to introduce me to the best food and assume it would captivate me. It did. And when we moved to Paris when I was ten, I took to accompanying my father when he went to the cheese shop, Barthélémy, the bread shop, Poilâne, the Patisserie Gérard Mulot, and the market on the rue de Buci. My father, with impeccable French and elegant manners, would take time to discuss the food with the shopkeepers. His seriousness was understood to be a sign of respect and was rewarded with generous discussion about such and such a cheese or the merits of a poulet de Bresse, the virtues of a particular Calvados, or the secret stash of *fraises des bois*. I had no idea how much I was learning.

But it was my mother who taught me to cook and to write. She will tell you she cooks by the book, but the margins of her cookbooks are marked with notes and changes. She will tell you she simply adds more of what she likes—more butter, more wine, more thyme—but in recreating the balance of a recipe, she always seems to improve it exponentially. She will tell you to come over and have a bite and several sumptuous courses later, you will still be feasting. When I was little, if I gave my mother something I'd written, she'd return it marked up in red felt-tip pen. Her editorial remarks were true to the *New Yorker*, where she writes, and the strange symbols seemed loopy and foreign to me, but what I understood was her dedication to the possibilities of language. I learned to ponder and question every choice I made, to reach for simplicity, and to never be less than precise. Today, it is with hungry anticipation that I give my mother what I write, knowing how very much I have still to learn from her.

London is now the home of two of my dearest friends, Nader and Alexandra Mousavizadeh. It is their house that has been my home away from home. Their immense generosity and friendship made this book possible. Their upstairs floor became my ground zero and their kitchen table conversation, my reward.

Every recipe in this book has been tested at least twice and made countless times for pleasure. My intern Chrissy Tkac proved indispensable. She has the precision of a true baker and the dedication of a real chef.

Numerous publicists helped me in London, but a very special thanks must go to Sophie Orbaum at Gerber Communications, Sarah Canet at Spoon PR, and Gemma Bell at Gemma Bell PR.

A first book is a leap of faith. While I'd written numerous screenplays and countless articles, I'd never tackled a book when my agents Eric Simonoff, Eric Lupfer, and Elizabeth Sheinkman at William Morris Endeavor took me on, believing somehow that if I could write a good thousand words, I could write a good eighty-thousand. I could not ask for a more loving, more enthusiastic, or more loyal team.

Of course, the biggest leap of faith was made by Ten Speed Press and, in particular, my editor Jenny Wapner. Jenny, with great straightforward and honest grace, has nudged where needed and given freedom where desired. With uncanny accuracy, she can pinpoint a problem before it is made, saving headaches and anguish. A true publisher, she moves seamlessly and brilliantly between the micro details of editing and the big picture vision of shaping a book. It has been a pleasure working together.

As a journalist, I've been privy to Kristin Casemore's book launches for over a dozen years.

No one does it better. What fun it is to finally be on the same team!

Assistant editor Clara Sankey answered all the silly questions of a first-time book writer with such graciousness that I never felt the least silly.

I've been a fan of creative director Emma Campion's work for years. When she agreed to take on this project, I knew I won the lottery. Watching her design this book has been quite thrilling. Somehow out of my inarticulate ramblings on aesthetics and vision, she made sense and turned it into art.

As did Sang An, whose photographs illuminate these pages. With the help of the wonderful food stylist George Dolese, Sang turned his elegant eye to the food, people, and places of London, giving visual life to this book. Their work may appear effortless, but they worked tirelessly to make it so.

Of course, there would be no book without the chefs here portrayed. Someone asked me when I started this book if I worried that chefs would refuse to give me their recipes. No, I answered, surprised. Great chefs create anew every day, dish to dish, as ingredients appear and ideas spark. They are fluid, energetic, and profoundly creative thinkers. And they are, by and large, a most generous lot, as eager to share their discoveries as to offer up an evening feast. But their hospitality (and lovely British manners) far exceeded all expectation. Nowhere have I received a lovelier welcome than I did at the restaurants in this book. It would seem, in cooking, that heart and talent are most always entwined, and that where the food is good, chances are the chef is a generous one. This book is about chefs, and it is for them.

Lemon Teabread
3.45

Chocolate Sug
3.

Carrot & Coconut
4.50

Lemon Pole
4.

RED HAMS. BACO

ABOUT THE AUTHOR

Aleksandra Crapanzano is the recipient of the James Beard Foundation M.F.K. Fisher Award for Distinguished Writing. Her work has appeared in several anthologies, including Best Food Writing, and she has written extensively for the *New York Times Magazine, Gourmet, Food & Wine, Saveur, Departures, Travel & Leisure* and the *Wall Street Journal*, where, for the last five years, she has written the dessert column "A Little Something Sweet." Aleksandra has spent much of her life in Europe. She now resides in Brooklyn with her husband, the novelist John Burnham Schwartz, and their son, Garrick.

INDEX

Library of Congress Cataloging-in-Publication Data
Names: Crapanzano, Aleksandra, author.
Title: The London cookbook : recipes from the restaurants,
   cafes, and hole-in-the-wall gems of a modern city / by
   Aleksandra Crapanzano.
Description: First edition. | Berkeley : Ten Speed Press, an imprint of the
   Crown Publishing Group, a division of Penguin Random House LLC,
   [2016] | Includes bibliographical references and index.
Identifiers: LCCN 2016012459 (print) | LCCN 2016020967 (ebook)
Subjects: LCSH: Cooking, English. | Cooking—England—London. |
   Restaurants—England—London. | LCGFT: Cookbooks.
Classification: LCC TX717 .C85 2016 (print) | LCC TX717 (ebook) |
   DDC 641.5942--dc23
LC record available at https://lccn.loc.gov/2016012459

Hardcover ISBN: 978-1-60774-813-7
eBook ISBN: 978-1-60774-814-4

Printed in China

Design by Emma Campion
Food styling and London location styling by George Dolese
Associate food stylist Elisabet der Nederlanden

10 9 8 7 6 5 4 3 2 1

First Edition